JEW SÜSS

Jew Süss
Life, Legend, Fiction, Film

Susan Tegel

continuum

Published by the Continuum International Publishing Group

The Tower Building	80 Maiden Lane
11 York Road	Suite 704
London	New York
SE1 7NX	NY 10038

www.continuumbooks.com

First published 2011

British Library Cataloguing-in-Publication Data
A catalogue record for this book is available from the British Library.

ISBN 978–1–8472–5017–9

Designed and typeset by Fakenham Prepress Solutions, Fakenham, Norfolk NR21 8NN
Printed and bound in Great Britain

Contents

*For
Peter*

Illustrations

Acknowledgements

Since 1945 several historians have written about Süss from whom I have greatly benefited, in particular: Barbara Gerber's *Jud Süss: ein Beitrag zur historischen Antisemitismus-und Rezeptionsforschung* (Hamburg, 1990) which examines the eighteenth-century response to his trial and execution, and in particular the legend of Jud Süss; the biography by Hellmut G. Haasis, *Joseph Süss Oppenheimer, genannt Jud Süss* (Frankfurt, 1998), which contains new biographical information, especially valuable since aspects of his private life feature both in his trial, the legend and the subsequent literature; and Peter H. Wilson, an historian of eighteenth-century Germany, whose work on Württemberg helps place Süss within context, important for understanding his achievements, failures and ultimately his demise.

I have used a number of libraries and archives over the many years since I first became interested in this subject. I am grateful to their staff who have been most helpful, in particular: The British Film Institute National Library; The British Film Institute National Archive; The British Library; the British Newspaper Library, Colindale; the Imperial War Museum, Film and Video Archive; the Wiener Library; the National Archives, Kew, the Bundesarchiv, Berlin; the Bundesarchiv-Filmarchiv, Berlin; the Stiftung Deutsche Kinemathek, Berlin; the Bayerisches Hauptstaatsarchiv, Munich; the Bayerische Staatsbibliothek, Munich; the Institut für Zeitgeschichte, Munich; the Staatsarchiv Hamburg; the Staatsanwaltschaft bei dem Landgericht Hamburg; the Deutsches Institut für Filmkunde, Frankfurt am Main; the Oestereichisches Staatsarchiv, Vienna; the Oestereichische Nationalbibliothek, Vienna; the US National Archives at College Park, Maryland. I also greatly benefited as a Visiting Scholar at the United States Holocaust Memorial Museum.

I would like to thank in particular those individuals who have either helped with my queries or with whom I have had fruitful discussions or who have provided me with useful information: Brett Bowles, Estelle Cohen, David Culbert, Edgar Feuchtwanger, Jo Fox, Isa Van Eeghen, Lucie Skeaping, Victor Tunkel, Cornelie Usborne, Roel Vande Winkel, Barbara Rogers and Susan Szeczetnikowicz. And finally I would like to thank my husband, Peter, for his help and advice throughout this very long process.

Preface

Since his death in 1738 Jud Süss, or Jew Süss, has lived on in legend, fiction and for the first half of the twentieth-century film, usually as a villain but occasionally not. When the villain he was a Jewish villain, though the nature of his villainy shifted according to the storyteller, the context and the intended audience. Jud Süss, that is *the* Jew Süss, is the name first given to Joseph Süss Oppenheimer in 1737 during his trial in Württemberg in south-west Germany and it is under that name that he has lived on.

Much of what we now know about Joseph Süss Oppenheimer (1698–1738) derives from evidence given at his trial which, in his own case, was under duress. Historians have tried to piece together this evidence, some with more success than others, but no one before 1945 did so without a strong inclination to present the case either for him or against him, and more frequently the latter rather than the former.

Some things we do not know about Süss because the evidence is simply not there or it is fragmentary. We do know, however, that he was a court Jew, a term used to describe Jewish merchants and financiers who acted in the service of the numerous German courts in the seventeenth and eighteenth centuries, that he worked mainly out of Frankfurt am Main, and at some point later for the Duke of Württemberg before the latter ascended the throne in early 1733 and then after his coronation, and that in 1735 he was summoned to Württemberg to act as his financial adviser. From that time on he was closely associated with unpopular policies, many of his devising; nevertheless, he was always acting on behalf of an unpopular ruler, a Catholic convert, in staunchly Protestant Württemberg. When in 1737 the Duke died suddenly and unexpectedly,

Süss was tried, convicted and sentenced to death. His execution the following year attracted huge crowds. An eighteenth-century media event, it stimulated the production of a variety of visual imagery and his life and death became the subject of books, pamphlets, broadsides and even plays.

Süss later became better known to a wider public not through the efforts of historians but initially through legend, then fiction, and finally also in the twentieth century in film. Two films were in fact made about him, the better known being the 1940 German film *Jud Süss* (*Jew Süss*). A notorious antisemitic propaganda film directed by Veit Harlan, it went into production several months after the invasion of Poland in 1939 and its premiere took place during the Battle of Britain the following year. Highly controversial, given its script, the context in which it was made and screened and the involvement of Propaganda Minister Joseph Goebbels in its production, there is some disagreement as to its precise relation to the Holocaust, in particular whether its underlying message called for the extermination of the Jews or only their expulsion from German territory, then government policy during the period the film was in production.

Less well known is the British-made film, *Jew Süss* or *Power* – the latter its American title. It opened in 1934 and was based on Lion Feuchtwanger's international best-selling novel of 1925, again *Jew Süss* in Britain, but *Power* in the USA – the same translation being published under two different titles. Feuchtwanger, a German writer of Jewish origin, had by that time been forced into exile. Unlike the novel, the film was not especially successful.

The 1940 German film, however, was a success at the box office. Widely screened, it had a stellar cast and lavish production values. Given this success – its subject matter and its links to government policy, the latter far from tenuous – its director, Veit Harlan, paid the price after the war, being the only German film director to be tried for crimes against humanity.

This study, however, does not begin with the film but with the subject of the film and his reincarnations over two centuries. It is also concerned with what might be termed the film's hinterland. Instead of concentrating on what appears on the screen, or how the film came to be produced (its production history), it goes back further in time to the early eighteenth century to the life and death of the historic Süss and the legend that began to grow after his arrest and in the immediate aftermath of his execution. It then considers how his story was retold in fiction in the nineteenth century as well as in the early twentieth century both by non-Jews and by Jews. Not all were hostile. It also considers how historians wrote about him, though until the third decade of the twentieth century they had only limited access to the archives. After 1918 the restrictions were lifted and a more complete and more accurate picture became possible. But within fifteen years the political context again changed – the Third Reich replacing the Weimar Republic. The Süss story returned again to centre stage; previous accounts were discredited, not only that by the Weimar historian, Selma Stern, who had made use of the recently opened archives or by writer Lion Feuchtwanger, but ultimately even that by the early nineteenth-century writer Wilhelm Hauff, the first to write a novella about him.

The book ends in 1950. Since that date the Süss story has still held an attraction for some playwrights and film-makers (potential or otherwise), mainly in Germany but in a sense – for which of course we should be grateful – life has begun to go out of the subject. Though the story can still be told, the angle is different, and indeed must be different since it is a post-Harlan story and that of course is a good thing. 1945 marks the military defeat, the *Stunde Null* or Year Zero for Germans, though it did not mark a watershed in every area given the inconsistent denazification process, which the Allies had hoped would force Germans to come to terms with the previous twelve years. And especially in the film industry, there was no Year Zero since many personnel continued to earn their living even while obviously film content altered in many respects, though less than one might have been led to expect. Denazification was intended to attach blame to those deemed to have benefited from the previous

system. In theory, they were expected to suffer penalties (from imprisonment to loss of earnings, career or job); in practice this often did not
happen. Many escaped through the net or got off lightly. Initially, Harlan,
the most successful of the Third Reich film directors, was one of the
escapees. His clearance during the denazification process led, unusually,
to a trial in which he faced the charge of crimes against humanity for
having made a film about Süss. Acquitted twice, he was able to return to
film-making, though never again would he achieve the success that he
had enjoyed during the Third Reich. The times had changed – admittedly not quite as fast as his enemies would have wished. His audiences
remained loyal but the lavish funding had dried up in a greatly weakened
German film industry.

Subsequently (and arguably, ironically), Harlan's name has begun to
attract, especially for his descendants, the opprobrium (even ignominy)
that had once been associated with the name of Süss. This is made clear
in the excellent 2008 Felix Moeller documentary *Im Schatten von Jud Süss
(In the Shadow of the Jew Süss)*. On the other hand, *Jud Süss, Film ohne
Gewissen (Jud Süss: Film without Conscience)* (2010), a feature film about
the making of Harlan's film, *Jud Süss*, focuses on the actor, Ferdinand
Marian, who played Süss. Admittedly, feature films are not known for
their historical accuracy, and some would even argue that film-makers
(like writers) are not beholden to the same rules as historians with
regard to 'facts', nevertheless, it is Marian who attracts opprobrium in a
story which deviates from what is already known. The post-war taboo
with regard to Harlan and his film is being broken. Süss is no longer the
devil as depicted (with a few exceptions) before 1945. Nor is it Harlan,
the man who directed the 1940 film about him (who was also one of the
scriptwriters). And now a German historian, a distant relative of Harlan,
has felt sufficiently confident to make a case for him: Ingrid Buchloh, *Veit
Harlan, Goebbels Starregisseur* (Ferdinand Schöningh, Paderborn, 2010).
Thus in Germany, where the story began, the story continues.

A word of clarification: to maintain a distinction between the
German-made film of 1940 and the British-made film of 1934, based

on the Feuchtwanger novel, the former will be referred to by its German title, *Jud Süss* (for non-German speakers 'Jud' means Jew) and the latter by its British title, *Jew Süss*. The historic character, however, will always be referred to as Joseph Süss Oppenheimer, or Süss or Süss Oppenheimer. The subject of the legend, on the other hand, will be Jew Süss. This is close to the German, though a more accurate rendering would be 'The Jew Süss' which puts the emphasis on the fact that Süss was a Jew, which was customary during his own lifetime and subsequently.

Joseph Süss Oppenheimer: origins and early career (1698–1732)

It was during his trial in 1737 that Joseph Süss Oppenheimer first acquired the name by which he would become best known, Jud Süss ('*the Jew*' Süss). Under interrogation he had given his name as 'Joseph Süss, Oppenheimer, von Heidelberg'.[1] His own name was Joseph Süss, but since it was customary for German Jews to add the name of the German town from which centuries earlier their ancestors had originated, in this case Oppenheim-on-the-Rhine, some forty miles north-west of Heidelberg, he was Joseph Süss Oppenheimer. Far from denoting aristocracy, the 'von' in the 'von Heidelberg', merely meant 'of', namely Süss himself was *of* or *from* Heidelberg.[2] To complicate matters of nomenclature, sometimes his father, as well as other relatives, referred to themselves as Süsskind, Süsskindt or Siess rather than Süss.[3] Jewish names, in this period, in contrast to Christian, 'slipped and slid'.[4] Less complicated, however, is the distinction between the historic character, Joseph Süss or Joseph Süss Oppenheimer and the Süss of legend, Jud Süss or *the* Jew Süss.

Heidelberg, where Süss was born in 1698, was then part of the Palatinate (Kurpfalz), or to be precise Lower Palatinate since Catholic Bavaria had acquired the Upper Palatinate at the Peace of Westphalia in 1648 which ended the Thirty Years War. The Lower Palatinate became a haven of toleration among the numerous German states. Its ruler, the Elector (*Kurfürst*) Karl Ludwig, grandson of King James I of England and son of the Winter King of Bohemia, had returned from exile in 1649. While living in the Dutch Republic he had been influenced by ideas of toleration and in Britain during the Civil War, to the discomfiture of his relatives (including his younger brother, Royalist General Prince

Rupert), he had developed sympathy for the parliamentary side. On his return to the Palatinate he invited Huguenots, Portuguese Jews as well as other German Jews to help rebuild his devastated land. His successors, who came from a Catholic rather than Protestant branch, did not abandon the tradition of toleration. In an edict of 1689 Johann Wilhelm von Neuburg granted the Jews of Heidelberg a special privilege, allowing them to own land in a particular location where they could also build their own houses.[5] That was nine years before the birth of Süss.

Nevertheless, conditions for the Palatine Jews, as elsewhere in German territories, were far from idyllic. If the ruler was, in principle, well disposed, the people were not. If for financial reasons the rulers wanted – and even needed – the Jews, their people did not. For them they were economic rivals, and even, according to Christian tradition, the embodiment of evil, the killers of Christ.

Süss was not born to a wealthy family but acquired wealth through astute business dealings – though ultimately not sufficiently astute since they helped make him unpopular, even notorious and that, in turn, cost him his life. An upstart, and an outsider, he would rise high and the higher he rose the greater the fall. Though ostensibly a member of the Oppenheimer clan, he was by no means a close relative of Samuel Oppenheimer who served as court Jew to the Hapsburg emperor in late seventeenth-century Vienna and who died in 1703. Until recently it was thought that Süss had had contact with these Oppenheimers.[6] Samuel Oppenheimer's son, Emanuel, who died in 1721, even worked out of Heidelberg for a time, though when he died Süss was only twenty-three years of age. The truth, however, is far more prosaic. Joseph Süss rose through his own abilities, taking advantage of every opportunity that came his way as well as those further afield.

His father, Issachar Süsskind Oppenheimer, was by occupation a trader, a designation then synonymous with 'Jew'.[7] Sometime between 1675 and 1688 he had come to Heidelberg.[8] He owned his own home, which became possible in Heidelberg shortly after his arrival and in 1703 became a tax collector for the Palatine Jews, responsible for Heidelberg.

This was a position of trust and indicated that he was a respected member of the small Jewish community.[9] Nevertheless, he was not well off, as borne out by the fact that when he died four years later his family was not well provided for.[10] Twice married, he had several children. Joseph was from the second marriage. From an earlier marriage he had two sons, one of whom, the eldest, Moses (Hebrew name Moyses) Süss, later converted and took the name Moses Süss Tauffenberg (*taufen* in German is the verb for baptize, ensuring that a convert could never hide his origins). It is likely that he made this move not for spiritual reasons or because he wanted to advance himself socially but solely because of the limitation placed on the number of Jews allowed to settle in Heidelberg which meant that (possibly due to his poor financial position) he was forced to leave the community. In 1717 he declared himself bankrupt.[11] Later he became a court factor at Hessen-Darmstadt,[12] though at the time of Süss' arrest he was apparently still living in Heidelberg as a Christian.[13] The second half-brother also converted: he may have been Abraham Christoph Tauffenberg who in 1719 in Jena took the name of Wilhelm Christoph Tauffenberg and wrote on Jewish law.[14] Süss seems not to have had contact with these two older half-brothers. He did, however, have close contact with his younger full brother, Daniel, with whom he often worked.[15] According to information provided by Süss at his trial, he had two sisters, one of whom died young.[16]

When in 1707 Süss' father died, it was Moses, as the eldest son, who settled his debts.[17] Joseph Süss was then only nine years of age. His young mother, born in 1677 and widowed at twenty-seven, was not well provided for.[18] Michal (Hebrew name) or Michele (as she signed herself) Chasan was the daughter of a prayer leader and choir leader at the Frankfurt am Main synagogue, Chasan denoting the Hebrew word for her father's occupation.[19] The maternal grandfather's career is the source of the legend that Süss was the son of a travelling player with a beautiful voice who attracted the attention of the Duke of Brunswick, when singing at his court.[20] Indeed, this is only one of the many legends concerning Süss.

Legend also has it that his mother was very pretty.[21] She had married young, probably at the age of eighteen.[22] Her only means of financial rescue from an impoverished widowhood would have been to make another marriage, most likely with a widower. This she managed to do very quickly and had another three sons. Just after the arrest of Süss she became widowed for a second time. Her second husband was Isaak Nathan Gabriel, a brother of the Ansbach court factor Isaak Nathan, and a trader from Wassertrüdigen, a small town some hundred miles east of Heidelberg. Gabriel also had older children of his own. She moved to Wassertrüdigen, leaving her own children from her first marriage behind in Heidelberg with the extended family of her dead husband who were to provide for them and bring them up.[23] After the death of his father and given the hazards of travel, the young Joseph is likely to have had only occasional contact with his mother.

This double loss of both parents at such an early age – the father's death followed by the loss of the mother through remarriage, move to a distant town and starting a second family – may help explain his legendary womanizing. On the day before his execution, which coincided with the anniversary of his father's death, Süss was aware of the date and chose to observe the Jewish custom of fasting.[24] Towards his mother, on the other hand, he may have harboured resentment, though we should not over-interpret since her remarriage would have conformed to normal practice for a Jewish widow, especially one in need of financial support. His womanizing went against Jewish codes of behaviour (and Christian too) – yet he chose to remain a Jew, though possibly this was also for business reasons since his contacts were mainly with Jews. On the other hand, such sexual licence was normal for rulers, the Duke he served providing a good example. Though his enemies made much of this, it was, in terms of court behaviour far from deviant, but then his enemies were also opposed to the court and the Duke. Therefore any attempt to provide a psychological explanation for this aspect of his behaviour must remain speculative; moreover it should also not be taken out of the historical context.

There is one slim piece of evidence to support the gossip that his mother was a frivolous and immoral woman. It derives from a report from 1710 by the chairman of the Heidelberg Jewish Community (*Jüdische Gemeinde*), Feist Oppenheimer, who had also been appointed guardian for the Süss children not necessarily because of any close family link or because he belonged to the Oppenheimer clan but in his capacity as chairman of the Heidelberg Jewish Community.[25] In this report he requests that the authorities expel Süss' mother from Heidelberg since her behaviour had offended the Jewish community.[26] According to this report, on the death of her husband and after being married for sixteen years (later mentioned in the same report as seventeen though neither is correct), and to the outrage of her children and all her relatives, she 'took up with two dissolute Jewish men'. Such behaviour prevented her from living with her parents in Frankfurt am Main as she had wished. She further offended Jewish ceremonial custom by giving birth two years later to an illegitimate child. Finally, she went off to Hamburg with a 'despicable, depraved Jew', her 'godless ways' outraging both Jews and Christians, especially the youth. After four years on the move the widow returned to her Heidelberg home, which now belonged to 'her three [*sic*], sons', claiming under a Palatine law of 1582 her right of use. The chairman of the Heidelberg Jewish Community disputed her claim, arguing that this particular law did not apply since she had not 'raised her children honourably' for after '17 years of marriage and seven children [*sic*]' and after undergoing an 'unpleasant change [in her ways]', she could no longer claim protection because she had neither paid the *Schützgeld* (a protection fee which Jews had to pay the state for a variety of reasons) nor contributed to the community. He requested that the government prevent further 'offence by issuing an order for her expulsion'. On 27 June 1710 that order was issued. It is likely, however, that she found supporters to enable her to begin the process again. Had the charges been true, namely her blatant violation of the Jewish – not to say Christian – moral code, her case would not have been treated with sympathy, though had non-payment been due to penury, her case would have been treated with more.

This report, cited as proof for the autonomy of the Heidelberg Jewish Community vis à vis the Palatine authorities, is a very slim piece of evidence on which to build a case against the mother's character.[27] Despite some errors, namely whether Süss' mother had been married for sixteen or for seventeen years – which if true, would have made her twelve at the time of her first marriage, since at the time of her son's trial she had given her birth date as occurring in the second half of 1679,[28] the document cannot serve as a reliable piece of evidence for her character but is nevertheless interesting. Excluding the negative – even slanderous – view of Süss' mother, recorded at a time when Süss was still a child, an alternative interpretation might be that the chairman simply got it wrong, and deliberately so, because the widow had dared to return to Heidelberg on a visit, stay with her sons and not pay the *Schutzgeld*. Perhaps she was in dispute with Feist Oppenheim regarding his guardianship of her sons but we cannot be certain of this.[29] Certainly, at Süss' trial no aspersions were cast on the mother's reputation, and if ever there was an occasion to do so, that was certainly one.

Being fatherless from a young age, and almost motherless, might account for Süss' free-thinking and loose ties to the Jewish community. Until his arrest the Jewish religion held little interest for him. He did not, for example, attend synagogue or adhere to the dietary laws – he kept two kitchens, one kosher for visiting Jewish contacts and one not.[30] But he neither attempted to convert nor deny his Jewish background.[31] There is no indication that he observed any rites or rituals, while his statements with regard to religion suggest that he was a freethinker. When questioned under interrogation about his religion, he replied that he was 'born a Jew but had the religion of an honourable man'. When asked whether he confessed to the Jewish religion, he replied 'yes'. When asked whether he had once publicly intimated that he was 'favourably inclined to all religions', he replied that by this he had meant that he had 'no passion against any religion and also that he was neither inclined nor ill-disposed'.[32]

Süss had a traditional Jewish education which his father's family would have ensured and mastered the cursive Hebrew script. This he used in his correspondence with his numerous Jewish business contacts, as was customary among Jewish businessmen to ensure that information was kept confidential.[33]

Shortly before his death, when already in his late thirties, which was late for practising Jews, Süss entered into negotiations to find a suitable Jewish wife.[34] Normal practice for better-off Jews was to marry off their sons and daughters at early puberty, with both sides bringing in a dowry. Marriage was a business transaction in which parents chose the partner and struck the deal, as made clear from the memoirs of Glückel von Hameln (1646–1724).[35] Another advantage of early marriage was to enable the reproductive years to be used to the full, given the Biblical injunction to be fruitful and multiply.[36]

Süss' own marriage prospects were blighted since he had two Christian convert half-brothers and no father to back him financially. He needed first to establish himself financially, especially if the prospective Jewish bride was to come from a wealthy family.[37] A decision to marry when already in his late thirties may have indicated a desire to mend his ways and settle down. On the other hand, it may have been a calculated business move, namely to secure his contacts with wealthy Jews and thus was merely another means of raising capital.

While the marriage negotiations were underway Süss was still living with his young mistress, twenty years his junior, Henrietta Luciana Fischer, known as Luciana, the daughter of a minor official of a very minor state, the Rhenish principality of Grumbach. He had met the motherless girl in Frankfurt am Main in 1736 and brought her to Stuttgart with the offer of a post as lady-in-waiting at the court while appointing her father to a position as government adviser. The lady-in-waiting post did not become available immediately and she was offered instead the position of acting as his housekeeper and given a special title.[38] Had he been as serious about finding a Jewish wife as with advancing his career and improving his financial position he would, one would assume, have made an effort to alter his behaviour, which should have alarmed the fathers of prospective brides. On the other hand, perhaps even with them business considerations overrode all others.

Legend has it – repeated by some historians and used by some writers to advantage – that Issachar Süss was not Joseph Süss' father but that his biological father was the nobleman Georg Eberhard Freiherr von Heidersdorf who also ended his life in ignominy, a generation before Süss, though he did not lose his life.[39] Like father like son. Aside from the Heidersdorf story sharing a few features with the Süss story, there are good reasons to reject this legend, which originated during his trial and which has been repeated subsequently in numerous accounts.[40] Two men, born a generation apart, active in the same south-west corner of Germany, and for a time even in Heidelberg itself, had fallen from a very great height, therefore it was concluded that that they must be related.

In 1693 during one of Louis XIV's eastward expansionist wars with incursions into German territory, Georg Eberhard Freiherr (Baron) von Heidersdorf, Teutonic Knight and Military Commander of Heidelberg, surrendered the city to the French without a fight. As a result Heidelberg was destroyed and burned to the ground. Louis XIV even had a medal struck with the words: '*Heidelberga deleta*'.[41] Heidersdorf was held responsible for the destruction. Court-martialled at nearby Heilbronn, then a 'Free Imperial City' (*Reichstadt*), he was sentenced to death, paraded before the entire army in a knacker's cart, had his sword broken across his knee and with one of the broken pieces had his face struck three times. The Habsburg emperor later commuted the sentence but Heidersdorf remained exiled from Habsburg territory and retired to a monastery at Hildesheim in north Germany where he died as a penitent Capuchin monk in 1719 or 1720.

Were Heidersdorf the father of Süss then conception would have taken place before the attack on Heidelberg in May 1693. That would have made Süss at the time of his death in 1738 several years older than the actual age he gave. Since Süss' mother was born in 1679,[42] she would have begun her affair with Heidersdorf when fourteen or thirteen years of age. Had she been mother to a child born out of wedlock, whose father was not a Jew, she would have been unable to marry a respectable member of the Jewish community, indeed she would have been ostracized.[43] Aside from also making her resident in Heidelberg rather than Frankfurt am Main, the story also begs the question as to how Süss' mother would have met Heidersdorf. Jews in Germany kept to themselves, indeed were forced to by circumstances. Even when slandered by the leader of the Jewish Community, Süss' mother was still accused only of consorting with 'dissolute Jews', *not* with dissolute non-Jews. In any case, it was never the custom for Jews to offer up their young daughters to men of high-rank – this was not the Ottoman Empire – and completely went against both religious and social custom.

This was by no means the only Süss legend. Another concerned Cabbalism, namely that Süss had used a horoscope to predict the future to the Duke of Württemberg, in particular that one day he would inherit the title.[44] Though Cabbalism may have figured in the downfall of other Jews – and in particular in that of a Heidelberg rabbi, Elkan Fränkel, in 1702, while Süss was still a child (the rabbi had a brother who was a court Jew to the Margrave of Ansbach and so Cabbalism and business were contained within one family though not within one individual) – there is, however, nothing to suggest that Süss himself had any connection with Cabbalism or any interest in the dark arts.[45] He was foremost a businessman and a banker, interested in material matters.

It was once thought that between the years 1713 to 1717, that is between the ages of fifteen to nineteen, Süss had travelled widely, spending time in Amsterdam, Prague and Vienna and in the last mentioned had made contact with the wealthy Oppenheimers. Samuel Oppenheimer, who had begun his career in Heidelberg as an agent for Carl Ludwig, the Palatine Elector, and who was later called to Vienna by the Emperor after the defeat of the Turks, had died in 1703 when Süss was still a child. His close relatives continued his work.[46] Süss' own activities during his late teens, however, remain obscure.[47] At his trial he mentioned having been to Prague,[48] but not having travelled widely, nor having been to Vienna, which suggests that he had no contact with the Oppenheimers, despite sharing with them a Heidelberg birthplace and a name denoting an origin in the town of Oppenheim some two centuries previously.[49]

Extensive travels, however, made Süss appear interesting and could explain his confidence, ease at court and meteoric rise, which his contemporaries found surprising as did those writing about him subsequently. Could his financial and business skills have been honed in such a confined geographic area? It was thus assumed (wrongly) that he must have undergone what later in the century became an aristocratic rite of passage, namely travel abroad. This, however, plays down his actual achievement since there is no evidence to suggest that he had lived and worked anywhere except first in the Palatinate, then in Frankfurt am Main, the leading financial centre, and finally Württemberg, where he met his end.[50] Süss was a self-made man – until his fall, a highly successful self-made man, aided only by his inherent abilities, drive and, it goes without saying, ambition.

2

Württemberg's court Jew (1733–1737)

Court Jews (*Hofjude*) rose to prominence after the end of the Thirty Years War (1648) and disappeared shortly before the French Revolution. They were mainly to be found in Central Europe, their absence elsewhere being attributed to an absence of Jews or an absence of economic opportunity or both.[1] In the aftermath of the Thirty Years War, German princes, unable to borrow from bankers now ruined by the war, turned to individual Jews who had been less affected, and indeed had often made fortunes as a consequence. Forbidden to own land, and exempt from religious strictures on usury, Jews had a long history of experience in money matters as well as access to a network of Jewish contacts across Europe, especially in the banking and commercial centres. They also had honed their skills in the jewellery trade, in particular with diamonds, since before the rise of stocks and shares their purchase and that of other precious stones was a form of insurance against harder times.[2] Moreover, they had knowledge of precious metals (gold and especially silver), which stood them in good stead with the coinage of money.[3] Jews had another important advantage: they were not tied to local interests, which made them suited to serving a ruler intent on strengthening his position at their expense.[4] They operated in an area of economy and society aptly described as a 'grey zone'.[5]

The term, court Jew, which described these mainly Jewish businessmen and financiers with access to the courts, was not a formal title. That might be court factor, war factor, cabinet factor, commercial factor, financial agent, court agent, or the slightly more important Resident. Such titles indicated that the individual raised loans for princes, provisioned armies, provided courts with luxury items (such as silks and jewels) or acted as correspondents in other states, keeping rulers informed about political and economic developments.[6]

Since Germany was far from united and indeed consisted of even more states (some 300) than a century later when calls for German unification were made, there were numerous opportunities – given the number of courts – for an ambitious Jew with a talent for business and finance. Süss already had role models. Often wealthy, some court Jews lived in style and, where possible, tried to reside outside the ghetto where Jews were usually compelled to live. By the early eighteenth century, Jews in Germany had ceased to wear a specific Jewish costume or to observe strictures against shaving.[7] Though no longer bearded or in traditional dress, court Jews remained practising Jews.[8]

Given their wealth and access to rulers, court Jews were not typical Jews. Most were poor, living on the margins, usually in prescribed areas and often denied rights of residence. Court Jews frequently disappointed their fellow Jews for which reason they were not always popular. They were even less popular with non-Jews but were protected by the rulers they served. If that protection was withdrawn, they fell swiftly and, as outsiders, had further to fall.

If court Jews were untypical Jews, Süss was an untypical court Jew – in style, personality and the extent of his activities.[9] Between the years 1717 and 1732, that is from the age of nineteen onwards, he worked, often with his brother Daniel, first from Heidelberg and then from Mannheim, the recently rebuilt and now newly designated residence city of the Palatine Electors who in 1718 had moved there from war-ravaged Heidelberg. In Mannheim Süss soon acquired a second place of residence and came in contact with prominent Palatine officials, including the president of the court of appeal and the court chancellor, both members of the Elector's privy council.[10] His clients included not only the princes, nobles and officials linked to the Mannheim court but also the Austrian princely house of Thurn und Taxis.[11] From 1723 to 1729 the Palatine concession for stamp paper (a state monopoly) was leased to him to manage. He was also made court factor.[12] From

Mannheim Süss then moved to Frankfurt am Main, the Free Imperial City (*Reichstadt*) and banking centre.[13]

In the autumn of 1732 Süss had been introduced to Prince Carl Alexander (1684–1737) at Wildbad, a spa in the Black Forest. He was by no means the first Jew that Carl Alexander had had dealings with and was introduced by another court Jew, Isaac Simon from nearby Landau, also known as Isaac Landauer.[14] Carl Alexander had recently become heir to the Duke of Württemberg whose only son had died the previous year, and grandson several years before that. Süss was asked to procure jewels, facilitate transfers of money and send reports, once the Prince returned to Belgrade where he was Governor. Carl Alexander wanted to be kept informed about the elderly Duke's attitude to him as well as that of the Estates, especially of any moves to bypass him as a Catholic heir to the throne and appoint instead his Protestant younger brother. He also wanted to be kept informed about developments in Frankfurt and Mannheim.[15]

On 14 November 1732 Carl Alexander appointed Süss 'Court and War Factor', a formal appointment which made it easier for him to travel on behalf of the Duke – he was sent on confidential missions to the courts at Darmstadt and Würzburg – and would even have been sent to Belgrade had the need arisen.[16] Unusually, the Duchess also made him her agent (*Agentenpatent*), mainly to provide her with jewels, money and clothes.[17]

Süss, however, was not working exclusively for the Duke nor did he confine himself to one particular kind of activity.[18] Already court and war factor to the Landgrave Ernst Ludwig of Hessen-Darmstadt, in February 1733 he was also appointed cabinet factor as well as *Admodiator* (lessee and manager) for the mint, though the mint proved unprofitable and he sustained losses.[19] Interestingly, though never previously commented upon, his elder half-brother Moses (the convert), was believed to have been working at Hessen-Darmstadt.[20] Clemens August, the Prince-Elector of Cologne, also made Süss his court and chamber agent, mainly to provision his army.[21]

One year after engaging Süss to act on his behalf, Carl Alexander inherited the Württemberg throne. His predecessor, Duke Eberhard Ludwig (1676–1733), who ruled for forty years, had been highly unpopular in sober Württemberg given his lavish life style. He built an enormous palace, in imitation of Versailles, at Ludwigsburg, just north of the then capital Stuttgart and had a thirty-year liaison with the influential Christine Wilhelmina von Grävenitz, Countess of Urach and Würben, while married to a princess from nearby Baden-Durlach. The relationship ended just two years before his death after which she was briefly imprisoned and her property, a gift from the Duke, confiscated. She fought back, however, and demanded compensation for having renounced the rights to land given her when in favour. She had powerful supporters, not only from the local nobility but also the Emperor and she later took refuge at the court of Frederick the Great.[22] Another cause of Eberhard Ludwig's unpopularity was his attempt to create a standing army.[23]

Eberhard Ludwig had inherited his throne when still a child. His uncle, was the father of Carl Alexander, who acted as regent. With little hope of succession, and without lavish means of support, Carl Alexander entered Habsburg military service in 1712–1713; he converted to Catholicism which caused offence in staunchly Lutheran Württemberg but he had much to gain thereby. After a number of military successes, especially in the wars against the Turks (the siege of Peterwardein in 1716 and the Battle of Belgrade in 1717), he was made, at the suggestion of Prince Eugene of Savoy, military governor of the recently conquered Serbian provinces. In 1727 he married the Austrian Catholic Maria Auguste, Princess of Thurn and Taxis (1706–1756), whose father held a lavish court at Brussels, Austria having only recently acquired the Spanish Netherlands. Süss numbered members of that family among his clients.[24]

Upon learning of his cousin's death, Carl Alexander left immediately, arriving at Stuttgart before the end of the year. Süss hurried to greet him and was soon rewarded.[25] Crowned at the beginning of 1734, Carl Alexander ruled for just three years and forty-three days, when he died suddenly. His short rule was stormy and at the eye of the storm was his Jewish adviser.

A middling German state with a population of under half a million, the Duchy of Württemberg or Alt-Württemberg (Old Württemberg), not to be confused with the Kingdom of Württemberg which, upgraded and enlarged by Napoleon, came into existence in 1806, nor should it be conflated with Swabia or the Swabian Circle within the Holy Roman Empire, of which it was only a part.[26] Württemberg was unusual. As the British Whig politician, Charles James Fox proclaimed on the floor of the House of Commons in 1770: only two states in Europe had constitutions, namely Britain and Württemberg, a statement requiring qualification since for Britain it was not one single legal document (nor, contrary to a popular view, was it 'unwritten') while in the Holy Roman Empire it was not just Württemberg but every constituent part had some kind of constitution.[27] Nevertheless, Württemberg did have a single legal document, which was effectively a constitution, and thus renowned, namely the Treaty of Tübingen of 1514 which, shortly before the Reformation, the then Duke had been forced to sign when the Württemberg Estates agreed to take on his debts. In exchange, they were granted certain political rights and privileges.[28]

Moreover, during the upheavals of the Reformation the nobility resident within Württemberg had seized the opportunity to withdraw altogether from Württemberg politics, opting for the status of 'Independent Imperial Knights' within the Holy Roman Empire and acknowledging only the Emperor as their ruler. Thereafter, the nobility played no role in Württemberg politics and were unrepresented in the diet.[29] Their place was taken by a devoutly Lutheran traditional local elite, known as the *Ehrbarkeit* (the honourable ones) – a term which they used to describe themselves, and which was a closed oligarchy of civil servants, clergy, and academics.[30] Neither a patrician class nor necessarily wealthy,[31] they dominated the Duchy's political institutions (including the diet), the Church and the Württemberg university Tübingen. With strong ties of kinship, having intermarried over generations, the *Ehrbarkeit* were

jealous of the privileges they had won for themselves and remained
united in their determination not to allow this —Duke (or any duke) to
gain the upper hand or impose his will.

The Estates met in a unicameral diet known as the *Landschaft* whose
representatives came mainly from the numerous small towns, most with
a population under 3,500 inhabitants. The 14 titular Protestant theolo-
gians for the former monasteries also attended *ex officio*.[32] Jealous and
proud of their privileges, unique in Germany, the full diet met – only
in times of crisis. The Small Committee (*Engerer Ausschüss*) conducted
its main business while another body, the Large Committee (*Grosser
Ausschüss*), was convened from time to time to discuss important matters.
Membership of both committees was drawn from the *Ehrbarkeit*. In the
early seventeenth century, another body, the privy council (*Geheime
Rat*), had been created to safeguard the constitution. Made responsible
both to the Estates and to the Duke, it also drew its membership from the
Ehrbarkeit. In contrast to elsewhere in Germany, the Württemberg ruler
could neither dominate the Church nor the Estates.

Though Württemberg born, Carl Alexander had spent most of his life
in military service outside the Duchy. His conversion to Catholicism
further isolated him. Before ascending the throne, he had been forced
to sign a document, the *Reversalien*, promising to stay out of religious
matters and not tamper with the religious arrangements. He first agreed
to this in 1727, well before ascending the throne and had to reconfirm
it on many occasions.[33] Lutheranism was guaranteed as the Duchy's
religion and control over matters pertaining to the Church was trans-
ferred to the privy council. Carl Alexander renounced his Episcopal
rights, and thus full control over church property and doctrine. This
meant that his position, if compared to that of his predecessor, appeared
weaker, though he still retained control in important areas unaffected by
the *Reversalien*, such as the court, finance and the military.[34] Certainly
his predecessors had been none too keen to share power with the Estates,
but he, if anything, given his years in colonial service at the frontier of the
Austrian empire, especially as military governor, was even less inclined.[35]

As soon as Carl Alexander ascended the throne, Württemberg was again at war, as Austria's ally against France in the War of the Polish Succession (1733–1735), supporting the Habsburg claimant against the French claimant. A military man, he was keen that Württemberg should be militarily prepared, especially since the Duchy occupied a vulnerable position between France and Austria and in previous wars had experienced French invasion. Nevertheless, Carl Alexander faced opposition when attempting to increase both military expenditure and the number of troops. This continued after the war when he wanted to retain more than 11,000 men on active duty.[36] This strengthened his resolve to weaken the Estates and seek a means of circumventing their control over funds.[37] Apart from military considerations, he was also keen to demonstrate his loyalty to the Austrian emperor since as a Catholic he would need his support in any future dispute. He was rewarded in May 1734 when the Emperor made him a Field Marshal.[38]

Additional funds for other purposes were also required. Carl Alexander was not, as long believed by historians though not according to the legend, an austere military man with little interest in personal luxury in contrast to his lavish-spending predecessor who had nearly bankrupted the Duchy. He collected precious stones, loved music and increased the number of court musicians. An enthusiast for opera, he had a Stuttgart theatre renovated to become Württemberg's first opera house. Many operas were also performed at the Ludwigsburg court where he laid out new gardens.[39] His wife too was a lavish spender, keen to emphasize her rank through conspicuous consumption.[40] Display at the Baroque court also helped maintain the Duchy's status as the leading power in the region.[41] But none of this went down well in sober Württemberg; the court's secular hedonism aroused strong objections. The emergence there of the Pietist movement had given Lutheranism a puritanical edge (Pietism shared some features with Wesleyanism, which developed in Britain later in the century).[42]

Carl Alexander's military background, as well as having been forced by circumstances to make his career outside Württemberg, predisposed him to regard rank in terms of achievement rather than status. This might explain his readiness to recognize the talents of an outsider like Süss and to work closely with him. The two men had a good relationship – the Duke's letters to Süss were warm, addressing him as 'Dear Süss' (Lieber Süss) in September 1734 to 'My especially dear Herr Resident', (Besonders Lieber Herr Resident) in March 1735, while the letters of Süss, in turn, had a respectful but never fawning or subservient tone.[43]

Süss was not the only outsider to whom Carl Alexander turned for advice. Spiritual, military and financial advice was in the hands of Württemberg outsiders, all non-Protestants, though the Habsburg military link was not particularly unusual for a Württemberg Duke.[44] To head the military he appointed the Catholic Austrian, Franz Josef von Remchingen (1684–1757), with whom he had fought in Serbia, an unpopular move but the Estates did not have direct control over the military. Remchingen set up an extraordinary committee in late 1735 to oversee a military plan and was later accused of organizing a military coup in 1737, cut short by the Duke's sudden death.[45]

Spiritual advice came from his old friend from Vienna days, the worldly Catholic Bishop Friedrich Karl, Count von Schönborn (1674–1746), who for many years had acted as Imperial Vice Chancellor and was now the Imperial Prince-Bishop of Würzburg and Bamberg. His magnificent Baroque palace at Würzburg, some ninety miles north-east of Stuttgart, would later astonish David Hume on his travels as even 'more compleat and finished' than Versailles.[46] An exponent of reformed Catholicism, which had a strong authoritarian element, the Prince-Bishop was keen to see Catholicism expand in south-west Germany, where the largest Protestant state, Württemberg, was now ruled by his old friend.[47]

For financial advice the Duke turned to Süss with whom he already had dealings. A financial adviser was unlikely to be popular, especially if recommending tax increases, and more unpopular if a Jew, compounded further by serving a Catholic ruler in a Protestant state. For obvious reasons, Süss played no role in military affairs, and despite rumours to the contrary, was not involved in any military coup. As court factor, he was already supplying the army (uniforms, weapons and provisions), hardly a controversial task. That was the extent of his military involvement and, it should be added, he was neither the army's most important supplier nor did this bring him huge profits.[48] Süss' activities were confined to the financial and economic spheres, which ultimately were also political.

Süss' ascent in Württemberg was rapid.[49] Shortly after the coronation, on 30 January 1734, he was appointed 'Cabinet Factor' and Württemberg *Resident* (a low level diplomatic post) in Frankfurt am Main.[50] One of the most populous and dynamic of the Free Imperial Cities, Frankfurt am Main also had the largest settlement of Ashkenazi Jews outside Prague. Forced to live in a specific area, the *Judengasse* (often referred to as a ghetto), they were locked up every evening – a practice which only ended in 1796. In the late seventeenth century 3,000 people were crowded into just 200 dwellings.[51] (The Rothschilds were not yet an important Frankfurt family since Mayer Amschel, the founder of the banking dynasty, was born six years after the death of Süss.)

Despite the insistence of the Frankfurt authorities, Süss did not want to be confined to the ghetto. Since 1730 he had been working from Frankfurt and had managed, without drawing too much attention to himself, to take up residence outside the ghetto.[52] Doubtless as a Palatine Jew he found such restrictions irksome, even humiliating but his insistence upon special treatment is also an indication of his character. He did not take humiliation lightly. The Duke made clear to the Frankfurt authorities that he wanted his Resident to 'enjoy unhindered' the same 'protection, help, privileges and prerogatives' of other Residents of other princes.[53] The authorities caved in and on 18 March 1734 Süss was formally sworn in, pledging his oath of loyalty to the Duke.[54] His commission was to report on important matters of interest and, if necessary, undertake special missions on behalf of the Württemberg government.[55]

By this time Süss had acquired material wealth but the post of Resident improved his status with the Frankfurt bankers and traders.[56] From there he continued to conduct his own business affairs and work for other rulers, providing minor princes with precious jewels, silks, credit and military supplies. His goal was to remain in Frankfurt, rather than go to Stuttgart. When he eventually made the move, contrary to legend, he was not a poor man.[57] He would continue to maintain a house and office in Frankfurt managed by his non-Jewish secretary and notary, Johann Nikolaus Leining.[58]

Süss never worked exclusively for Carl Alexander, though it was Carl Alexander who became his most important client. An early assignment at the outset of the War of the Polish Succession was to arrange the delivery of tents for the Württemberg army. He also organized the bullion supply for the Württemberg mint and advised the Duke on financial matters, in particular about raising money, given the hostility of the Estates. Another early task was representing Carl Alexander in the financial negotiations begun by Eberhard Ludwig with his dismissed but once powerful mistress, Christiane Wilhelmina von Würben, Countess Grävenitz (1686–1744). Initially, Carl Alexander had hoped to win popularity and save expense, by reopening the case, arresting members of her clique and even reviving the charges of witchcraft and treason. But after Prussia intervened on her behalf, he decided against wasting more money fighting her by drawing attention to the abuses of his predecessor and the matter was brought to a speedy close.[59] Later, however, Süss would be accused of having given away too much to this unpopular woman.[60]

Like his predecessors, Carl Alexander tried to exclude the Estates: in June 1735 he set up a Cabinet Ministry to curtail the influence of the privy council.[61] Summoned to Stuttgart in June 1736, Süss was appointed Privy Councillor for Finance (Geheim Finanzienrat), sometimes translated as confidential financial adviser, with a salary of 2000 florin. He was also named Cabinet Treasurer (Kabinettsfiskal).[62] Now the Duke's most important adviser, especially with regard to finance, he was never actually finance minister, for which reason he has recently been described as a 'quasi-minister'.[63] He was also not actually a civil servant.[64] He never wanted to be a part of the formal bureaucratic hierarchy and his actual title came from outside the hierarchy of offices.[65] But according to a ranking order established some thirty years previously in 1718, he is assumed to have ranked twenty-seven out of 145 in the court hierarchy.[66] He was not represented in the Cabinet though his voice carried weight. Thus he always acted as a private adviser, though admittedly the public–private boundary is blurred if the advice concerned increasing income through raising taxes and is given to a ruler wielding 'absolute authority'.[67]

Since Württemberg law prevented non-Württembergers and non-Lutherans from holding certain positions, a formal appointment would have been an affront to other office-holders as well as to the Estates.[68] Even without such a formal appointment Süss' position was an affront. In any case, appointment to a specific office should not be confused with the actual exercise of power, especially in a state where the style of rule – as distinct from a formal structure – was absolute. Far more important than any actual formal title or appointment to a specific position was access to the ruler and influence. Since Süss enjoyed both, it makes it more appropriate to describe him as a 'favourite', namely someone whose power derived from his special relationship with the Duke.[69] Serving him in a private capacity as confidential adviser, he could remain outside the formal bureaucratic structure at a time when the Duke was determined to maintain his power over (and against) the Estates.[70]

Yet the legend persists that Süss was a minister, a finance minister rather than simply an adviser. Writing during the Weimar period an historian considered his titles to be empty while an historian who began his research during the Third Reich insisted on the opposite.[71] In the Nazi propaganda film, *Jud Süss*, Süss is addressed with emphasis and in a sarcastic tone – the words almost being hissed – as 'Herr Minister'. He is shown to have abused his office and the implication is that he acted according to character or 'race' since appointing a Jew to an office of state is, by definition, a transgression and thus he was only acting in character. Such a view has a long history and makes its first appearance in print at the time of his execution.[72] If, however, Süss merely acted as adviser, others become implicated, especially the Duke, and this weakens the case against him.

Carl Alexander did not attack the Estates over their control of direct taxation but circumvented their control either by raising indirect taxes or by introducing new ones such as surcharges on property, cattle, legal transactions, testaments, inventories, salt, firewood, drinks, the production of playing cards and stationary. Collection was farmed out to speculators, usually not from Württemberg (often Jewish firms from Frankfurt), in exchange for lump payments to the crown giving them exclusive rights.[73] To supply the army, Süss found others, usually but not always Jews, though he himself also had a small share.[74] The tobacco concession, a minor monopoly, went to Palatine Jews who obtained concessionary rights but they sold these on to a business rival of Süss, the Spaniard Don Barthelemi Pancorbo d'Ayala et Guerra, a fiscal adventurer. This venture also failed due to under-financing.[75] The monopolies established in salt, tobacco, linen and leather also foundered either because of insufficient capital or because they were sold onto others.[76] Most of the liquid capital in Württemberg remained with the *Ehrbarkeit* who had close links to the guilds. Staunch Lutherans, they were disinclined to usury and favoured the just price.[77] Such ventures were anathema to them.

In July 1734 Süss was given control of the mint, which he exploited in order to guarantee the Duke an increase in revenue.[78] Such a position allowed him a guard in livery. That also caused offence.[79] Later he was accused of having debased the coinage, but a ducal commission concluded that the accusation was unfounded. Even during his subsequent trial no charges materialized, despite a re-examination of the evidence several times.[80] Other mints had also been in trouble, given the monetary crisis.[81]

Shortly before Süss' arrival in Stuttgart Carl Alexander had ordered all government employees to contribute one eighth of their annual salaries to the *Rentkammer* (Ducal Treasury), while all new and future employees were to contribute 25 per cent of their first-year wages, later increased, with a proportion going direct to Süss.[82] This salary tax became known as the 'Jew's penny' (*Judengroschen*), a good indication of its reception.[83]

There were other failures: the setting up a trust fund, the so-called *Pupillenkasse*, to control the property of orphans was extended to the orphans of civil servants; it foundered on the hostility of the Estates as an intrusion into privacy.[84] Impressed with the Bank of England, established four decades earlier (1694), and the Vienna *Stadtbank* (City Bank) founded the following decade (1703), Carl Alexander called for the establishment of a Württemberg state bank under the direction of the mint then headed by Süss. This never materialized: civil servants were opposed as were moneylenders, who feared being undercut.[85]

An attempt to set up a lottery in Württemberg was also unsuccessful. Lotteries had done well in Venice, Milan and Rome and were not unheard of in German territories (Hamburg, Frankfurt, Dresden), but games of chance were anathema to devout Lutherans. Süss leased out two lotteries to himself but then sold them on. Accusations that he had enriched himself, however, proved unfounded: he sold at a loss.[86]

Also anathema to Württemberg Lutherans was Carnival, a Catholic holiday preceding Lent, introduced, not by Süss but by the previous Duke at the behest of his mistress in 1715.[87] Alcohol, the wearing of masks and an erotic element offended Protestant moral and religious sensibilities. All officials were ordered to attend; few dared disobey. An exception was the constitutional jurist Johann Jakob Moser who refused and then decided to leave Württemberg service.[88] He would later criticize Süss' death sentence.

Perhaps most controversial of all was the creation of two new departments.[89] The Gratialamt, an office to collect, 'donations of gratitude', was set up in October 1736, headed by Jacob Friedrich Hallwachs who would later be imprisoned for eight years. The Gratialamt offered a sale of offices to prospective applicants, especially the newly created local and central government posts.[90] Depending on the size of the gift, the Board recommended an appointment: the greater the contribution and the more glowing the recommendation, the more prestigious the

appointment. Positions ranged from an overseer at the public bathhouse
to the Bürgermeister of Stuttgart.[91] The selling of offices was at this time
official in France and Austria for the highest positions in the army.[92] This
new development threatened the dominant position of the *Ehrbarkeit*
which had held the monopoly on offices, since jobs were now being
offered to individuals outside their network. To great outrage, traditional
exemptions based on rank were no longer to be taken into account.[93]

The second department, the Fiskalatamt (Fiscal Office), aptly described
as a kangaroo court, was especially notorious.[94] Created from another
body (the *Landesvisitation*), which earlier in the century had been set
up to supervise civil service efficiency, local government finance and
deal with public complaints,[95] it offered, in exchange for payment, to
suspend criminal proceedings against officials for tax evasion or other
irregularities.[96] Rather than wait for the officials to come forward, denun-
ciations were invited, resulting in charges being laid against mayors and
local officials. A former Tübingen law professor, Dr Johann Theodor
Scheffer (1687–1748), now director of the Duke's Cabinet, was put in
charge. Money was extorted from civil officials otherwise exempt from
taxation; in some cases their heirs were being charged, which led to cries
of extortion.[97]

These new offices were subject to abuse; Süss himself lined his own
pockets benefiting from the fees, bribes and profits.[98] His enemies found
such payment from cuts or commission unacceptable.[99] Nevertheless, that
was the terms of business since any salary he drew for specific appoint-
ments was likely (in his mind) to have been of a temporary nature.[100]
Some posts, however, did come with a form of payment (Resident in
Frankfurt at 500 guldens annually and confidential financial adviser at
2,000 florins).[101] In a sense, Süss was merely a salesman, peddling advice
(the adviser) or peddling goods (the merchant) and taking his cut when
feasible.

One of Süss' achievements was to help change the system so that the
inhabitants, once regarded as members of vested interest groups, were
now to be regarded as individuals.[102] Nevertheless, his policies remained

mercantilist, according to which the treasury formed the heart of the state with money being the driving force.[103] His talents lay in extracting wealth, rather than in accumulating wealth or in investing capital.

Süss enabled Jews to settle in parts of Württemberg which had been forbidden by the constitution. Before the reign of Carl Alexander they had acquired the right to reside (as opposed to settle) in a few small towns on land which the then Duke had donated to his mistress Countess Grävenitz. She had also obtained permission for her court Jew, Landauer, to reside in Stuttgart. In 1736 Süss enabled two Jewish families also to reside in Stuttgart as well as six families in Ludwigsburg under the jurisdiction of the Duke.[104] Until then, residence for court Jews had been the exception.[105] In January 1737 the Duke extended the privileges and Jewish immigration began immediately. Given the attitude of the inhabitants of Württemberg to outsiders and in particular to Jews, such measures, so closely associated with Süss, were especially unpopular.

Süss was not without allies in Württemberg. They included those who had loosened their ties to the *Ehrbarkeit* such as Scheffer and the Prelate of Hirsau, Philipp Heinrich Weissensee, whose daughter Magdalena Sibylle was a poet, and who kept Süss informed about Landschaft opinion.[106] Other allies were those who did not come from Württemberg who, without ties to the *Ehrbarkeit*, suffered disadvantages as a consequence. Süss did not mix much socially, but felt able to with Caspar Pfau, a non-Lutheran, a Calvinist from Dessau whose father originated from Saxony-Anhalt, and who had promoted the interests of Countess Würben. In his house faro was played, a popular card game of chance.[107] Against deviant individuals, the conservative Württemberg elites formed a united front and on the death of the Duke would take their revenge and claw back power. Pfau too would take his own revenge after he learned of Süss's alleged relations with his wife and daughter.[108]

As early as October 1735 Carl Alexander had approached the Emperor about granting his financial adviser a title of nobility. Süss claimed that a rise in his status would improve his marriage prospects.[109] It would also improve his status, since noble holders of office had an advantage over non-noble holders.[110] Not surprisingly, the request was turned down. Aside from having earlier made an enemy of the Württemberg envoy to the Vienna court, Christoph Dietrich von Keller, who was involved in the decision, Süss had not considered conversion, and it was unheard of at this time for a non-Christian to be ennobled.[111] This would not be possible before 1789 and even after this date it was exceedingly rare.[112] Nevertheless, such an unprecedented request is evidence of Süss' boundless ambition as well as revealing just how far the Duke was prepared to go on behalf of his adviser.

Süss lived in style: his servants wore livery; he owned precious objects – jewellery, expensive furniture, objets d'art such as Dresden porcelain and Delftware and other costly objects, as well as wine, including champagne.[113] According to an inventory produced for his trial he had over 4,256 engravings, including portraits of European rulers and Roman emperors, various officials and dignitaries. Many were copies of famous works and may in fact have partly been 'stock', since Süss dealt in works of art and the collection has been described as to having been 'formed indiscriminately, without specific direction and also without specific Jewish content'.[114] He had an extensive library, mainly in Frankfurt, with books on law, history and judaica, as well as works by the renegade Roman Jewish historian Josephus and the converted Jew, Christoph David Bernard – the latter he would meet in his prison cell shortly before his execution.[115]

At the time of his arrest Süss had three houses: two in Württemberg and one in Frankfurt. His last Frankfurt residence, which he had been renting since 1735, had thirteen rooms.[116] In June 1736 the Duke provided him with a seven-room house in Ludwigsburg near to the palace, from which several months later Süss offered to move to make way for porcelain manufacture. He then rented a house across from the palace park.[117] Since government business was conducted in Stuttgart, a larger place was required there. Initially, he rented the second and third floors from the Stuttgart mayor, but this proved inadequate. In the autumn of 1736 he bought a grand town house inclusive of furniture and with a large garden from Field Marshall Johann August von Phul. He moved in just eight weeks before his arrest.[118] That house had to be purchased through an intermediary (the government adviser Philipp Jacob Lautz, who came from Mannheim) since Jews, as elsewhere in Germany with the exception of the Palatinate, were forbidden to own land with the proceedings being initiated by the administrator for Stuttgart who following year would be given the task of supervising the execution.[119] The Stuttgart home was by far the grandest with an orangerie, gardens and greenhouses. As with the Duke, even more so with his adviser, such display caused offence in Württemberg but conspicuous consumption enhanced his reputation as a businessman.[120]

Though Süss had become the Duke's most important adviser, the extent of his power has been exaggerated, partly because, as recently pointed out, the sources for this view derive from his trial when it was in the interest of his enemies, intent on clawing back power after the Duke's short and unpopular reign to paint Süss in the darkest of colours. The extent of his room for manoeuvre, however, was carefully circumscribed.[121] For obvious reasons he was excluded from church affairs and maintained that he was neutral in matters of religion. He was also excluded from military affairs, hence he played no role in the Catholic plot which planned a coup (though the plotters managed to destroy at the time any incriminating documents).[122] His sphere was confined to the economic which was also political.[123] Even here, the Duke, decidedly not a weak character, was ultimately always in charge.

That Süss was a Jew was not the only problem, though it was unheard of for one to rise so high, to be so close to the centre of power, and to be entrusted with symbols of office, i.e. of the right to rule, such as a seal and a sword. Such symbols were forbidden to Jews whose status was not only low but also anomalous since they were outside Christendom.[124] He also acted as courtier, a role never before associated with a Jew and which could suggest social disorder – a topsy-turvy world. But he was serving an unpopular Duke, one who had few local ties, who had abandoned Lutheranism, who had pitted himself against the entrenched conservative Estates and who had turned to outsiders for advice. Süss, an outsider, also promoted unpopular policies – or more to the point, unpopular with those that mattered, namely the *Ehrbarkeit*.

Concerned with the security of his position, Süss was careful to obtain a written order for every undertaking and to have everything counter-signed.[125] In the last year, his relations with the Duke are believed to have cooled, though views differ on this.[126] He felt it was time to leave, though apparently as early as 1735 he had been requesting his release.[127] Aside from his growing unpopularity and exclusion from the Catholic plot, he also wanted to pursue his business interests elsewhere. By January 1737, he had begun to wind up some of his Württemberg activities, in particular his private business with the Duke.[128]

On 12 February 1737, precisely one month before the death of the Duke, and after repeated requests, Süss finally obtained his Absolutorium.[129] This was published in the official government paper, which envoys to the Imperial Reichstag in Regensburg would have noticed.[130] As its name suggests, the Absolutorium absolved him of responsibility for his actions on the grounds that he had always been carrying out the Duke's orders.[131] A deed of settlement of his business affairs is dated 8 March 1737, retrospective to July 1735.[132] He would have been free to move on. Four days later the Duke died; the Absolutorium was ignored.

3

Trial and execution (1737–1738)

The death of Duke Carl Alexander occurred on 12 March 1737. It was sudden and unexpected. He was at his Ludwigsburg palace and had been planning to leave the next day for a military inspection tour of the Württemberg fortresses, after which he was to visit a doctor in Danzig whom he had consulted earlier about a wound to his foot. Feeling unwell during the farewell banquet he was hosting, he withdrew early from the celebrations.

The cause of death may have been an embolism on the lung,[1] or a stroke[2] or 'Steckfluss',[3] a common diagnosis at the time, akin to dropsy or choking catarrh, though, given the then-state of medical knowledge, we cannot be certain. According to legend, however, his death was brought on when his valet increased his dose of aphrodisiac; or because a new ballet dancer or singer paid him a visit;[4] or because a visiting Landschaft deputation, which he had turned away, had put him in a violent rage;[5] or because playing cards with his financial adviser had excited him too much.[6] Chroniclers also mention omens which appeared during his final evening: stormy weather with rain, hail and snow while the sun still shone, and the sighting of bats and witches in flight.[7]

Joseph Süss Oppenheimer was at the Ludwigsburg palace at the time of the Duke's death, having journeyed there in a coach from Stuttgart with another non-Württemberger, Philipp Jacob Lautz, a lawyer from Mannheim.[8] Süss returned immediately to Stuttgart, on this occasion sharing a coach with Heinrich Reinhard, Baron von Röder, with whom until then he had worked closely.[9] In a few hours the baron would turn against him. Towards midnight Süss visited the Duchess to pay his condolences while Röder waited for him. It was at this point that the latter ordered the guard to make the arrest though he had no arrest warrant but much to gain. Having worked closely with Süss, he would need to be on the right side of the Estates in the likely event that they tried to wrest back control from the next ruler. Otherwise he too could face arrest. His action would be memorialized in songs and poems. Süss was taken to his elegant Stuttgart residence on the Seegasse and placed under house arrest.[10] His sword was taken from him.[11] One story, often repeated in the accounts, is unfounded, namely that he had tried to escape, reaching the vineyards of Kornwestheim on the Stuttgart outskirts, where Röder arrested him after which the crowds set upon him.[12]

During his planned absence in Danzig the Duke had arranged for control of the government to rest with his wife, along with several trusted men. Süss was not one of these men, though those selected were then friendly to him. In addition to Röder and Lautz, they included the Austrian General Franz Josef von Remchingen and the former Tübingen Professor of Law Scheffer, whom Süss had earlier appointed to act as Oberkanzler (head of the Cabinet) to oversee the legal aspects of government, and Caspar Pfau, a non-Wüttemberger as well as non-Lutheran who earlier had belonged to the clique promoting the interests of Wilhemina von Grävenitz, Countess Würben, the one-time mistress of Carl Alexander's predecessor. As a Württemberg outsider he had been happy to socialize with Süss, another outsider.[13] However, after Süss' death, Pfau, who had returned to Dessau service, is alleged to have published an unflattering portrait of Süss, doubtless motivated by revelations during the trial that both his wife and daughter had been involved with Süss.[14] Apart from Röder, who also from time to time met Süss on social occasions,[15] and Scheffer, none of these men originated from Württemberg. Nor were any, as yet, enemies of Süss', though this would soon change with Röder and later with Pfau.

Rumours were rife. The *Ehrbarkeit* feared a Catholic putsch during the Duke's absence; some apparently even expected another St Bartholomew's Day Massacre which in the late sixteenth century had led to the death of thousands of French Protestants.[16] What the Duke intended is not known, possibly merely the introduction of a *Simultaneum* (the granting of equal rights to Catholics alongside Lutherans), though that in itself would have upset the religious order as established with the Treaty of Westphalia in 1648.[17] Fear and paranoia was so great that the Duke's friend, the Prince-Bishop of Würzberg, Franz von Schönborn, believed that an agent of the Estates had poisoned him.[18] Hatred against Süss also intensified,[19] though as a Jew he would have had little interest in the issue of Catholic rights. According to legend, the members of the guild of smiths had been hard at work forging weapons to defend themselves against a Catholic coup.[20]

The day following the Duke's death the Estates took action: the lead was taken by the privy council, which earlier the Duke had pushed aside. The Duke's will was read out. Since his heir, Carl Eugen (1728–1793), was only nine years old and thus under age the Duke had designated both Schönborn and his wife, the Duchess Maria Augusta, to act as co-regents, along with a distant cousin, the elderly Protestant Carl Rudolf of the Württemberg-Neuenstadt line (1667–1742), a retired general who had spent many years in Danish service. The privy councillors seized the opportunity to overturn Carl Alexander's will: against his express wishes, they excluded the two Catholics, leaving Carl Rudolf to act as sole regent (Landesadministrator). He would give the Estates a free hand.[21] The Duchess protested but to no avail.[22] Indeed, she was even prevented from holding a full Catholic funeral for her husband.[23] She turned to Remchingen to intervene but he prevaricated; one week later on 19 March, along with seventy others, he was arrested and imprisoned.[24]

Having ignored the Duke's express wishes and thus broken the law, the privy council now sought evidence to justify their actions. Additional arrests were made. Süss was not the only one to be imprisoned, though he would be the one most harshly dealt with and the only one to lose his life. The small number of Jews then living in Stuttgart, many too lowly to ever have had dealings with Süss, were accosted.[25] The cashier from the mint, Isaac Samuel Levi, who lived in Süss' grand Stuttgart house, was arrested as were Süss' Jewish secretaries and non-Jews suspected of dealings with

Süss.[26] Not every Württemberg inhabitant supported these actions: the recent changes had been welcomed by some who did not belong to the *Ehrbarkeit* who were pleased to see some privileges disappear.[27]

The confiscation of Süss' property began on 13 March, the day following the Duke's death. It was not yet clear, however, how things would develop.[28] Also arrested were Scheffer and three former officials, low in the hierarchy who had worked closely with Süss in the new financial administration: Johann Friedrich Bühler, Johann Albrecht Metz and Jacob Friedrich Hallwachs, the last mentioned having been brought to Stuttgart by Süss to head the hated Gratialamt and preside over the sale of offices. On 20 March they were moved, along with Süss, to the hill-top fortress of Hohenneuffen some fifteen miles north-west of Stuttgart.[29] Süss' house was sealed, his papers confiscated. His correspondence written in the cursive Hebrew script was turned over to the former rabbi, now Christian convert, Christoph David Bernard, the lector in Oriental Languages at the Württemberg university Tübingen for translation. Bernard's books could be found in Süss' library in Frankfurt am Main.[30] The two men would eventually meet the day before the execution in the condemned cell; Bernard would write and publish a vivid account of that meeting.[31]

A decree was published inviting all subjects to lodge any complaints against Süss or his accomplices (Metz, Hallwachs, Bühler and Scheffer) with the Duke Administrator.[32] These accomplices, though not in Süss' pocket, had broken their ties with the *Ehrbarkeit* by showing a willingness to support Carl Alexander's reforms.[33] Several months later, in September, Remchingen appeared in court, giving his word of honour to return after settling some Imperial business in Vienna. He then absconded, protected by the Emperor, who refused to send him back.[34] Scheffer was eventually released and even allowed to take up his Tübingen law professorship the following year. Metz and Hallwachs got off lightly by testifying against Süss, who later accused them of betrayal while Bühler, whom Süss did not curse, remained in prison for a further eight years.[35] Süss was the only one to lose his life in what would be referred to post-1945 as a case of judicial murder.[36]

Until 21 March Süss had been addressed with respect as Herr Finanzienrat Joseph Süss Oppenheimer. On that day he was addressed as 'Jud Süss Oppenheimer' (the Jew Süss Oppenheimer) and subsequently simply as 'Jud Süss', the name by which he would thereafter be best known.[37] The judicial tribunal remained at Hohenneuffen until 11 April.[38] Süss' interrogators included his personal enemy, Johann Christoph von Pflug, a government adviser (Regierungsrat), and Court Lawyer (Hofgerichtsadvokat) Dr Philipp Friedrich Jäger plus two court assessors (Johann Jacob Dann and Wilhelm Eberhard Faber).[39] During the interrogation, which lasted from 28 March to 1 April, Süss was asked to respond to 170 questions ranging from taxation to personal matters.[40] Initially the charges were vaguely formulated: Süss and his accomplices had perpetrated 'fraudulent, godless acts of violence and schemes ruinous to the country'.[41] At this stage he seems not to have grasped the precariousness of his own position since he requested an audience with the Duke Administrator and also offered to advise him in future.[42]

The interrogators were not solely interested in Süss' relations with the Duke or his financial and political activities. They took an unusually long time in extracting details about his sexual contacts. Süss himself divulged nothing.[43] The puritanical burghers may have had a prurient interest but such evidence also served their purpose since it provided an opportunity to expose behaviour which contravened Württemberg moral codes, perpetrated by a Jew serving a Catholic ruler. On a deeper level, it was also a Jew defiling Württemberg women, well before the term *Rassenschande* (race defilement) had been coined and even if 'race' was not yet an issue, the Jew was still the other and a transgression had occurred.

Luciana Fischer, Süss' mistress of just over one year, was arrested. Questioned frequently and at length about their sexual relations, she remained loyal to Süss throughout. Despite a medical examination when almost five months pregnant, she succeeded in concealing the pregnancy up until the delivery of a son in prison in September.[44] This may seem surprising but given the then-state of medical knowledge and taboos about males examining females an accurate diagnosis of such a common condition was not always possible.[45] She was kept in a house of correction where the child, described as sickly, died a few months after his birth and one month before his father's death, his frail constitution hardly helped by prison conditions.[46] Later released, Luciana disappeared. Despite rumours to the contrary, also repeated by historians,[47] Süss had no living descendants.

Rape, as opposed to seduction, was another topic to interest Süss' interrogators. Catharina Agatha Reyher, recently widowed at the time of her interrogation, had before her brief marriage been advised by an official to see Süss to put in a personal plea on behalf of her betrothed who had been in danger of losing his job. Süss had met her in his dressing gown and nightshirt, she finally admitted to her interrogators, and had thrown her on the bed and 'had his way with her'. Despite this, she paid him several more morning visits, when he still continued to use force but also promised to help her betrothed with his debts, which he then failed to do. These meetings took place five or six weeks before her wedding.[48]

Christina Dorothea Hettler, daughter of an official from the village of Berg near Stuttgart, recently married in October 1737 to a government secretary by the name of Johann Friedrich Faber, confessed after intense questioning to having sexual relations with Süss but also, unusually, only after the examining judge Jäger decided to visit her in her own home for the interrogation. Given the threat to her honour, position and self-esteem, she finally broke down, admitting to sexual relations with Süss and providing details such as that he had practiced *coitus interruptus*.[49]

Both stories would provide material for the Veit Harlan film. Christina Dorothea becomes Dorothea (the first name doubtless being dropped because she was played by Harlan's wife Kristina Söderbaum). She marries a character whose last name is Faber (the last name of Hettler's husband and also of one of the court assessors, probably the two were related), but he is arrested before their marriage is consummated. She visits Süss to plead on his behalf and is met by him in his dressing gown.

When his attempt at seduction fails, he throws her on the bed and rapes her.

Another incident also later surfaced in the film: this concerned a mother and daughter. In February 1737 during Carnival (the court celebration introduced by the previous Duke), shortly before the Duke's death, two masked women arrived at Süss' grand town house 'soliciting'. The wife of a government clerk, concerned about payment owed to her husband, consulted a Jew in contact with Süss who advised that she see Süss in person. She chose to send her daughter instead, either to Süss at his home or at the masked ball which he was organizing. The daughter, who was shy, arrived at Süss' house, accompanied by a maid. Süss invited the daughter to step into his office, unaccompanied, to discuss her request. The office (or so the story goes) also doubled as his bedroom. At this point, full of remorse, the mother rushed in. Having confessed to her husband that she had given permission for their daughter to attend the masked ball (but not about the soliciting then taking place at Süss' quarters), she was told sharply to bring the daughter back.[50] In the Harlan film, the mother persuades the father to allow the bashful daughter to attend the masked ball at which Süss procures her not for himself but for the Duke.

Since the Terra film company had sent the first scriptwriter and the dramaturge to the Stuttgart archive, where these documents are housed, and their visit was exceedingly brief (one day), it is highly likely that even if no specific request appears in the letter dated 23 February 1939, the archivist would have been well aware of the kind of material likely to interest a scriptwriter, namely Süss' sexual activities rather than his tax policies.[51] Though extensive historical research is not the norm for historical films, it is nevertheless of interest that in this particular case some research was actually undertaken, even if hardly extensive, limited in scope and prescriptive in nature.

The criminal proceedings against Süss began on 22 May 1737 in a specially convened court linked to the privy council and under the chairmanship of a privy councillor, Ernst Conrad von Gaisberg. The

other examining judges included the four men involved in the interrogation plus two court assessors Eberhard Ludwig Bardili and Johann
Georg Georgii. Two Tübingen professors of law were appointed to advise
on the legality of the sentence: Dr Georg Friedrich Harpprecht Senior
and Professor Dr Wolfgang Schöpff.[52] From this point onwards it looked
highly likely that Süss would be condemned to death.[53]

On 30 May, Süss was moved, along with the other prisoners, to
another fortress, Hohenasperg, some twenty miles south-east of Stuttgart,
thought to be more secure. There had been fears that Süss, in particular,
through bribery, might escape.[54] It was there that the specially convened
trial began on 4 June and ended on 11 September. Over 1,000 questions
were put to Süss with the sole aim of extracting a confession. Acting on
behalf of the Estates, the prosecution was eager to undo the damage they
believed had been done by Carl Alexander. What we know about Süss'
own role during his four-year association with the Duke derives from
the answers he gave to those questions framed and put to him by his
enemies.[55] It was safer for the *Ehrbarkeit* to blame the Jew, the outsider,
rather than the hereditary ruler. Süss became the scapegoat and his trial
has aptly been described as a 'show trial'.[56]

Once Süss realized the hopelessness of his situation, he began to lose
his self-confidence.[57] When a confession was not forthcoming, living
conditions were made less agreeable. Confined to a damp, unheated cell,
he was put in chains, his right arm shackled to his right foot. Torture,
it was claimed, was not used, though it was generally used against Jews
in the German territories at this time.[58] The interrogators, however, had
been instructed to ensure that no reference to torture appeared in the
record.[59] In any case, the discomfort of the chain should qualify as a form
of torture.[60] An officer was with Süss day and night; he was forbidden
visitors, letters, books or writing material. He refused to take any food
not prescribed by his religion, eating only eggs, white bread, tea and
sugar. For two or three days a week he also fasted.[61] He began to pray in
Hebrew and read books in Hebrew. He lost weight; smaller handcuffs
had to be obtained. By September these chains were removed at the

request of his jailer, who feared that they might cause the death of his greatly weakened prisoner.[62]

At the beginning of August, and unknown to Süss, his recently widowed mother was arrested and also held in Hohenasperg: her offence was to have briefly entered Württemberg territory without paying the charge for Jews when on a journey to Heidelberg to visit a son from her second marriage. Since her son was imprisoned, she feared the worse, but her fears proved unfounded: she was released after three days and never even questioned about him or his activities.[63]

The relations of mother and son were apparently strained but the mother also appears feisty. She expected business to come her way (or rather her second husband's way), once Süss was in a position to help and was disappointed when this did not happen. From his perspective, Süss may well have found his mother an embarrassment and thus bad for business.[64] A few weeks before his execution she returned to Stuttgart hoping to obtain from the Württemberg state, which had confiscated her son's property, a sum she believed Süss owed her late husband for business undertaken on his behalf. Summoned to court in early January 1738 to explain her case, she even dared refuse to attend on that day because it was the sabbath. She finally appeared before the examining judges on 14 January, now also putting in a claim for the old Heidelberg house, declaring that it had been her property and requesting that the documents which related to the original sale be returned to her. According to the judge, the documents could not be found – they were in fact then in Süss' Frankfurt office. In any case, Süss claimed the ownership of the house, though he did try to ensure that payment be made of the amount owed to his late stepfather. In the end, the mother had little choice but to settle for the reduced sum on offer from the court.[65]

Süss' mother also put in a request to visit her son, pointing out that it was 'natural' for a mother to want to do this. At the same time she was careful to distance herself from him, given his 'transformation' and 'unjustifiable behaviour'. Though she agreed to the presence of an escort during the visit and to speak with her son only in German rather than in Yiddish, her request was eventually turned down, after which she left, keen to be out of Württemberg before the day of execution.[66]

Süss maintained his innocence throughout: he had done nothing without the Duke's knowledge or authorization and claimed protection from the Absolutorium.[67] He also promised to make good any loss or damage caused to anyone as a result of his role in the two hated offices: the Fiskalatamt, responsible for the kangaroo court, and the Gratialamt, responsible for the sale of offices. Ultimately, the real charge was that Süss had got above himself: an upstart, who had wielded power, a Jew who had behaved freely with the Duke and with Christian women, who had exploited his subordinates, overstepped both written and unwritten laws and, finally but possibly the most damning, introduced changes unpopular with the *Ehrbarkeit*.[68]

Assigned to defend Süss was a Stuttgart lawyer, Michael Andreas Mögling, though Süss had requested that his defence lawyer not come from Württemberg. As a Jew he also had the right to make an appeal to the authorities outside the Duchy (in Wetzlar as well as Vienna), but this was disallowed, despite a request put in by his brother Daniel to the authorities. The Württemberg government maintained that they could deal with 'this much talked about Jewish matter'.[69] Mögling was merely expected to go through the motions: important documents were withheld and even access to Süss was, at times, denied him.[70] Süss himself expressed outrage at the legal irregularities when everything that he had done had been at the Duke's express wishes for which the Absolutorium was proof. But this was a sham trial.

Aware that his influential contacts had abandoned him (the Duchess, and the rulers from the courts at Hessen-Darmstadt and Cologne), Süss requested a visit from a Catholic or Protestant clergyman, possibly from outside Württemberg, someone who was above suspicion, who could act on his behalf and who would, if possible, also secure him an audience with the Duke Administrator.[71] He was made to wait three months before his request was acted on and then on 4 December, shortly before the court reached its unsurprising verdict, Georg Conrad Rieger, a gymnasium teacher and Lutheran clergyman of the devout Pietist persuasion, who preached from a Stuttgart church and whose sermons were often published, appeared at Hohenasperg, sent on behalf of the Estates. He was intent on persuading Süss to convert which would not have saved his life, but merely his soul, which for Rieger, if not for Süss, was no minor matter. It was normal practice to hand a Jew over to a Christian pastor for a 'battle of religions to take place' and to provide the pastor with a unique opportunity to fulfil a long-standing dream of conversion. Generally, Jews were willing to convert if their lives were spared but the authorities were unwilling to grant that concession.[72] It is purely speculative what Süss would have done had there been the slightest chance that conversion would have saved him. But this was never a possibility; it could not have absolved him of the serious crimes of which he was accused. After the execution Rieger published an account of the meeting. He quotes Süss as saying to him: 'I am a Jew and remain a Jew. I would not become a Christian even if I could become Roman Emperor. To change one's religion is a matter for a free man and ill becomes a prisoner.'[73]

That Süss returned to the Jewish religion is likely to have been for psychological comfort. Earlier when seeking ennoblement, he had not considered conversion when it certainly would have been to his advantage. Nor did he now when facing death. This suggests that he had never abandoned his religious identity as distinct from religious practice, and that no matter how high he rose or how much he appeared the cavalier, he had no intention of embracing Christianity (unlike his two half-brothers who may not have had a choice). It may also have been a matter of pride. Moreover, conversion for a 'libertine' might not have run smoothly. Being a Jew was part of his identity even if, when times had been good, he had chosen not to practise the religion. In reply to one of the questions put during his early interrogation, he had described himself as a freethinker. It may also of course have been to his financial advantage to have remained a Jew since his business had mainly been with other Jews, while not practising also opened doors socially. Now abandoned by those whom he had hoped would come to his aid, he turned to the religion he had stopped practising, doubtless for solace. Only extreme prison conditions had made possible his religious awakening which suggests that he had never wholly abandoned it.

A number of charges were mentioned during the trial but proved difficult to substantiate: debasement of coinage due to a lack of evidence; crimes against the ruler as too vague; high treason as inapplicable since Süss did not come from Württemberg; blasphemy since he was not a Christian. On 13 December 1737 the verdict was simply guilty of the 'perpetration of detestable abuses on gentlemen and people' with the penalty being death. The mode of execution was to be hanging as befit someone of low status; the body was to be displayed in an iron cage, an even greater stigma – 'a monument to infamy'.[74] The judges' decision had been unanimous and had the full backing of the privy council, though one nineteenth-century Württemberg historian would claim that one judge, Professor Georg Harprecht, had dissented, on the grounds that, although Süss deserved death, there was no provision for this in the penal code. This error would be repeated in subsequent historical accounts.[75]

On 25 January 1738, after some hesitation, the Duke Administrator, Karl Rudolf, who had qualms but was under considerable pressure, finally agreed to sign the death warrant with the oft-quoted remark: 'It is a rare occurrence for a Jew to have to pay the bill for Christian scoundrels'.[76] And the distinguished Württemberg-born constitutional jurist, Johann Jacob Moser, who had left Württemberg service two years before Süss' execution, and who later returned only to come in conflict with Carl Alexander's son, Carl Eugen, and then suffer imprisonment, observed that 'circumcised as well as uncircumcised, and for the most part worst scoundrels than Süss, still go about as honest men, free and unpunished'.[77] Such punishment fell mainly on outsiders and individuals of low status.[78] Süss was an outsider to Württemberg and, as a Jew also of low status. His execution might even function as a 'sacrificial rite that purged society'.[79]

Süss did not hear the verdict. His jailer at Hohenasperg merely informed him that he was to be moved to Stuttgart. Given an elegant scarlet taffeta coat (customary for the condemned), a waistcoat and new stockings in the same colour, as well as a three-cornered hat, he was put back in the chains, which seven weeks earlier had been removed. On 30 January he travelled in a carriage to Stuttgart, accompanied by grenadiers – two seated beside him, two on the driver's seat with others acting as escorts.[80] This was a reversal of the victor's triumphal procession, derived from Roman ritual and now part of Baroque ceremonial. It functioned as a procession of humiliation, the Jew at last made subordinate with order restored. When earlier, a few days after his arrest, Süss had been transported to Hohenneuffen turbulent street scenes occurred: Süss was showered with pig's excrement and hit in the face with a pig's tail, hardly desirable for anyone, but this was intended as a grave insult for a Jew for whom the pig was unclean.[81] The third procession of humiliation, which Süss would undergo, would be to the site of execution. [82]

Messengers announced Süss' arrival in Stuttgart; he was led to the condemned cell in the *Herrenhaus* where the diet met, overlooking the main square.[83] He refused all food and, at first, also all drink. A tin beaker he found insulting, demanded his silver one and finally agreed to drink water from a jug, but for the next six days, until his death, he refused to eat.[84]

On the following day, 31 January, Süss was brought before the court and told to prepare himself for execution in the next four days, though he was not told the manner of death. Asked if he had anything to say he replied:

> I will die a Jew. I am wronged. An injustice is being done to me. I have not yet been properly cross-examined and no external counsel has been brought to defend me as was done for the other defendants. I am to be offered up as the sacrifice for the whole of Württemberg to the privileged interests of a few families. I appeal to

my judges before the judgment-seat of God. In all my deeds I have only sought to promote the well-being of the country.[85]

He was led back to the condemned cell.

Offered the services of either a Protestant or a Catholic priest Süss refused both. His preference was a rabbi from Frankfurt am Main or Mannheim, failing that, no one; he wanted to die a Jew.[86] Against his express wishes, that evening two Stuttgart clergymen appeared in his cell, both from the same Stuttgart church: Vicar Immanuel Hoffmann and Deacon Christoph Conrad Heller. Visits from clergymen were not uncommon and all to the good if the prisoner recanted or, as in this case, converted, since another soul had been saved. Hoffmann paid many visits and proved most persistent.[87] (The day before the execution a greatly weakened but exasperated Süss even threatened to hit him, if he did not stop his entreaties.)[88]

Süss remained firm; he wished to die a Jew and refused to be drawn into any theological questions.[89] Undeterred, Hoffmann told Süss that he had committed many crimes, including adultery, punishable by death, which he claimed covered any sexual relations, even if both parties were unmarried or widowed and that this was also a crime in Jewish law.[90] This seems to have been the source for the belief, often subsequently repeated, that in Württemberg a law existed, though then no longer in force, forbidding sexual relations between Christians and Jews.[91] In fact such a law did once exist, but capital punishment had been replaced by banishment and after the middle of the seventeenth century even that had died out.[92] In the 1939 film, which had its premiere five years after the introduction of the Nuremberg Laws, the infringement of this law is cited as the reason for the execution of Süss (as in the 1934 film though in Lion Feuchtwanger's novel it was described as in abeyance).

Süss requested a Hebrew prayer book and a visit from Jews. Two Jews were brought to him on 1 February: Marx Nathan, a court factor, resident in Stuttgart for over thirty years, then in his late sixties, and a leading figure in the tiny Jewish community.[93] He had testified against Süss, though Süss did not know this. The second Jew was Soloman

Schächter, a slaughterer, who would later publish a pamphlet about Süss depicting him as a martyr to the Jewish faith.[94] Süss' relations with such Jews had been ambivalent: he did business with them but lorded it over them and, presumably, drove hard bargains from a position of strength.[95]

Accompanying Nathan and his son-in-law was the Christian convert Bernard from Tübingen University, whose books could be found in Süss' library. Shortly after Süss' arrest he had been brought in to translate his business letters written in Hebrew. It was in these last four days that Süss and Bernard finally met. Bernard was decidedly anti-Jewish. Previously a rabbi in Poland, he had arrived in Germany penniless and soon converted. Anti-Jewish propaganda provided him with a livelihood.[96] His presence, however, was merely to ensure that Süss said nothing untoward to his Jewish visitors in either Hebrew or Yiddish.[97] Yet Bernard seems to have been moved by Süss' piteous state when writing about his meeting:

> It is almost unbelievable … how ghastly I found the sight of this wretched man. Once so splendid and handsome, what remained was scarcely more than a hovering corpse soon to be totally decayed; pain and fear, not worms, had gnawed his flesh, and in any case, his dissembling face had become even more repellent because of the growth of a thick black beard like moss on a skull. The once alert eyes were like two extinguished candles and their remaining movement so strange that it was impossible to gauge the various emotions. The rest of his attire contributed further to this extraordinary and extreme transformation. The stubble on his head he covered with a green cap. A silk handkerchief was wound around his neck. About his body hung a short and wide coat that some time ago, during his imprisonment, had come to ruin as he himself had. In short, he looked to me more like a slave who, freed at last from harsh servitude, carried about him the signs of his previous wretchedness to awaken Christian compassion.[98]

Had Bernard's new-found Christian compassion been awakened? Or was he merely attempting to show how the mighty are fallen – how Süss, the Jew, had not escaped his destiny for which he was now paying a terrible price? After the execution he wrote an account of his meeting with Süss in which this passage appears. Though never deviating from the correct line, it is apparent that the lowly scholarly convert felt the sheer force of Süss' personality as well as some awe in his presence.[99] After the execution he forbade Jews to mourn him after one of the two Jews whom he had escorted had issued a manifesto calling on fellow Jews to honour Süss' memory as a martyr to his faith. That ban is evidence that Bernard had no intention of jeopardizing his livelihood and had not been overwhelmed by compassion.[100]

Despite his piteous state, and without legal training, Süss was still able to point out the legal irregularities to his visitors, one of whom included the secretary, responsible for recording the judicial proceedings, Johann Philipp Pregizer. The judges, according to Süss, should have included three men from Württemberg (Lutheran), plus six from outside – three Catholic and three Calvinists, though when informed that this was not possible, he had reduced this to at least three from outside Württemberg. He also offered to relinquish all his property and hand over 100,000 Reichstaler to the poor.[101]

Four days later and early on the morning of 4 February, Süss, his chains now removed, was led back to the Herrenhaus where a large crowd had assembled. Some 1,200 soldiers kept the marketplace clear. While the judges wore black, Süss wore scarlet. A chronicler records that as soon as Süss entered the courtroom he fell on his knees, begging for mercy. The executioner told him to be quiet; Süss replied that he was fighting for his life.[102] The chairman broke in three a thin white stave, flinging one of the pieces at the feet of the prisoner. That indicated death. Protesting his innocence, Süss raged at the injustice. The judge asked the executioner if he had understood the sentence; replying in the affirmative he then tied up his prisoner before taking him back to his cell to be given his last meal. Despite the attempt to produce a meal in accordance with Jewish dietary laws, Süss refused the food and now also the water.[103]

Shortly thereafter, Süss was taken to the place of execution on the outskirts of Stuttgart, travelling in a gallows cart, seated on a chair next to the executioner. Grenadiers marched at the front, rear and side.

Crowds lined the road. Larger crowds, estimated at between 10,000 and 12,000, awaited him at the iron gallows, the highest in the German Reich, originally constructed in 1596 for the execution of an alchemist from Moravia.[104] Contemporary illustrations probably do not exaggerate.[105] The judges arrived before him to take up their privileged vantage point in the specially constructed viewing platform – they had left the courtroom as soon as the sentence had been pronounced. Three additional viewing platforms were also erected for other privileged observers.[106]

At the foot of the gallows, Süss' shoes were removed along with his neck scarf, the latter replaced by the rope. Four hangmen pushed and shoved him up the forty-nine-rung ladder. Struggling to defend himself, he lost his hat half-way up, his wig also fell to the ground.[107] After reaching the top of the ladder, the executioner shoved him into the large iron cage, recently constructed by the guild of locksmiths, painted in red and gold stripes. Hanging twelve metres above ground and extending beyond the main wooden gallows by two metres, it was linked by a plank which Süss was forced to cross.[108] Once in the cage, the rope was pulled tight: Süss was throttled rather than hanged. Fifteen minutes later, once there were no signs of life, the rope was removed and replaced with a chain. The cage was then shut and locked in three places with a thick chain added for good measure.[109] Süss' corpse, hanging high above the gallows, was now on display.

Chroniclers mention that while ascending the ladder Süss had accused others of intriguing against him (the prisoners, Hallwachs and Bühler and his business rival Don Barthelemi Pancorbo d'Ayala et Guerra). The drummers were ordered to beat their drums to drown out his voice.[110] Other accounts mention that he was praying loudly.[111] At the foot of the gallows stood the two Protestant clergymen, Hoffmann and Heller (a Catholic priest was also in the vicinity, though not by the gallows). Before Süss breathed his last, Hoffmann taunted him: 'You stubborn Jew … Jesus whom you have denied will be your judge.'[112] Süss' last words were the final words of a Hebrew prayer, namely *Adenoy echod*, which means 'the Lord is one'. The crowd below, it was said, misunderstood the words, believing they sounded like the German *nicht allein*, which means 'not alone'.[113]

That Süss was executed in a cage gave rise to several legends: he was now a bird in a cage, an appropriate form of punishment since a crude German word for the sexual act is *vögeln*, deriving from the German word for bird (*Vogel*),[114] or that it referred to a joke that Süss is alleged to have once made: 'They cannot hang me higher than the gallows'.[115] There were rumours that the Jews of Fürth, a small town in Franconia near to Nuremberg, some 140 miles to the north-east of Stuttgart, also had their own legend: on the day after the execution some of their number had come to take down the body and replace it with another.[116]

Aside from displaying the corpse, the cage also ensured that the body could not be removed.[117] It remained on display for six years. Once Carl Alexander's son, Carl Eugen, came of age and the regency ended, Süss' body was taken down and buried at the foot. Several decades later in 1788, on the eve of the French Revolution, when Carl Eugen was still on the throne, the gallows were finally removed, in response to complaints – an indication perhaps that after a half-century a new sensibility was emerging in Württemberg.[118]

1. Portrait of Joseph Süss Oppenheimer, by Ferdinand Stenglein, likely to have been taken from a formal portrait commissioned by Süss himself. Now in a prison cell he gazes at the viewer. Below in an inset appears the gallows with the cage suspended above and a statement that this is a true likeness, that he was hanged in his fortieth year and that his execution was witnessed by a huge number of people.
Württembergisches Landesbibliothek, Graphics Collection, Stuttgart.

2. The main Stuttgart square where crowds gather to watch the procession to the execution site. The insets show Süss at the height of his power and then as a prisoner. Below: the execution site where huge crowds watch Süss being dragged up the ladder. Guards and two members of the clergy stand beneath. Artist, Jacob Gottlieb Thelo; Engraver, Lucas Conrad Pfanzelt.
Württembergisches Landesbibliothek, Graphics Collection, Stuttgart.

4

The legend

In his own lifetime Joseph Süss Oppenheimer was much discussed, occasionally admired (by those who benefitted from his advice), but more often reviled. His trial and execution aroused interest well beyond the frontiers of Württemberg: to 'almost half of Europe', according to one contemporary observer.[1] The legend began shortly after his arrest, when he acquired the new name of Jud Süss (in English *the* Jew Süss).

Unlike myth, which is wholly fanciful, legend suggests a grain of truth and in this case there had been an historic figure, a court Jew, whose ascent in Württemberg was sudden and swift. Beyond that, however, much would be untrue. Nevertheless, the legend would endure for more than two centuries. Many would subsequently try to tell his story – for good or ill – failing to separate legend from fact.

Rumours of Süss' illegitimacy first surfaced during his trial. In his account of his prison meeting with Süss, the Christian convert Christoph David Bernard wrote that 'some say his father was an officer'.[2] Johann Heinrich Zedler's *Grosses Universal-Lexicon*, the only encyclopaedia of its kind in the German language, accorded nine columns to the entry on Süss in the 1744 edition, as extensive as that for Emperor Charles V, considerably more than for Galileo, and a third longer than for Charlemagne, though to put this in perspective recent events were deemed important and Carl Alexander was accorded even more space (twenty-three columns). Süss was a 'bastard of a Christian' but his father was not identified.[3] The author was the scholarly Michael Ranfft who had published the entry on Jews in the encyclopedia's 1735 edition; his source for claiming Süss' illegitimacy was the Süss 'biography' by the pseudonymous Arnoldus Liberius published in 1738 which had claimed that Süss' mother had begun an affair during her marriage rather than before.[4]

One of the examining magistrates, Philipp Friedrich Jäger, apparently also produced an account which was more specific, though he may only have been writing down what had already become common currency when he stated Süss' father to be the notorious Freiherr (Baron) Georg Eberhard von Heidersdorf who in 1693 (several years – rather than months – before the birth of Süss) had surrendered Heidelberg to the French.[5] A satirical poem about Heidersdorf's paternity was also already in circulation in the year of the execution.[6]

Thus some time after the arrest of Süss, his spectacular rise and even more spectacular fall became linked with the somewhat less spectacular fall – but hardly spectacular rise (given his noble background) of Heidersdorf who in 1693 had surrendered the fortress of Heidelberg to the French. Heidelberg also happened to be Süss' birthplace, though Heidersdorf's removal occurred several years before his actual birth, if we accept the birth date which Süss gave at his trial. Initially, it was suggested that Süss' mother had begun her affair with Heidersdorf when a married woman, but this then changed (for obvious chronological reasons) to having occurred before she married.

In any case, whether before or after, the problem remains that after 1693 Heidersdorf was no longer in the area and free to conduct an affair. His paternity therefore was only possible if several years could be added to the age, which Süss gave at his trial, as well as a convincing motive for why he found such 'deception' necessary. Vanity was an explanation put forward at a much later date.[7] It was never questioned why, when fighting for his life, nor earlier when seeking ennoblement, he had not claimed noble (though illegitimate) descent when it could have proved an advantage. Without a plausible explanation for why such information had been withheld, aristocratic parentage could not be established nor a link between two men, born a generation apart, each active in the same south-western corner of Germany both of whom met an ignominious end.

When during interrogation, Süss was asked his age he replied that he had been born in February or March 1698 – such vagueness being explained by the fact that he used the Jewish lunar calendar. This information was not challenged.[8] Moreover, beneath a portrait of Süss produced shortly after his death the words appear: 'executed before a large crowd in Stuttgart, on 4 February, in his fortieth year'.[9] We can therefore assume that up until the time of his arrest, as well as during the early stage of his incarceration, his birth date had not been in dispute, even if earlier there was some disbelief that a Jew could be so at ease at court. That helped feed doubts about his parentage, namely that his father could not have been a Jew. Once his name was linked with Heidersdorf's, his actual age was disputed.

Süss' reversal of fortune – his life, trial and execution – became an eighteenth-century media event, the subject of books, pamphlets and broadsides, the last mentioned telling his story in both images and text as well as drama.[10] Artists, writers and publishers seized the opportunity, publishers especially encouraged by the large turnout for the execution.[11] The production of prints (engravings and woodcuts) began appearing shortly after Süss' arrest to coincide with the Easter fairs in Frankfurt and Leipzig – the first publication appearing as early as Easter 1737, just a few weeks after the arrest. Such material was produced quickly and in large numbers as the events unfolded.[12] Most were available by 1738, the year of the execution.[13] The broadsides were sold by street traders in cities like Vienna or by hawkers at annual fairs.[14] The places of publication went well beyond the borders of Württemberg and south-west Germany to include Prague, Breslau (then part of Poland), Amsterdam, Basle, Bologna and Antwerp.[15] They depicted Süss' rise and fall, especially the latter – his incarceration, sentencing, route to the gallows, execution and finally his corpse suspended in the cage. Such images, one would assume, were popular with the illiterate.[16] But as they were usually accompanied by text, it is clear that they were also intended for a literate market and would provide moral instruction.[17]

From the Reformation to the eighteenth century, the topical event proved to be a favourite subject for illustration and instruction for the

general populace, informing them about extraordinary natural events
such as a comet or of the ceremonial events of Baroque culture.
Especially popular in the eighteenth century was 'the world upside down',
an inversion of the social order, which included disruptions to the social
order such as criminal activity. This also fed the taste for sensationalism.
Süss illustrated well this inversion or disruption to the social order since
he was a Jew who fell from high office *and* a criminal, not only because
he was tried and executed but also because it was assumed a Jew was
inherently criminal.[18]

The extant prints consist of portraits of Süss, narrative accounts of
his life and execution as well as allegorical compositions. Repeated in a
number of the broadsides is one particular image, which suggests that it
was based on an official portrait, possibly one originally commissioned
by Süss himself – two portraits are listed in the inventory of his property
which was produced for the court.[19] An elegant Süss, in three-quarter
pose, wears a wig and a heavily embroidered jacket. With posture erect
and an alert look he gazes out at the spectator (or artist). His face is
full, somewhat puffy, his eyes large, his brows thick and dark and his
nose straight. This portrait, unadorned, appears as the frontispiece to
an account, which has been described as 'completely neutral', unlike
others published at the time.[20] The author was the Lutheran clergyman
Georg Conrad Rieger who in December 1737 had visited Süss in his cell
on behalf of the Estates. The artist Elias Ba(e)ck (1679–1747) was also
the publisher.[21] In a sermon shortly after the execution, Rieger found
something good to say about Süss:

> This Süss did not die as an Epicurean, he believed in God and the Holy Ghost [*sic*], the
> immortality of the soul and eternity. Was he not in this far better than many … numbered
> among the multitude of Christians? Take heed lest this Jew do not damn you at the
> Judgement Day. He called on the name of the Lord with every breath until the end.[22]

The same face also reappears in some of the broadsides, but accompanied by a small inset or cartouche where normally one might find

a coat of arms, but is now replaced by the gallows as in that by the Augsburg engraver Mathias Deisch (c.1718–1789) which appears as the frontispiece for two of the published accounts.[23] In addition to a cartouche, the same portrait sometimes appears framed by devils, rabbis, iron chains, padlocks and sacks of money.

The same face appears in B(a)eck's own series – he was not only a copper plate engraver and publisher, but also a painter and had made the journey to Stuttgart from Augsburg, a centre for engraving some 100 miles east. Along with other artists, he was present at the execution but, unusually, also the sentencing.[24] Nevertheless, he had no access to the condemned cell to witness Süss' final breakfast, despite his claims to have drawn from nature an 'accurate' image of Süss, showing him seated on his bed as though for his portrait, well-fed, wearing what purports to be informal dress (a three-quarter length robe and a floppy cap). Next to a pile of books on a low table before him, dishes are laid out with their contents listed. Not only did no artist have access to Süss in prison but this particular image also contradicts the wasted Süss in Bernard's account of his meeting with him three days before his execution.[25]

Emphasizing its didactic purpose, one portrait appears accompanied by the following description:

> The great lord who misused favour through evil advice
> As this insolent Jew Süss Oppenheimer did
> Whose spirit and arrogance taken with debauchery
> Who must like Haman finally go to the gallows.[26]

The Jew has become the evil Haman, the one-time enemy of the Jews, according to the Book of Esther. Lutherans knew this story – Martin Luther had included the Book of Esther in his version of the Bible and had identified Protestants with the Israelites.[27] (This of course did not interfere with his attack on the Jews.)

Such images, it is interesting to note, were not in themselves negative: no visual distortions or exaggerations, no clues that the subject is a villain, aside from one extant example where he appears in flames, obviously in hell, half-dressed as a savage (the other): conch shells hanging from his neck and his wig at his feet. Even if some images have been lost, this particular one is untypical.[28] Instead, villainy is usually emphasized by the accompanying text, or the cartouche, or the symbols which frame the image. This follows a tradition of depicting criminals and differs from medieval paintings, where Jews were easily identified by their exaggerated features or from the antisemitic imagery of the nineteenth and twentieth centuries.[29] Some broadsheets illustrate Süss' downfall, almost comic-like, step-by-step, in multiple images, not dissimilar to William Hogarth's 'A Rake's Progress', which had appeared in print form three years prior to Süss' execution. Admittedly that was on a different artistic level since the images of Süss are often quite crude.

Artists also used their imagination. In one engraving published in Basel Süss' female mourners weep at the base of the gallows. Overhead ravens circle the suspended cage as Süss' mistress, Luciana Fischer, flies to him on a devil's pitchfork with a billet doux in her hand.[30] (A popular belief was that prostitutes were transformed into witches.)[31] One of the mourners, singled out by her dark robe and wimple, is dressed like the Virgin Mary at the crucifixion, lamenting her son.[32] One might assume this to be dangerous territory for an artist but apparently Christian iconography was permissible even if conflating the Virgin Mary with one of Süss' mistresses might undermine the message.

Images illustrating the reversal of fortune accompany one of the early Süss 'biographies'. Four images appear together on one page: the portrait; the procession to the gallows; the corpse in the cage; and the goddess Fortuna atop a globe. Süss (on Fortuna's right) in eighteenth-century dress (three-quarter length jacket, breeches and three-corner felt hat) ascends the globe. She offers him a helping hand and the caption reads: 'Here Jud Süss climbs to the top for the view'. But to her left he topples headlong, arms akimbo, the gallows visible in the distance and the caption reads: 'Here he falls to the rope'.[33] As elsewhere, the text reinforces rather than contradicts the image.[34]

Just three months after the execution in May 1738, a play about Süss in the Underworld (also published that same year) was being performed in Württemberg.[35] Drama could reach the illiterate – a feast for both eye and ear, though its reach was dependent on the availability of travelling players.[36] In Saxony the following year a play with the same title was also being performed (possibly the same play).[37] *Des justifizierten Juden* (*The Justified Jew or Joseph Süss Oppenheimer's Ghost in the Elysian Fields*)[38] is likely to have been inspired by a line in one of the best known publications in which the anonymous author has Süss declare: 'My life, as it was nothing but a tragicomedy, will undoubtedly provide posterity with material for the theatre'.[39] He appears along with fictional characters – the mixing of fictional characters with real contemporary figures was already a feature in early eighteenth-century German Baroque comedy as well as in the more didactic Protestant *Schultheater* (School Theatre).[40]

Two social types are contrasted – the religiously justified and the religiously unjustified – through two stories running in parallel – the fall of Süss and the fairy tale-like rise of Jean, the poor orphaned Christian kitchen boy. The prologue announces that 'the righteous who are raised and the wicked who fall are both the work of God. Only he, not blind Fortune, can will that at the end all will go well for the god-fearing', as will be the case with Jean, which will serve as an example to others.

In Act One, Charon transports Süss to the Underworld where he is assigned to the Elysian Fields for eternity. In conversation with other Jewish spirits in the kingdom of the dead, we learn of his deeds, how he had aimed for wealth and success and offers the advice that 'he who wishes to be rich should not weigh matters on the golden scale of conscience but rather see which way the wind is blowing'.[41] Süss represents the blindness of the Jew while the stock Commedia dell'arte character, Harlequin, represents the blindness of the fool. However, it is Süss who will prove the greater fool because social mobility goes against God's order. He will be cruelly punished while Jean, in contrast, submits to God's will, accepts his place in the scheme of things and is rewarded by being raised to the nobility.[42]

The numerous publications about the life of Süss were usually published anonymously. The authors were most likely to have been civil servants or officials (the *Beamte*), or former officials who had resigned their positions to try and earn their living through writing – 'the aristocracy of the pen'.[43] Not only had they an axe to grind, since Süss' policies had endangered a system which had ensured their livelihoods, but they also had the writing skills which enabled them to vent their dissatisfaction. In a rigid status-based society, they had obtained their position, not through the advantage of birth, but through ability and education. Acutely sensitive to the gradations of hierarchy, they did not welcome a Jew, who by definition lacked status and thus devalued their own achievement.[44]

None of the roles Süss performed for the Duke were safe from attack. Initially, he was engaged for his financial and business skills and ability to deliver desirable goods, but his responsibilities soon expanded into the realm of politics. His appointment as *Resident* at Frankfurt was in practice political, which makes it appropriate for his contemporaries to have described him as a *politicus*, that is someone with a professional knowledge of the state and of political economy, a cross between a statesman and a political economist which after Machiavelli also suggested a new calculating type.[45] Once summoned to Württemberg to provide expertise on a wider range of issues he took on another role, namely that of courtier, since serving the Duke involved attendance at court. He soon became the Duke's 'favourite', a term closely associated with the role of courtier. His lavish life style as well as his relations with women suggested yet another role, namely that of cavalier or gallant. None of these roles was compatible with his status as a Jew. Each provoked a reaction and provided material for writers.[46]

The anonymous authors knew a good story and took their revenge. One of the better known is the biography, *Leben und Tod des Berüchtigten Juden Joseph Süss Oppenheimers, aus Heidelberg* (*The Life and Death of the Infamous Jew Joseph Süss Oppenheimer from Heidelberg*), published anonymously in 1738 in Frankfurt and Leipzig in several editions. Its author has been identified as the Swede Johann Casparson who had once worked in the Hessen Post Office at Giessen, when he had known of Süss, when the latter was working out of Frankfurt and travelling in the area.[47] Though not directly affected by Süss' policies, Casparson is likely to have felt that this Jewish upstart posed a threat to his own status and was an affront to the system.[48] But he also will have found this a good subject to write about. Perhaps it was a little of both.

Unlike his fellow authors, Casparson's attitude to Süss was not wholly negative: he conceded that court Jews provided an important service.[49] Other writers, in contrast, used the case of Süss to attack court Jewry.[50] Casparson also did not claim that Süss had arrived in Württemberg a poor man (possibly because he had known about him before his arrival in Württemberg).[51] Süss had not made his fortune in Württemberg but merely enhanced it. His appointment had been the result of having a reputation for providing good financial advice as well as desirable goods. He was therefore not quite the vampire of legend, nor did he suffer such an extreme reversal of fortune.

One author who retained his anonymity was the pseudonymous Arnoldus Liberius, whose work also appeared in 1738. He makes his position clear not only by the accompanying image (discussed earlier) and the title, *The Complete History and Description of the Life of the infamous and notorious Württemberg Adventurer, Jew Joseph Süss Oppenheimer*, but also by its lengthy subtitle:

> whose good fortune it was to be raised to Financial Adviser at the Württemberg Court, afterwards, however, through his own self-sought misfortune, given his deceptions and evil machinations ruinous to the country, well deserved his death by hanging outside Stuttgart on 4 February 1783 and being locked in a very strong six and half shoe high iron cage.[52]

Süss also appears in a popular genre, the *Dialogues of the Dead*, influenced by the Roman satirist Lucian. The Leipzig-based David Fassmann, a former civil servant turned writer, arguably Germany's first journalist, however, claimed Fontenelle as his inspiration and, between 1718 and 1739, produced 240 imagined dialogues between rulers and important individuals with political or military influence, relating the events of the individual's life to contemporary events.[53] Süss was mentioned in number 225 during a conversation between the recently deceased Duke of Württemberg with the recently deceased Ferdinand, Duke of Courland.[54] He was also discussed in another (anonymous) Fassmann work in the same genre.[55] He also appeared as a character in another anonymous publication in the same genre: *Curious News from the Realm of the Circumcised* which linked the rise and fall of Süss to that of the self-proclaimed Jewish messiah, Sabbatai Zevi (1626–1676), who later converted to Islam. Süss and Zevi, both notorious Jews born some seventy years apart and obviously with very different careers, converse on a number of topics relating both to their achievements and failures.[56] Casparson also contributed to the popular genre: he has Duke Carl Alexander converse with the Duke of Tuscany about Süss.[57]

Rieger, the first clergyman to visit Süss in prison, who published an account of that meeting, did not do so for financial reasons.[58] One of his sermons delivered shortly before the execution, entitled 'Good Work Brings Splendid Rewards' was also published.[59] As a Pietist he disapproved of Süss' worldly success since human destiny rests with God, happiness cannot be sought in this world, and one's status in society is 'god-given'. The execution, Rieger informed his parishioners, was only of value were a Christian lesson to be drawn, namely the importance of piety. Pietists, were hostile to Baroque Court culture, especially annual events like Carnival, which they believed was only celebrated by atheists, Jews, Papists and 'faithless Lutherans' hiding behind their masks. They saw the hand of God in the demise of both the Duke (closely associated with high living) and Süss (a 'Satanic figure on the world stage').[60]

The convert, Christoph David Bernard, published two works relating to his contact with Süss: one described his meeting which took place three days prior to the execution while the other warned the Jewish community not to turn Süss into a martyr.[61] Marx or Marcus Nathan or Mardochai Schloss (he went by several names), Elias Hayum (a court Jew) and a Rabbi Loew from the Freudenthal enclave helped the Stuttgart Jewish slaughterer, Salomon Schächter, who had visited Süss in prison, publish anonymously in Fürth, where the Jewish community had a Hebrew language publishing house, the only account of Süss' life and death written by a Jew and from the Jews' perspective.[62] It was in 'mixed Hebrew and Jewish German' and was an attempt by Jews to create their own Süss legend, presenting Süss as a scapegoat for Christians but holy for Jews. But they heeded Bernard's warning: they suppressed the pamphlet and did not mourn Süss openly.[63]

Not all publications contributed to the legend. The serious press, then in its infancy in Germany, gave the trial and execution only brief coverage since their purpose was to be as factual as possible and create a distance from the popular and moralizing publications.[64] One merely reported that the Duke had died of a stroke, did not mention who had ordered Süss' arrest, nor the reason for his execution, possibly because in their view no valid one had been given. Significantly, they made no mention that Süss was a Jew.[65] Another publication merely described Süss as the 'well known financial adviser' and also did not mention that he was a Jew.[66] His position was presented as dependent on the Prince's favour and his fall was attributed to a change in court politics.[67] Confined to the factual, such coverage was brief, since facts, unlike opinion (and fantasy), were hard to come by.[68]

Even the political journals, more learned than the newspapers, which usually covered dynastic events, Cabinet politics and military activities, were also cautious and did not mention either religion or morality.[69] One publication, *Historische Jahr-Buch*, put the trial in a political context and interpreted it as a revolt of the Protestant Estates. Though it expressed no criticism of the Estates, it did not ignore Süss' expressions of innocence or the partisan nature of his trial and concluded that it was his misfortune to have been caught up in a change of rule, which left him (the Jewish courtier) unprotected, while the others under arrest were dealt with less harshly.[70]

By 1739, media interest in the rise and fall of Süss had peaked. After 1740 publication on the subject almost ceased.[71] The counter-revolution of the *Ehrbarkeit* had resulted in a grotesque trial and execution, inspired an outpouring of hate-filled literature and imagery and created a villain whose villainy would live on for more than two centuries. Though Jews and sympathizers would try to tell the story differently, it was the tale of the all-powerful Jew, lascivious and dangerous, who had got above himself, which had the enduring appeal, doubtless because the devil gets the best tunes.

5

Wilhelm Hauff's Jud Süss

Almost a century passed before the life of Württemberg's court Jew became a suitable subject for literature. Not quite ninety years after the execution, Württemberg-born Wilhelm Hauff entitled his 1827 novella *Jud Süss* (*Jew Süss*), the name by which Joseph Süss Oppenheimer had become best known (except of course to Jews). Despite the choice of name, Hauff was trying to move away from the Süss of legend. His novella belonged to the new genre, the historical tale.

This was not, however, Süss' first literary appearance. That had occurred a generation earlier in 1781 in the work of another Württemberg writer – a minor and fleeting appearance in the work of a major writer, Friedrich Schiller. Born and raised in Württemberg, Schiller had attended the elite military academy in Stuttgart, the Karlsschule, where ultimately he came into conflict with the then Duke, Carl Eugen, the son of Carl Alexander, who ruled for over half a century. Schiller's first play, *Die Räuber* (*The Robbers*), originally published anonymously in the summer of 1781, was performed shortly thereafter in January of the following year in Mannheim by which time he had fled Württemberg.[1] The performed version underwent a number of changes, at the behest of Friedrich Dalberg, the theatre's *Intendant* (General Director), much to the regret of the twenty-one year old Schiller (to avoid controversy Dalberg had insisted that the play be moved back in time to the late middle ages).[2] The passage relating to Süss, however, remained unchanged. In Act 2 Scene 3, the hero Karl Moor declares: 'This diamond I took from a counsellor for finance (*Finanzrat*), who sold honours and offices to the highest bidder and turned from his door the sorrowing patriots'.[3]

It is in Hauff's novella, *Jud Süss*, however, that Süss makes more than a fleeting appearance. It is also the first literary work to appear under that title. And over a century later the first script submitted for the 1940 film was advertised as being based on the novella.[4]

Though barely known in the English-speaking world, Hauff was a well-known German Romantic writer whose popularity only declined at the beginning of the twentieth century. Following in the footsteps of the brothers Grimm and influenced by E. T. A. Hoffmann's theory of the uncanny, he was admired for his collections of folk or fairy tales, where he displayed a freer hand than the Grimm brothers.[5] Transforming many popular Württemberg tales, he published two volumes of stories, while a third appeared posthumously. It was, however, his historical novel *Lichtenstein*, set in sixteenth-century Württemberg and published the year before *Jud Süss*, which established his literary reputation.[6]

Hauff was born in Stuttgart in 1802, just over 100 years after the birth of Süss, to a government civil servant and his wife. Duke Carl Eugen had been dead only nine years. Shortly after his birth, the reigning Duke switched sides (from Austria to France) for which Napoleon suitably rewarded him by giving additional territory (mainly the hitherto autonomous enclaves within the Württemberg borders) and elevating the Duchy to Kingdom.

Both Hauff's maternal and paternal ancestors had belonged to the *Ehrbarkeit*, the hereditary urban elite towards which Hauff himself, as is apparent from the novella, feels some ambivalence. His maternal grandfather had been a high court judge and his paternal grandfather a *Landschaftskonsulent*, that is someone able to make legal representations in Vienna on behalf of the *Landschaft*, which he did in its dispute with the Duke at the time of the arrest of the distinguished jurist Johann Jacob Moser.[7] (Interestingly, it was this same Moser who had opposed the decision to execute Süss and earlier had refused to attend the Duke's Carnival celebrations, prompting him to leave Württemberg for a period.) The paternal grandfather served as a model for the father of the novella's hero.[8] Hauff's own father, August, had also been in government service. Shortly after marrying in 1800, he was arrested along with others suspected of pro-French sympathies. Accused of wanting 'to establish a German republic', he was incarcerated for six weeks in the fortress of Hohenasperg, where Süss himself had spent several months.[9] After his release he was rehabilitated, partly because the Duke had switched sides and being pro-French was no longer a crime. He died when Hauff was aged six, his death hastened, according to a nephew, by the effects of imprisonment.[10] Hauff then lived with his maternal grandfather along with his mother and younger siblings, while his elder brother lived with the paternal grandfather. This is not an irrelevant biographical detail since it was the grandfather he did not live with who served as a model for the father of the novella's hero.[11]

Hauff himself died in Stuttgart in late 1827 just two weeks short of his twenty-fifth birthday. Intended for the Lutheran clergy, he turned to writing when still at university where he belonged to the *Burschenschaft* (the nationalist student fraternity). After university he worked as a tutor. On 1 January 1827, he took over the editorship of the literary side of the *Morgenblatt für gebildete Stände (Morning Paper for the Educated Classes)*, a Württemberg weekly cultural journal published by J. G. Cotta, the publisher of Schiller, Goethe and Herder. Its then elderly director was Johann Friedrich Cotta, a friend of the Hauff family, though initially Hauff was keen to keep his distance from him.[12] The novella was first published in serial form in that journal beginning in July 1827, in a heavily censored version (the original manuscript for this has now been lost) and in a separate edition after his death in 1828 by the Stuttgart book and newspaper publisher Gottlob Friedrich Franckh (five years later he was arrested and imprisoned for participating in a republican conspiracy).[13]

In the spring of 1826, before taking up his post as editor, Hauff undertook the equivalent of a grand tour for a provincial young German with literary interests. His travels took him to Paris, Normandy, Belgium, Göttingen, Bremen, Hamburg and finally Berlin where he spent one month. In Berlin he met prominent literary figures such as Chamisso and Hoffmann and in Dresden Ludwig Tieck.[14] Berlin was a world away from provincial Württemberg. It is more than likely that Hauff had some social contact with Jews and would have been made aware of the influential role played by Jewish women such as Dorothea Schlegel (1764–1839), daughter of Moses Mendelssohn whose second husband was the writer Friedrich Schlegel, or the literary salon hostesses, Henrietta Herz (1764–1847) and Rahel Levin-Varnhagen (1771–1833), the latter married to the writer and diplomat Karl August Varnhagen von Ense.

During the Revolution French Jews had been granted equal rights, later extended to German Jews during the French occupation but rescinded after the defeat of Napoleon. Hauff was thirteen at the time of Waterloo and reached maturity after such concessions had been withdrawn. A contemporary Jewish publicist, Saul Ascher, characterized this period as dominated by *Germanomanie* (his term). This covered two distinct phenomena: revolutionary conservatism which declared the German state to be Christian and integral nationalism, based on the *Volk* which was hostile to alien elements within or without.[15] Hauff was seventeen in 1819 when the popular wave of attacks on Jews, the Hep Hep Riots, spread to several German cities. The issue of Jewish emancipation did not disappear, though the number of Jews resident in Württemberg was tiny. A few months after Hauff's death, a law, which had aroused controversy was passed which would permit Jews public worship.[16] Haunting the debate would have been the ghost of Süss, the bogeyman of the popular verses, songs and stories. Indeed even outside Württemberg the ghost of Süss haunted debates on Jewish emancipation.[17]

Well before the Holocaust, Lion Feuchtwanger had described Hauff's *Jud Süss* as 'naively antisemitic';[18] more recently it has been accused of 'advancing an antisemitic narrative';[19] of being the 'progenitor of the antisemitic Süss tradition'[20] or even that given the Holocaust it should *not* be read.[21] Certainly, the novella is qualitatively different from at one end chronologically, the Süss of legend, and at the other, the Süss of the Veit Harlan film. It needs to be placed in context in order to understand what he might have been trying to do by telling this story with this title in fictionalized form.

An important influence on Hauff was Sir Walter Scott; along with many other Germans he had read him avidly.[22] In *Ivanhoe*, published in 1819, which later appeared in more than one German translation, the character, Rebecca, is the beautiful and noble Jewess, the daughter of the moneylender and merchant, Isaac of York. In love with the hero, Ivanhoe, she realizes this is forbidden, does not renounce her faith or marry and eventually escapes with her father to Grenada, then under Moorish rule, a happy end of sorts for there, prior to the *reconquista* Jews, Muslims and Christians had lived on good terms. In Germany there had also been great interest in Shakespeare, in part due to August Wilhelm Schlegel's translations – his *Merchant of Venice* was published in 1799. There the Jewess Jessica escapes her father, Shylock, to marry Lorenzo but she will no longer remain a Jew, a happy end of sorts for her, if not for her father, whom she has defied.

In the Hauff novella, the beautiful Jewess, Lea, is loved by the diffident hero, Gustav Lanbek, a young lawyer (*Aktuarius*) and son of a *Landschaft* councillor, who is a fierce opponent of Süss. Though she displays some awareness of the insurmountable difficulties facing the couple, the hero displays a greater awareness, torn as he is between his love of his fatherland, specifically Württemberg (rootedness in a particular region, nationalists claimed, was a precondition for being considered German), respect for his father and hatred of Süss, Lea's brother, responsible for the changes he believed to be destroying Württemberg.

It would have been difficult at this time to make a male Jew a positive character. Female, on the other hand, proved easier since females were excluded from the public sphere, enabling the author to humanize the Jew without entering dangerous territory. An exception was a decade earlier in the farces of Julius Voss, where the female was also a target.[23] Her appearance, whether positive or negative, was not unrelated to a public debate about Jewish emancipation.[24]

The beautiful Jewess was an ingredient in this variant of Orientalism; she was also chaste. In contrast to Scott's Rebecca, Hauff's Lea is not entirely positive: blind to her brother's faults, she is flippant about religion and, at one point, concludes that Protestants are closer to heretics, since they are like 'we Jews' and unlike Catholics, as both have no 'head of church'.[25] On the other hand, the hero's younger sister makes similar simple-minded comments, as befits the inferior sex. If compared to earlier popular accounts of Süss, the novella does attempt to humanize the Jew, even if female rather than male. Father and son debate Württemberg's politics, as do other characters – son with father's friends, with his own friends and with his sisters. The serious discussion is confined mainly to the men, but it is the hero's older sister who displays some grasp of the issues. Aside from religion, gender here plays a role.

On the other hand, the depiction of Süss is extremely negative while Lea's main moral failing is her partiality towards her brother and incomprehension as to why people hate him. For this reason, her relationship with the hero is doomed. Being female and dependent on her brother, conveniently twenty years her senior, she occupies, in some respects, an ambiguous position more like his daughter but, unlike Jessica in *The Merchant of Venice*, she has no wish to escape his control. Her lack of independence, which would then have been the norm for women, suggests that they cannot be moral beings. Süss, in contrast, embodies the negative characteristics associated with one of Schiller's despots rather than a villain with specific Jewish features; nor is he the grotesque of the previous century's broadsides, popular biographies and contemporary plays. Apparently Hauff had read the broadsides, chronicles and newspapers, as well as questioned his grandfather and other elderly Württembergers whose parents and grandparents had provided them with eyewitness accounts.[26]

Hauff makes use of the legend in a number of ways. Süss is described as a 'Minister' and made solely responsible for all the evils that have befallen Württemberg. A number of his policies are mentioned, along with the Absolutorium, the announcement of which opens the novella, absolving Süss (to great outrage), of all responsibility for his acts. His powers, as in the legend, are greatly exaggerated: he is even presented as deeply involved in the Catholic plot. The Duke makes no appearance, doubtless because this would not have passed the Württemberg censor. Thus he is spared from criticism and the author from accusations of sedition. Yet danger lurks since it should not have escaped the notice of either reader or censor that it was the Duke who had appointed Süss and then failed to intervene to protect his subjects.

One element in the legend not alluded to are the rumours concerning Süss' illegitimacy, possibly because this would have muddied the waters, making it difficult to draw a clear distinction between good (natives of Württemberg) and evil (those considered not native, e.g. Jews and even Catholics). This would have complicated matters in this first fictional retelling, especially as the novella appears to be less about Süss, despite its title, and more about tragic love between two young people, the sister of Süss and the son of a leader of the *Landschaft*. Süss is not humanized while the character of the sister enables the author to advance a view, then tendentious, that perhaps not *all* Jews are bad, though where exactly a female fits into the scheme of things is left unexplored. Hauff's readers will have known that the story *must* end badly while simultaneously they enjoyed vicariously, though fleetingly, the pleasures of forbidden love between Jew and non-Jew.

The novella incorporates elements from *Romeo and Juliet* – the warring families, the Lanbeks and the Süsses replacing the Montagues and the Capulets – as well as the story of Pyramus and Thisbe, set in Babylon as told by Ovid, itself possibly an inspiration for *Romeo and Juliet*. Pyramus and Thisbe meet over the garden wall, but their parents forbid their marriage and both die tragically. Süss and his sister live in a property next to that belonging to the father of the novella's hero. Hauff's paternal grandfather's house shared a border with the large property that Süss occupied in the last months of his life.[27] Hauff himself when growing up may even have entertained adolescent fantasies about a beautiful Jewess residing in the house next to his grandfather's once inhabited by the notorious Süss. This of course is pure speculation but the young Hauff had known where Süss had once lived and, though he lived with

his maternal grandfather and his older brother with the paternal grandfather, he will have visited the paternal grandfather.[28]

Following Schiller, Hauff's Süss remains the despotic minister, but
he is also a Jew. He is given a beautiful and almost completely virtuous
sister, whose only moral failing is her desire to save her evil brother.
The 'beautiful Jewess', by no means a stock character, was not Hauff's
invention.[29] Her moral failing, not unexpected given her sex, is her
willingness to sacrifice principle to save her brother while the hero,
in contrast, upholds principle for which he will never find personal
happiness. There is no happy end: Süss remains the villain, the despot,
the outsider, bent on destroying Württemberg.

The Süss story, according to Hauff, begins with Carnival 'never so
brilliantly celebrated as in 1737', making it difficult to believe that this
could be 'strict, serious Württemberg [made] even stricter through an
earnest, often ascetic, Protestantism' (an allusion here to Pietism).[30] Süss
is in charge (though the Duke's non-appearance relates to censorship),
the entrance fee being described as an indirect tax, going straight into his
pocket.[31] Described as the 'Cabinet Minister' and 'Finance Director', he
is celebrating his birthday and now also the Absolutorium granted him
that morning, 12 February, by the Duke who had 'given him many gifts
… but now the most welcome gift of all, the edict bearing that day's date
absolving him of all responsibility for past and future'[32]:

> Crowding the steps and besieging the anteroom to wish him luck were those
> countless people of different status, belief or age [appointed by Süss] as well as
> many honest officials who, through fear of bringing misfortune on their families,
> were driven to kiss the hand in the house of the Jew.[33]

Süss appears with a masked woman, described as the 'beautiful Oriental',
her identity is unknown. Everyone present is in mask. Some speculate as
to which of Süss' women she could be, perhaps even a daughter of 'many
a wretched father, as whispered, who sends his daughter to the Jew with a
request'.[34] That Süss has a sister is known only to the hero, Gustav, dressed

as a Saracen, his turban the same colour as hers. Gustav enters a second room where Süss is playing cards. The gold coins he has won are stacked in front of him; the expression on his face remains unchanged. Having never seen him before at close range, he concedes that:

this man's face was well and beautifully formed, that even his forehead and eyes had acquired something imposing through the habit of domination, but there between his eyebrows where the bare forehead joined the beautifully formed nose, lay hostile, forbidding furrows. The moustache could not hide the hint of malice about the mouth. And the forced laughter of the Jewish minister that accompanied the loss and profits struck the young man as truly gruesome.[35]

A man dressed as a peasant enters the room, rests his head on the stick he holds in his hand and says in the local dialect: 'You have a great deal of money there, Sir! … have you earned it all yourself?' to which Süss replies: 'Good Evening, Countryman'. 'I am not exactly your countryman', exclaims the farmer: with a sarcastic play on the word, *mauscheln*, which means to speak Yiddish as well as to fiddle. Nonplussed, Süss responds: 'You are witty, my Friend.' 'God help me!', the farmer retorts, 'Were I your friend, Herr Süss … I would not be in shabby clothes with a moth-eaten hat since you make your friends rich.' Replying in a 'hoarse, unpleasant voice' Süss declares: 'Then all Württemberg must be my friend for I make it rich' and mentions his business activities such as supplying the army and the manufacture of playing cards. The conversation continues as he plays cards but on hearing laughter his face darkens. Another man, similarly attired, appears. The farmer, addressing him as Hans, asks him why his beard is so pointed since it makes him look completely Jewish. Hans replies: 'It is the fashion since the Jews are masters in the land; soon I will look completely Jewish' at which point a distinct voice from the crowd shouts: 'Wait yet a couple of weeks, Hans, then you can be Catholic.'[36] Süss leaps from his chair, demanding to know the speaker's identity and orders his arrest in the name of the Duke. He then hears the words: 'Maskenfreiheit, Jude' (freedom of the mask, Jew), which entitles the wearer the right to speak freely.[37] (A version of this scene will appear in the 1940 Veit Harlan film.)

The farmer and friends disappear, the crowd disperses and Gustav, lost in thought, feels someone take his hand. He turns to see the 'Oriental' who, in a trembling voice, asks the origin of the rose on his hat and is told 'The Sea of Tiberius'. She invites him to follow her quickly through the crowd to a quiet corner of a room where they can speak freely ('only her turban points the way'). She is concerned about her brother because 'The people here whisper his name. I do not know what they say but I think it not good … Ah, I know well, these people (*Menschen*) hate our people (*Volk*)', a deliberate choice of words, doubtless because Hauff is emphasizing that the Jews are a *Volk* (not to be confused with the anodyne English term folk) and thus a people apart.[38]

An embarrassed Gustav refrains from mentioning that prayers are being offered: 'God save us from all evil and the Jew Süss' but he does mention the recent incident with the mask. He tries to calm her. She tells him of her nightmares and fears that misfortune will befall her brother. He begs her to spare him an hour alone to talk, as she had promised. She offers Sara, her nurse, to stand guard at the entrance.[39]

They find a room. They take off their masks. He gazes in delight at Lea The description of her physical perfection makes clear that she is beautiful, though qualified by being a beautiful 'Oriental':

> One might say her face was the perfection of oriental features. The symmetry of these finely chiseled features, these wonderful dark eyes shaded by long silky eyelashes, these arching eyebrows, shining so black, and the dark locks that fell on the white forehead and beautiful neck, in such pleasing contrast, all these lovely features met in the tender red lips that enhanced the even more delicate white teeth … the turban entwined with her curls, the precious pearls wound about her neck, the alluring and yet modest costume of a Turkish lady … created such an illusion that the young man believed he was seeing one of those wondrous apparitions, as described by Tasso, that the stimulated imagination of the traveler painted on his return.

'Truly', cried Gustav 'you are like the sorceress Armida, and so I imagine the daughters of your race when you still lived in the land of Canaan. Such was Rebecca and the daughter of Jephtha'.[40]

Lea then tells Gustav how lonely and unhappy she is in her brother's house, unlike earlier in Frankfurt where she had friends (obviously from the Jewish community); now she is forbidden to meet the guests and must remain pious and pure, so that her soul can serve as a sacrifice for his. 'Mad superstition' exclaims the young man, 'you poor child, all joys of life refused you',[41] and advises her to have nothing to do with her brother's friends, assumed to be drawn from the demi-monde, or to attend his parties. This incidentally, is the only passage alluding to Süss' mistresses. The childlike Lea suggests that Gustav bears a grudge against her brother at which point a commotion is heard outside the room. Voices shout and Gustav recognizes his father's. Planting a kiss on Lea's forehead, he rushes to his father's side. A group of five older men are in dispute with Süss' secret police. 'Grab the Turk!' (this being Gustav) shouts a policeman, 'he's the one!' Tellingly, Gustav does not remove his mask to reveal his identity to his father, though this could have helped him since 'he feared his father's anger more than the Jew's power'.[42] Here is an embryonic generational conflict. Yet despite fearing his father, ultimately he knows in his heart that his father is right.

It is Gustav, however, who is arrested. Süss visits him in prison, trying to discover the identity of the two masked men. When Gustav proves unforthcoming he is asked if he cannot recognize the voice of his own father. He denies that his father is a rebel and claims that he has always been loyal to the Duke, a telling distinction.[43] Süss then mentions that his sister fell on her knees begging him to spare Gustav.[44] Embarrassed, young Gustav replies that they have committed no offence, words which the worldly Süss finds amusing but he then announces that he is appointing Gustav to a well-paid junior legal position (*Expeditionsrat*) which Gustav tries to decline on the grounds that there are older and more deserving men but refrains from adding that he does not wish to appear as Süss' favourite.[45]

Süss also takes the opportunity to propose marriage with his sister, adding that he will provide well for her. Gustav refuses:

> He thought of his proud father and the reputation of his family, and so great was his fear of disgrace and so deeply rooted at that time were still the prejudices against those unhappy children of Abraham that even his tender feelings for the daughter of Israel were overwhelmed.[46]

Lea, he tells Süss, can have no warmer friend than he but she has misunderstood the nature of their relationship and adds insult to injury, by pointing to religious differences.[47] An angry Süss, speaking on Lea's behalf, declares religious differences pose no impediment, accuses Gustav of playing with her feelings and his father of having committed a serious crime. Gustav is released, given four weeks to bring his father round, take up his new post and marry Lea or his reputation will be ruined and his father imprisoned.[48]

Sometime later at home, father and son discuss the present state of Württemberg in the presence of Major von Röder, the man who did indeed turn on Süss and arrest him.[49] Now Hauff sticks more closely to the historical record, or rather what he would have assumed to have been historically correct. Appalled at what has happened since 'Alexander has come on the throne', the father mentions the sale of offices and the 'five scoundrels' (the five men later imprisoned with Süss, three of whom he mentions by name – Römchingen (*sic*), Hallwachs, Metz), as well as the first mentioned's alleged request to the Archbishop of Würzburg for troop reinforcements.[50] Gustav is shocked that the Duke has dared do this.[51] Father and son now look to the emperor in Vienna for protection.

The Duke's plan to inspect the military fortresses the following month will provide the rebels with their opportunity. Gustav's new position of trust provides welcome cover and he pledges his father his support. Both men embrace. Now committed to the conspiracy to defend Württemberg, he is nevertheless worried about Lea's fate, once her brother has been dealt with.[52] Keen to confess to his father the 'scandal' of his relationship before it is too late, he becomes paralysed when he recalls Lea's 'pure, innocent, interesting features', or 'deep expressive eyes' at which point the authorial voice interjects that he does not know what draws Gustav to return to their meeting place, whether it is 'vanity, madness, love or even … magical power, allegedly still possessed by the daughters of Israel since the days of Rachel'.[53] Whether she is called Rachel or Rebecca, such figures for Hauff suggest the uncanny.

Gustav and Lea meet again over the palisade dividing the properties. She tells him that since she begged her brother to release Gustav his attitude to her has changed and he now treats her as though she were an adult.[54] She asks Gustav to introduce her to his sisters whom she has observed at their window, at which point the couple are discovered first by Süss and shortly thereafter by Gustav's outraged father. The latter threatens to disinherit Gustav for the shame he has brought on the family.[55]

Later when the father announces they must arm themselves to rid Württemberg of the terrible enemy, he agrees to forgive his son his 'madness' on condition he does not see Lea:

> With unending melancholy Gustav thought long about the unhappy creature whose heart belonged to him and whom he ought not to love. He shared all the strict religious views of his time but shuddered at the curse which persecuted a homeless branch of humanity.[56]

Hauff then adds: 'He found no excuse for himself and his forbidden attraction to a girl who did not share his faith but drew some comfort in subordinating his own destiny to that of a higher order'.[57] Father and son are now reconciled.

The debate about Jews is now put into the mouths of females: the two sisters discuss Lea. The younger one, having observed Gustav's meeting with her, declares that she has never seen anyone so 'beautiful and graceful' and that she too could have fallen in love with her to which the older, sensible sister, responds: 'How can you talk such nonsense! Whatever she is, she is and remains only a Jew'.[58]

The conspirators, including Röder, arrive at the Lanbek house. The sisters eavesdrop (in the Harlan film it is Süss and secretary who will do the eavesdropping). The childlike younger sister fears that if the plot fails they will be forced to become nuns (expressing her fear and ignorance of Catholics) while the older, wiser sister comforts her with the thought that they are 'the daughters of a man who will do what is best for our fatherland'.[59]

Hauff now reflects on history, providing a Hegelian gloss. (Hegel came from Württemberg but since 1818 had held the chair of philosophy in Berlin from where his ideas on history were disseminated). He justifies rebellion just as Hegel had justified the French Revolution:

> In the life of the state there are individual moments when a century later the attentive observer will say that at that point in time there had to be a crisis … In all times there have been men whether led by their own genius or by study of history – who understood and had the courage and strength to take on the role. History has long decided about the short rule of Carl Alexander's minister. It does not curse the dead; otherwise the tears and sighs of the Württembergers would become harsh words against the author of their misfortune in the year 1737.[60]

The rumours circulate about the Duke's planned journey – here Hauff is relying heavily on the legend. It is 11 March 1737, the night that the Duke will die. Lanbek senior conspires with his son and the captain, the son's friend, (previously his prison guard), who is now engaged to the sensible, older sister. 'With tears in his eyes' Gustav tells his father, 'God, that I should abandon you in this crisis and that I am perhaps guilty of your unhappiness'. When the younger sister intervenes he enquires why Gustav must leave so quickly, and her father replies: 'Because I do not want a Jew for a daughter' (in the Harlan film a similar line will be delivered by the patriarch – 'I do not want Jewish children'.[61] The father had discovered Lea's note to Gustav which he had promptly returned to Süss. Father and son are now reconciled and the father bids his son farewell.

The young men ride through the night. In a scene redolent with a sense of the uncanny they pass the iron gallows where once an alchemist had been hanged. Ravens gather and caw, in anticipation of their new prey. Gazing up in silence, Gustav then lowers his eyes, as he imagines a grieving Lea beneath the gallows.[62] Here Hauff, perhaps inspired by the popular eighteenth-century image of Süss' female mourners gathered beneath the gallows, has inserted the chaste Lea. Perhaps she is replacing the female in the dark robes akin to the grieving Virgin Mary.

Reaching Ludwigsburg in the dark, Gustav recognizes 'the proud but somewhat anxious voice' of Süss declaring that he is on his way to the Duke. Röder informs him that the Duke has just died. Süss mentions his Absolutorium but is told: 'Now your rule has come to an end, Jew!' In a dreamlike trance Gustav follows his fellow conspirators, who lead Süss through the village. They again pass the gallows with the circling ravens, Gustav has a 'premonition of Lea's unhappy fate'.[63]

Playing with fact and fiction, Hauff mentions that two-thirds of offices had been sold,[64] but that only one individual was dissatisfied with his appointment, namely his fictional character Gustav who is then given the unwelcome task of prosecuting Süss. Though he is not pleased, he does his duty as a good lawyer and as the son of his father.[65] Visiting Süss in prison to interrogate him, he takes no pleasure at the sight of 'a pale, wasted man in rags' and can hardly hold back the tears when Süss uses the opportunity to mention the 'unhappy, innocent girl that we both know'.[66] But Hauff quickly crushes any sympathy for the victim since Gustav later learns that Süss had lied about his wealth in Frankfurt, though he allows Gustav to be unable to banish the thought of Lea 'abandoned and unfortunate'.[67]

Several months later in the autumn, Lea visits Gustav's sisters, asking to see Gustav to plead for her brother's life. Gustav does not think Süss' life is in danger but Lea then mentions an incriminating letter which she begs him to ignore. This he cannot do, forbidden by his honour and good name, though he offers to help her with her claim on her brother's property outside Württemberg. They part. With tears in his eyes, Gustav gives her a 'pained look', realizing that this will be the last time he will see her. She gives him a 'loving look'.[68]

Sparing the reader the details of the trial on the grounds that it would be 'too exhausting',[69] Hauff concludes that there is a temptation to accuse the Württemberg of that time of the most terrible barbarism. But the men who lived then often mentioned that Süss had to die on the scaffold, not merely for his grave crimes but for the terrible deeds and plans of more powerful men who go unnamed. They were saved by relationships, respect and secret promises, but no one could or wanted to save the Jew who had to pay the price for others.[70] Though Hauff has Gustav say these words, it was the regent who in fact said something similar, when declaring that Süss was paying the price for 'scoundrels'.[71] The Duke, however, had said nothing about 'relationships' or 'secret promises'. That was Hauff alluding to the *Ehrbarkeit*.

Elsewhere in Hauff's writings, there are more overt negative comments about Jews. In his tale, 'Abner, der Jude, der nichts gesehen hat' ('Abner, the Jew who saw nothing'), the comic, dwarf-like figure Abner plays only a small part in the eponymous tale, mainly at the outset, where the narrator comments:

'Jews, as you know, are everywhere and everywhere there are Jews: cunning, with falcon's eyes for the slightest advantage, crafty, the more crafty, the more they are mistreated, aware of their craftiness, and somewhat conceited about it.'[72]

Hauff tried to take the Süss legend beyond its early eighteenth-century origins. No longer the demon, Süss is a despot as in Schiller and lacks specific Jewish characteristics. To a great extent, however, he remains in the shadows since the novella, despite its title, is more about Lea and Gustav. By no means a heroine, Lea is presented as an object of love, beautiful though a mere Oriental beauty – desirable yet forbidden. Unable to betray his father or his country, Gustav does not rebel but retains his honour by doing his duty when accepting the role of Süss' prosecutor. Justice is done. Süss is executed. Lea dies, lost without her brother, her protector, whom she (wrongly) wanted to save. Gustav lives to a ripe age but never marries. Nor does he ever smile again. It was said that he had once loved a girl who had drowned herself in the River Neckar.[73] For Gustav, virtue is not rewarded, which suggests that Hauff felt some unease with the verdict. Thus inventing a sister for Süss did more than create a love interest. The Jewess could be – to some extent – the acceptable face of the Jew.

6

After Hauff

On the eve of the revolutions of 1848, two decades after the death of Wilhelm Hauff, a play entitled *Lea* opened in Koenigsberg in East Prussia. When published much later it claimed to be, according to its title page, 'after Wilhelm's Hauff's novella *Jud Süss*'. The playwright was Albert Dulk (1819–1884), an active revolutionary. During the opening performance he had taken to the stage to announce that revolution had broken out in Paris.[1] The author of several plays, almost all unperformed, this one, his second and most important, had productions in German cities and apparently also in the USA, doubtless because of its subject matter as well as Dulk's reputation.[2]

A radical and freethinker, Dulk officially broke with the Protestant Church, and left Koenigsberg to participate in the revolutions which continued beyond Prussian borders after which he fled to Egypt where he travelled and even for a time lived in the Sinai Desert. Eventually he moved to Switzerland near Lausanne, remaining there for ten years, finally settling in 1858 in Württemberg, in Stuttgart. Highly unconventional, he lived in a ménage à trois and at one point, apparently even à quatre.[3] Later he joined the newly founded Social Democratic Party, campaigning twice as a Reichstag candidate for Stuttgart (in 1878 and 1881) and twice for the Württemberg Landtag (in 1876 and 1882) during the 1878 election campaign was arrested for comments made and charged with infringing the recently introduced Anti-Socialist Laws. He spent one year in prison which seems to have damaged his health which until then had been robust – in his mid-forties he had swum across Lake Constance (from Römershorn to Friedrichshaven), a six-and-a-half hour swim. When he died suddenly five years after his release, 10,000 people attended his funeral in Erfurt. It had been his wish that his body be sent for cremation to Germany's only crematorium.[4] In 1893, his complete plays were published posthumously in three volumes by the Social Democratic Stuttgart publisher J. H. W. Dietz.

Dulk was an extraordinary man for his time, a colourful character, a life force. Having obtained his doctorate (in pharmacology), he failed to obtain his *habilitation* (an advanced doctorate), refused him by the Prussian authorities on political grounds. It is likely that he identified with the outsider Joseph Süss Oppenheimer which may have inspired him to rework the Hauff story as drama. Süss was now the hero, punished for being clever and different. In 1848, Dulk's target was Protestant conservatism and its close identification with the state. As a freethinker, he waged war on religion which also made Süss a suitable subject. Dulk had frequented the circle of radicals and democrats in Koenigsberg – Johann Jacoby (of Jewish origin), then a democrat, later a Social Democrat, had been a family friend. He was also familiar with the Jewish milieu and able to capture some of the humour: in the play the occasional Yiddish word crops up.[5]

Dulk also introduced other characters which do not appear in Hauff: the ministers Bilfinger and Scheffer; a clergyman, as well as Süss' servant, the last mentioned taken from the chronicles. He digresses considerably from Hauff in a convoluted plot in which Süss is more than a shadowy figure, even a tragic hero. Lea's role has been enlarged, not surprising given the title; one of Gustav's sisters, the elder one who supported her father, has been eliminated, while the younger, Käthchen, who was sympathetic to Lea, is retained to become her dear friend.

All traces of the novella's antisemitism have been expunged for this is a philosemitic play. Süss is a smart and sympathetic individual, intent on sorting out the mess in Württemberg while his enemies appear highly unsympathetic. His execution is presented as a miscarriage of justice since there were no apparent grounds. Reworking the Hauff story, Dulk expunged anything negative while expanding on what the novella, in a subtle way, had dared, almost tentatively, to criticize. His target is the officials: Röder is made the villain, presented as having fallen foul of the Duke from their time in Serbia fighting the Turks.[6] In court, Süss makes a strong defence and only in the last few pages does it become clear that he will be executed. Gustav pleads on his behalf, namely he should at most be banned or imprisoned but not executed. In gratitude, Süss calls him his friend while Röder calls him the Jew's 'brother-in-law' (*Judenschwager*).[7] Lea goes mad – a not-uncommon danger facing heroines at this time – and dies, though no reason is given. To compound the tragedy, Gustav throws himself on her body and also dies. 'I cannot believe', declares Süss, 'that just judges should condemn me to death because I am a Jew and spare the others … as though I were worth less.' Another character describes the people's hatred as 'animal-like' since they demand that he should be hanged higher than the gallows,[8] while Süss himself jokes that this would not be possible. As he is about to ascend the special gallows, Dulk has a clergyman deliver the parting line, attributed in the chronicles to Vicar Hoffmann: ' … damned Jew, stubborn evildoer'.[9] Käthchen, Gustav's sister, who had befriended Lea, exclaims that everything is 'horrific' while her father moans that 'we are also victims, because God wills it'. The minister Bilfinger (who often appears in the few pro-Süss versions as a positive character) retorts: 'Not God! Man dares do much ill in the name of humanity; inhuman ill for the glory of God; I see not God, only the people, Christianity'.[10] And so ends the play.

In 1897, *The Prime Minister of Würtemburg* (*sic*) was published by Wm. Andrews and Co. in London. The author's name was Eller, a pseudonym, according to the British Library catalogue entry, for Anne Elizabeth Ellerman.[11] But her actual identity is not clear. On the title page she is described as the author of *Ingatherings*, another work also published in London in the same year by the same publisher, a collection of prose and poetry, some 'original', some by Goethe. The author's anonymity may have been for protection, given the extent of plagiarism,[12] helped also by the fact that Hauff, now dead seventy years was out of copyright and whose work would have been unfamiliar to an English readership. Considerably longer than the novella at 170 pages, the novel retells the

Hauff version, with the additions of a date or two, an umlaut or two (e.g. Neüffen) and Süss being renamed Siece.

Several other stories or plays about Süss appeared during the course of the nineteenth century and up until the outbreak of the First World War. Some were based on the pamphlet literature, most were by authors with links to Württemberg. Almost all were tainted with antisemitism.[13] A novel by Württemberg writer, Theodor Griesinger, was serialized in his Württemberg journal *Die Schwäbische Hauschronik* (*The Swabian House Chronicle*).[14] A reviewer in the then only journal for German Jewry found that it far surpassed any other example of Jew-baiting, and using the word *Schwabenstreich*, a play on the word for Swabians (speakers of the Swabian dialect spoken in Württemberg), concluded that one would want to avoid 'this scribbler' whose novel was full of 'historical distortions and ignorance about Jewish customs and religious practice'. Tellingly, however, the critic added 'not that we want to defend the all-powerful finance minister, but the novelist presents him as a blank sheet on which to smear Jews and Jewry and drag them through the mud'.[15]

Inspired by Hauff, and perhaps as a riposte to Griesinger, Jews also began to offer a fictional retelling. In 1872 author and Orthodox Rabbi Markus Lehmann (1831–1890) published a novel about Süss: *Süss Oppenheimer: eine jüdische Erzählung (Süss Oppenheimer, a Jewish Tale)*, which was serialized in the weekly for German Orthodox Jewry, *Der Israelit*, in 1872 and also published separately as a book.[16] He had founded the weekly in 1870 at the time of German unification when Orthodox Jewry felt threatened by the advance of secularization as well as by the threat to Orthodoxy from the reform of Jewish religious practice. He edited it until his death after which his son took over the editorship.[17]

A skilful storyteller, Lehmann provided a charming but highly inventive Süss story – a tale of rags to riches – which contained a clear moral for his orthodox readership concerning the limits of integration. This might account for the fact that it was still being published as late as the 1950s in Hebrew and Yiddish.[18] Depicted as highly talented, but headstrong, Süss makes his mark against all odds in a world which conspires against him. To his credit, and despite his transgressions, he never abandons his Jewish faith, insofar as he never converts. However, he does not practise, which in orthodox terms mean he cannot be considered a good Jew as he neither adheres to the dietary laws nor attends synagogue. These are not his only failings: womanizing and a taste for luxury are also mentioned, though it is the latter which gets greater emphasis. Surprisingly, Lehmann takes from the eighteenth-century legend Heidersdorf's paternity which Süss' Jewish contemporaries, who presented him as a martyr, had not referred to.

The story begins at a splendid ball (as in Hauff) hosted by Heidersdorf and attended by his beautiful wife, the countess, believed to be an Italian, though in reality she was not his wife but his mistress since she had refused to convert, nor was she Italian. Their liaison had begun when Heidersdorf and some of his troops had been billeted on the parental home (not in Heidelberg but in the fictional Bunzlau). Having become pregnant, she chose to leave the family home with Heidersdorf on his departure. Unprotected by her brother, then studying in Prague for the rabbinate, he finally finds her at the ball. He learns that Heidersdorf loves her dearly, also that they have a son and that she not only had refused to convert but also insisted that her son be circumcised. Thus she could not marry; moreover her son is a Jew. After Heidersdorf's fall from grace, she eventually returns to the family home with her son. In poor health, she soon dies. The uncle, now a rabbi living in Oppenheim, takes over his nephew's education but the unruly and headstrong Süss runs away, eventually reaching Amsterdam. Fortunately, the uncle has seen to it that he has been trained to perform circumcisions which provides the penniless, wanderer with his lucky break. As surgery must take place on a certain day after birth to ensure a Jew's covenant with God, he steps in to substitute for a 'surgeon' who has been delayed. (This is one Orthodox twist to the story.) Having now made the first of his good contacts, he begins to make money.

Eventually, Süss meets Carl Alexander; he funds the future Duke, even arranges his marriage with the Duchess, goes off to Belgrade with him after his appointment as Governor and returns with him to Württemberg on the death of the reigning Duke. The inhabitants hate Süss for his policies which fill the Duke's coffers but Süss has little choice since the Duke is incapable of economizing and indeed becomes furious at the very mention of the subject: he is a spoiled man whom Süss must indulge. The uncle learns of Süss' whereabouts and travels to Stuttgart to beseech him to mend his ways. But the nephew refuses on the grounds that he is too implicated to be able to leave freely. On the journey to Stuttgart the uncle, at one point, had the good fortune to share a coach with Bilfinger, who proves a useful contact after Süss' arrest. The Duke dies at his palace in Ludwigsburg the night before beginning his journey to Danzig to see a doctor about the wound to his foot. Süss is not with him but has remained in Stuttgart. Süss' friends arrange for his escape which would entail abandoning his wealth, even that which he had brought with him to Württemberg. In the end, he decides not to run away on the grounds that this would make him appear guilty and remains to defend himself; he is promptly arrested and charged. The uncle, learning of this, travels to Stuttgart. He calls on Bilfinger who arranges for Süss to be removed from a less dank and dark cell.

Süss meets his accusers in court. The prosecutor is the young Lanbek, the character invented by Hauff, who cries out: 'What insolence this Jew has.' He is described as a young man whom Süss himself had promoted and whose motive is 'to gain favour with his father'.[19] No more is said about Lanbek but aspersions have been cast on his motives and this is a sufficient reminder to those readers familiar with Hauff. Bilfinger allows the uncle to remain with Süss until the execution not because he is a relative but because he is a clergyman. Since both men observe the law there can be mutual respect. This also sends out a message to the Orthodox Jews of Germany just after unification about the limits to integration but also as a warning about the need to observe the laws of the land.

It is a chastened Süss who goes to his death. According to his uncle, he has more than atoned for his sins, given his harsh prison conditions. Near to the scaffold are trees. Atop sit Jews, dressed as peasants. As he goes to his death, Süss hears their prayers. This comforts him and they then pray together. The uncle returns to Oppenheim to a happy end of sorts, at least for a rabbi, since his daughter, whom Süss on a visit earlier had been smitten with, marries someone who meets her father's approval and provides him with offspring whom he can teach.

This tale of rags to riches to rags provided moral teaching for Orthodox German Jews. Among Süss' many failings in their eyes, aside from all forms of non-observance, which included his non-adherence to the dietary laws, was their belief that he had refused to help his fellow Jews. However, during his lifetime and subsequently, his enemies always claimed the opposite. Other failings which had made the lives of his fellow Jews even more precarious included his conspicuous life style, behaviour and close association with an unpopular ruler. Since in the end Süss recognized his transgressions and atoned, he had, in a sense, died a good death, making his story suitable for an Orthodox retelling. During his own lifetime the choice would have been between Orthodox obser-vance or conversion, though Süss (unusually) did neither. The attempt to reform Jewish religious practice came later in the next century. Thus Lehmann's task was to convince an Orthodox readership that Süss' story was suitable for retelling and that lessons could be learned.

The popular Prague Jewish novelist Salomon Kohn (1825–1904) also provides a new (neo-Orthodox) interpretation of Süss for a bourgeois reading public.[20] His novel, *Ein deutscher Minister, Roman aus dem Achtzehnten Jahrhundert* (*A German Minister: A Novel from the Eighteenth Century*) was published in 1886 by Bloch publishers in Cincinnati, Ohio where a number of German Jews had emigrated, though not Kohn himself (Cincinnati had become the headquarters for American Reform Jewry even though Kohn himself was not a Reform Jew). Aside from its length (two volumes and over 400 pages), Kohn's novel was quite different from Lehmann's, and certainly less pious. At the outset Süss is presented as an innocent eighteen-year old living in Württemberg with his poor, blind, widowed mother. It is 1710 (thus Kohn preferred the 1692 birthdate). Süss gives violin lessons to the two daughters of the local baron (taking from Hauff the two sisters who are contrasted in their response to Süss, though both are smitten with him). One sends him a note to meet one evening in the garden; the other intercepts the note and takes the place of her sister; in the dark nature takes its course: the young Süss though 'pure, moral and noble ... was a man ... in his veins the blood began to course.'[21] He flees Württemberg. The pregnant sister marries, her husband unaware that the child is not his. Within a few pages twenty years pass: it is now 1732 and Süss has become the Duke of Württemberg's adviser, having first made his acquaintance in a forest while playing his violin. Shortly after that Carl Alexander inherits the throne. Kohn's Süss is an incorruptible prime minister and finance minister who protects the people from unjustified taxes, calls for unity against the hereditary enemy, France, and opposes the privileges of the Estates, thus being presented as a man 100 years before his time, and in many respects a National Liberal.[22]

By the early twentieth century, interest in Hauff had declined and his particular version of the Süss story had become less familiar. Fritz Runge's 1912 play was a psychological study of Süss, which combined Kohn with Griesinger's antisemitic story. Schoolteacher and journalist Eugen Ortner wrote an antisemitic play in 1911 but was forced to wait nineteen years for it to be performed – Breslau in 1930 and Fürth in 1933.[23]

Since Hauff had become less familiar to a German readership, as well as conveniently having fallen out of copyright by the late nineteenth century, films could be based on his work. Feuchtwanger revived the interest in the subject but Hauff could be used free of charge. In the late Weimar period and again in 1939 there were announcements that films based on his novella were shortly to be made. The first never materialized; the script for the second underwent such a transformation that very little of Hauff remained in the final version.

7

The historians

In the third decade of the nineteenth century, many writers, inspired by Sir Walter Scott, were drawn to the historical tale. Until then writing about the past had been, for the most part, the preserve of historians. In Germany the discipline of history was also undergoing a transformation. In 1824 the great German historian Leopold von Ranke (1795–1886) published his first book in which he argued for the importance of a critical evaluation of the sources (*Quellenkritik*).[1] He did not join in in the praise for Scott.[2] Quite the contrary, after reading him he affirmed that 'historical truth is infinitely richer, more interesting, and more beautiful than … imaginary events, however suggestive they might appear.'[3] In that same year which was three years prior to the publication of Wilhelm Hauff's novella, Christoph Wagenseil (1756–1839), the editor of a Württemberg weekly for the 'educated classes', wrote about the need for 'a complete life of Süss Oppenheimer … based on the documents.'[4]

In the very year that Hauff published his novella, Karl Friedrich Dizinger, an *Oberjustizrat* (Higher Legal Counsel), which in Württemberg also meant that he was a legal official, was granted access to the Royal Private Library and the Royal Archives.[5] Seven years later he published a short account of the period 1734–1744 which covered the reigns of Duke Carl Alexander and his son Carl Eugen, when the latter was still under age.[6] Its subtitle indicated that the study was, to a large part, based on unpublished material, in particular those documents relating to the trial of Süss. It is also evident that he made use of eyewitness accounts of both the trial and the execution published at the time.[7] He claimed to be 'strictly non-partisan' and emphasized that nothing had been taken either from 'reprehensible' sources or witnesses.[8] Nevertheless, Süss was referred to as 'the Jew', as in 'all bowed and trembled before the Jew', the 'sly Jew' or the 'crafty Jew',[9] and the Duke as his dupe. Dizinger also mentioned the testimony taken from the women assumed to have had relations with Süss.[10] For it was not just Süss' economic power which had been feared but also his sexual power, especially since that was a threat to the social order. And both would later be emphasized in the 1940 film.

Though Dizinger's study was based on archival material, he rarely adopted a critical stance towards his sources, nor did he question the criminal proceedings, which had resulted in Süss' conviction and which two centuries later (after 1945), would be characterized as a miscarriage of justice, even judicial murder.[11] It should come as no surprise that Dizinger's work did not contribute to a reassessment of Süss. Moreover, he was responsible for an error which over the next two centuries crept into subsequent accounts, namely that one of the trial judges, Dr Georg Friedrich Harpprecht, had declared, that although Süss had 'well deserved' the death penalty, he did not believe that the penal code stipulated capital punishment for his crimes.[12]

Following Dizinger, several years later, the Württemberg historian Carl Pfaff devoted some forty pages to Süss in his lengthy history of Württemberg first published in 1839, second edition in 1850.[13] Referred to as 'the Jew',[14] he is described as knowing how to tap sources for money with a 'genuine Jewish delicacy and shamelessness',[15] and elsewhere: 'Thus spoke a Jew, who had no advantage other than a boundless lack of shame and the appalling dexterity of the most skilled cutpurse,' who satisfied his 'lust' by resorting to 'all manner of persuasion, threats and violence',[16] and who, for reasons of trade, allowed in such an influx of Jews that within a short time he had found it 'advisable to stem the numbers'.[17] Pfaff also repeated Dizinger's error, namely that Harpprecht had declared that the penal code did not stipulate the death penalty for Süss' crimes.[18] Perhaps by this time (both Dizinger and Pfaff felt slightly uneasy about the penalty and it was this which persuaded them to reconsider the merits of the decision, though it was the penalty rather than the guilty verdict which concerned them. Combined with disparaging references to Süss (and to Jews generally) and given the overall tone in both accounts, the conclusion is inescapable that at this point in time in Württemberg a sea change had not yet taken place, despite allowing a limited access to the archives. Half a century later, in 1902, another Württemberg historian, Christian Belschner, was still referring to Süss as 'the Jew'.[19]

A break with this tradition, however occurred with the publication in 1874 of the doctoral dissertation by a Württemberg Protestant clergyman, Manfred Zimmermann (1841–1900), a son of (Balthasar Friedrich) Wilhelm Zimmermann (1807–1878), a Württemberg Protestant clergyman, historian and democrat, who had sat on the extreme left in the Frankfurt parliament – the parliament which had granted basic rights to Jews.[20] Twenty-five years later in 1873 at the public unveiling of a monument to the Württemberg poet Ludwig Uhland, he complained about 'the new Empire's lack of complete freedom'.[21] His son would have been working on his doctoral dissertation at this time.

Both the father's politics – as well as choice of career – are likely to have influenced the son whose study had the revealing subtitle: 'a piece of Absolutism and Jesuit history'.[22] (Absolutism, a term only coined in the 1830s to describe absolute authority, for example, as wielded by Louis XIV, was in this case used to describe rule east of the Rhine.)[23] The Württemberg authorities did not grant the young Zimmermann access to the state archives, forcing him to rely on the defence documents which were housed at Tübingen University. He also made use of the contemporary chronicles. His limited use of sources was one weakness; another was the absence of footnotes.[24]

Breaking with the custom of referring to Süss as 'the Jew', Zimmermann presented him merely as an adviser to a despotic ruler, who in order to maintain his despotic rule was forced to rely on the Jesuits. The Estates came off no better, portrayed as dominated by a corrupt oligarchy pursuing their own selfish interests. Blaming the Jesuits in Protestant Württemberg was acceptable, even timely: this work appeared three years after unification and during the *Kulturkampf* (struggle for culture), launched by Bismarck against German Catholics whom he suspected of disloyalty to the new state.

Zimmermann rejected the negative view of Süss, pointing out that he had never been a minister, nor part of any constitutional set-up: 'He was not a minister and his rule rested solely on the unconditional trust of the Duke who took his advice'.[25] He too alludes to Süss having had a Christian father and gives his birth date (wrongly) as 1692.[26] He also describes him as having 'oriental traits', but does not elaborate, along with 'Christian traits', as well as the 'manner of a cavalier'.[27] Nor was he taken for a Jew.[28] Most importantly, however, he declared that Süss was not 'the fundamentally contemptible personality for which the unreason of religious antipathy still takes him to be'.[29] Moreover, it was Carl Alexander's 'Catholicism and military despotic character', which Württemberg feared.[30] Like the radical *Achtundvierziger*, Albert Dulk, Zimmermann's view of Süss was far from negative. (His was the historical study which Lion Feuchtwanger mentioned as having consulted.)[31]

The entry for Süss in the 1894 edition of the comprehensive multi-volume biographical dictionary, *Allgemeine Deutsche Biographie*, was highly negative: Süss was described as the Jew who knew how to play on the Duke's moods with 'typical Semitic slipperiness'.[32] The author was the archivist and literary scholar Rudolf Krauss (1861–1945). Several years later in a scholarly Württemberg journal he would identify the reference to Süss in Act 2, Scene 3 of Friedrich Schiller's drama, *Die Räuber (The Robbers)*.[33] Whether Krauss ever revised his views after the publication of Feuchtwanger's novel in 1925 stimulated interest in Süss, or after the 1940 film again stimulated interest (though now orchestrated by the state), is not known. Perhaps discussions with his anti-Nazi son, Werner Krauss (1900–1976), not to be confused with the actor of the same name who took a leading role in the 1940 film, jogged his memory. Also a literary scholar (a Hispanicist), the son could not obtain an academic appointment (given his anti-Nazi views), later joined the anti-Nazi Communist-influenced resistance group, *Rote Kapelle*, for which he was sentenced to death in 1943, commuted to five years in jail.[34]

Krauss senior died in 1945; Krauss junior survived to take up academic posts in East Germany.[35] What this does tell us, however, is that this kind of description in an important reference work was acceptable in Wilhelmine Germany.

Jews too began to write about Süss – even if defensively. What is significant is that they now felt able to. In his history of the German Jews Adolph Kohut conceded that Süss had lined his own pockets.[36] In another account based mainly on Zimmermann's findings published a few years later in a yearbook for Jewish history and literature, he concluded that Süss had been 'a poor victim of medieval *raison d'état*, personal hatred' and 'contemptible intolerance'.[37]

The following year Theodor Kroner, a Stuttgart *Kirchenrat* ('church' councillor, ie a member of the Stuttgart Jewish Council), discussed Süss in the German Jewish journal *Im deutschen Reich*.[38] He claimed to have been granted access by the Württemberg king 'to additional archival material under certain limiting conditions',[39] though it was Kaiser Wilhelm II's intervention, apparently, which had enabled this.[40] His aim, he declared, was a desire to 'correct the image of Oppenheimer' as the 'evil spirit', familiar from the contemporary pamphlets and literature.[41] Zimmermann, he conceded, had at least made an attempt to present an historically faithful portrait of Süss but chided him for his 'subjectivity', lack of footnotes and the fact that he had been unable to compare the defence documents with those of the prosecution, alluding here to the fact which he must have known that Zimmermann, unlike Dizinger decades earlier, had been denied access, though even the latter had not been granted full access.[42] Doubtless it was Zimmermann's credentials (or his father's *Achtundvierzig* credentials) which had set alarm bells ringing among the officials. Given this, as well as the Kaiser's intervention, Kroner will have found it prudent to distance himself from his predecessor.

Interest was also developing at the turn of the twentieth century in the extensive contemporary material – pamphlets, book, broadsheets and images which was fast becoming collectors' items, doubtless for prurient reasons (some of this material was also housed in the Württemberg archives). Reports about this material, though intended mainly for bibliophiles, still tells us about the growth of interest in the sexual aspects of the Süss legend.[43]

The publication of Feuchtwanger's best-selling novel, *Jud Süss*, in 1925 created additional historical interest. Dr Curt Elwenspoek, who had known Feuchtwanger at university in Munich, produced a short popular study of Süss, which was published the following year.[44] Feuchtwanger arranged for the English translation as well as a British publisher, an indication that he was not ill-disposed towards Elwenspoek nor did he see his study as competition for his novel – possibly even the reverse: it could stimulate interest in the subject.[45] Based on little archival study – the sources were mainly a selective use of the eighteenth-century pamphlet literature. Despite claiming to have used the archives, fully open since 1918, Elwenspoek dismissed such material with the revealing comment that 'depressing masses of mouldering files tell us little about the man himself'.[46]

Feuchtwanger did, however, take exception to the work of Selma Stern (1890–1981). Her scholarly study, based on an extensive use of the archives, appeared in 1929 entitled *Jud Süss* ('his' title and not 'Joseph Süss Oppenheimer' as in earlier studies by Jews or by Zimmermann). He is unlikely to have forgotten her dismissive review of his novel published five years earlier, in the recently established German Jewish journal, *Der Morgen*.[47]

One of Germany's first female historians, Stern received a doctorate at Heidelberg in 1913. The subject of her dissertation Anarchasis had been Cloots (1755–1794), a Prussian philosophe and supporter of the French Revolution, guillotined by Robespierre.[48] Her choice of topic already indicated her interest in the outsider, though not yet to Jewish history.[49] She decided against pursuing a *habilitation* since it was unlikely a woman would ever obtain an academic position.[50] When the war ended she turned from German history to German Jewish history after being appointed a research fellow at the newly founded institute, the Akademie für die Wissenschaft des Judentums in Berlin, a secular research institute for the study of Jewry, the first of its kind in Germany. Her mentor was the director Eugen Täubler (1879–1953), whom she married in 1927. In 1925 she had published the first volume of a history of Prussian Jewry, the same year that she criticized Feuchtwanger's recently published novel while in the course of reviewing another historical novel by Max Brod. Brod did not 'transform or distort historical reality in contrast to the apparently successful novel by Feuchtwanger' in which 'specific Jewish suffering is absent' and where Süss appears at 'the centre of a courtly state novel (höfischen Staatsromanes) from the eighteenth century'.[51]

In 1927 Täubler was appointed professor of ancient history; just married, Stern moved to Heidelberg, the birthplace of Süss, which was also geographically convenient for a trawl of the nearby archives in Mannheim, Frankfurt, Stuttgart, Tübingen and Hessen-Darmstadt.[52] Two centuries earlier Heidelberg Jews, unusually, had not been confined to a ghetto but had even been allowed to own property, though the case of Süss suggested – contrary to the underlying thesis in Stern's recent study of Prussian Jewry – that any optimism about the gradual integration of Jews into German society might be misplaced.[53] (That optimism related to her disagreement with on the one hand the Zionists and on the other the antisemites as to whether the Jews belonged in Germany.)[54] The case of Süss, in her view, had been only a temporary rupture, a view harder for her to maintain after 1933 and even harder after 1939 when her last piece, presented for publication, fell victim to the censor.[55]

Stern's study of Süss was published in 1929. The following year Feuchtwanger reviewed it harshly in the Berlin newspaper, the *Berliner Tageblatt*. Like other liberal papers it was then providing a platform to authors of best-selling biographies like Emil Ludwig (*Goethe, Bismarck, Wilhelm II*) and Stefan Zweig (*Marie Antoinette*).[56] Such books, Stern believed, satisfied a contemporary 'longing' to read about 'great leading personalities'.[57] They also provided some competition for the institutionalized, conservative historical profession or at least challenged their authority.[58] According to Feuchtwanger, Stern had failed to capture the man, unlike her predecessors, though conceded that, despite her obvious lack of 'artistry', her work was still a 'model' for a 'precise biography'. It is unlikely that he had forgotten her earlier review of his novel, though she had not been dismissing the genre per se but rather his failure in the genre. Characterizing three earlier studies based on archival research as 'readable (Zimmermann), 'cautious and anodyne' (Kroner), and well-written in the style of Ludwig which, though at times 'misleading', still provided a 'rounded picture' (Elwenspoek), Stern's was a 'masterly example' of an accurate biography. But there was also the romantic biography which had reached its peak with Lytton Strachey, André Maurois and Ludwig as well as the historical novel. The battle rages with those in the first group, 'usually the poorest writers screaming the loudest'. No one could object to an exact portrait of Elizabeth of England, 'more effective than Schiller's or Lytton Strachey's'. But a good portrait is not like a photograph, he concluded, but its opposite.[59]

Stern herself, given that she was female and not attached to any university but to an institution unallied to a university, remained outside the academy. Moreover, she was writing a biography about Süss and biography occupied a lower status in the eyes of academic historians. Nevertheless, she was a scholar, the focus of her work was the state which was also the focus of most academic studies. In her work on the Jews in Prussia the state had been the 'subject' and the Jews the 'object'.[60] In her study of Süss he became the 'subject'.[61] But she was not producing popular biography since her concern was to illuminate an historical problem as the subtitle makes clear – 'a contribution to German and to Jewish history'.

For Feuchtwanger, however, she had failed to capture the man, unlike her predecessors Zimmermann or Elwenspoek, though conceded that despite her obvious lack of 'artistry', her work was still a 'model' for a 'precise biography'. He then delivered the coup de grâce, complaining that she offered 'meat but without gravy'.[62] For 'gravy', he presumably meant poetic licence. It is unlikely that he had forgotten her dismissive comments about his novel five years earlier.[63] More importantly, she was not dismissing the genre but rather his failure in the genre.

Feuchtwanger's displeasure with a scholarly study appearing on the same subject as his best-selling novel under the same title was understandable. Even if Stern's aim differed from his, namely to relate the life of an individual to a wider historical problem, and even if, unlike Elwenspoek, to use the latter's own turn of phrase, she had managed to wade through 'depressing masses of moldering files', Feuchtwanger still felt called on to defend the historical novel, especially when it was an author who had earlier dared to criticize him.

Stern refrained from replying to Feuchtwanger, though her husband wrote him privately on her behalf, a good indication of her marginal status. He pointed out that her study had been conceived as a contribution both to German history and to Jewish history and in particular with the integration of the Jews, rather than with 'an unusual destiny' or the 'unique' or the 'personal' as in 'the loves and adventures of a great financier and gallant adventurer', an allusion to Elwenspoek's catchy subtitle which he pointed out, would 'not have illuminated the historical process'.[64]

After 1933, Stern experienced difficulty in publishing the second volume of her study of Prussian Jewry and it finally appeared in 1939.[65] In the spring of 1941, her husband was invited to take up a post at the Hebrew Union College, in Cincinnati, Ohio, where American Reform Jewish rabbis had their training. There, in 1945, Stern obtained the newly created post of archivist and in 1950 published a study of court Jews, translated into English, of which Süss comprised only a small part. By then she had another critic.

Heinrich Schnee (1895–1968), no relation to the Governor of German East Africa, Heinrich Albert Schnee (1871–1946), began his research on the court Jew during the 1930s, a suitable subject for an historian keen to emphasize the deleterious influence of Jews in German economic life. He claimed to be seeking archival evidence in support of the controversial thesis of Werner Sombart about the role of Jews in economic life. Sombart's

Die Juden und das Wirtschaftsleben (*The Jews and Economic Life*) had been published in 1911, purportedly developing a theme touched on – but not elaborated on by Max Weber in his *The Protestant Ethic and the Spirit of Capitalism* (1905).[66] Sombart, however, had gone much further, arguing that the influence of the Jews had been wholly negative.

Schnee first published his findings in article form in 1941 under the title: 'The Jewish Question in History and the Present'.[67] His six-volume study, *Die Hoffinanz und der moderne Staat* (1953–1967), appeared after 1945,[68] published by the respected Duncker and Humblot, which earlier had published Sombart and whose director from shortly before the outbreak of war in 1914 until 1936 had been Ludwig Feuchtwanger, a younger brother of Lion Feuchtwanger.[69]

Schnee never obtained a university position: he always taught history in a *gymnasium*. Born in that part of Silesia which went to Poland after the 1921 plebiscite, he moved to German territory, joined the Catholic Centre Party but later welcomed the Nazis, though as a practising Catholic could not become a full party member until 1938.[70] He became one of the historians involved in scholarly research on the Jews.[71] Under a pseudonym in 1936 he published a book on 'race and history'.[72] Under his own name he published studies of the two major Austrian antisemites, the Mayor of Vienna Karl Lueger, and the Pan German Georg Ritter von Schönerer.[73] He then turned to the court Jew, publishing essays on the subject in 1943 and 1944 – one in Nazi ideologue Arthur Rosenberg's journal was on an ancestor of Heinrich Heine, who had been a court Jew.[74] For Nazis believed that court Jews, by obtaining privileges for themselves, had been advancing the cause of Jewish emancipation.

Schnee's scholarly apparatus is deceptive although it is undeniable that it was a work of scholarship, unlike that by lawyer Peter Deeg whose 500-page study of the court Jew had been published in 1938 by Julius Streicher's publishing house, *Der Stürmer*. It went through twelve editions up to 1943, its subtitle giving a good indication of its contents: 'Jews, Jewish crimes and Jewish Laws in Germany from the past to the present'.[75]

Doubtless, Deeg took his lead from the few words Adolf Hitler devoted to the subject of the court Jew. In *Mein Kampf* he writes: ' It is thanks to the German princes that the German nation was unable to redeem itself for good from the Jewish menace'. He refers to their 'ensnarement' which leads to their 'ruin', and as 'their relation to the peoples loosens ... [and] they cease to serve the people's interests', they 'become mere exploiters of their subjects, a process the Jew ... tries to hasten'. Through 'vilest flattery' he encourages them in their 'vices', making 'himself more and more indispensable'. 'With his deftness, or rather unscrupulousness, in all money matters, he is able to squeeze, yes, to grind, more and more money out of the plundered subjects ... Thus every court has its "court Jew"'.[76]

In the fourth volume of his history of the court Jew, Schnee writes about Süss at length but elsewhere also discusses his activities, mainly those outside Württemberg.[77] Though keen to present him in as negative a light as possible, Schnee did not go beyond what the evidence could support. His work on the court Jews is still regarded as indispensable.[78] Nevertheless, his tone is antisemitic, no Jew ever appears in a favourable light, least of all Süss. The German-born British historian Francis Carsten noted at the time of publication of the first volume that 'the author's antisemitic bias makes the reader wonder whether the date of publication is 1953' and expressed surprise at the high praise coming from the German professors cited in the book's prospectus: had they actually read the book, he asked, or was 'such praise ... symptomatic of the standard of historical scholarship in Germany today'.[79] Schnee's bias, Carsten pointed out was revealed in an assumption about Jews, namely that they had always made considerable profits.[80] As often pointed out, 1945 did not mark a *Stunde Nul* (Year Zero) for German historians.[81] That Schnee persisted with the view that the Jews had done untold damage to the German economy and society should come as no surprise, given that he first began his research in the 1930s and tried hard to join the Nazi party.

Schnee, however, would appear to have ignored Nazi guidelines on the race question. He mentions Süss' lack of a specific Jewish appearance, about which Süss' contemporaries had commented, and which, combined with other elements in the legend, led him to accept the paternity of Heidersdorf.[82] Thus while buried in the archives, it would appear, he had failed to notice the introduction of the yellow star in October 1941 precisely because physical appearance had proved such a poor guide to racial origin. Despite Nazi teachings on the subject of 'race', with which he should have been familiar, given that he had even written (under a pseudonym) a book on the subject, he still subscribed to an earlier view.[83]

One of Schnee's aims had been to refute Stern. Keen to find fault, he indicated that she had not always read the documents with care.[84] Both Schnee and Stern were scholars; both belonged to the same generation (Schnee was five years younger) but one had undertaken her research during the Weimar era and the other during the Third Reich. That explains one major difference; the other was quantity: Schnee produced a six-volume study of court Jews of which Süss formed only a small part while Stern produced a one-volume biography and two decades later a one-volume study of the court Jew translated into English for an English-speaking readership. Though both published after 1945, both had begun their research before and, in the case of Stern, research and publication mainly before 1933. For neither did 1945 represent a *Stunde Null* (year zero) on the subject of Süss. Moreover, at no point in Stern's later work did the Holocaust, that rupture to German Jewish integration, seemingly intrude. Not surprisingly, it also did not for Schnee.

Since 1945, more information about Süss has been uncovered, though mainly about his personal life or about Württemberg politics.[85] But this would take us beyond our story. The Süss historiography reflects the debate on the position of Jews: in the 1830s a growing awareness that perhaps something was not right with the penalty though not the actual verdict; with the revolutions of 1848 support for Jewish emancipation; shortly after German unification disaffection and the coining of the term antisemitism to suggest that Jews belonged to the 'semitic race' because they spoke a semitic language, namely Hebrew, for which reason they could never be German; the Weimar Republic with its constitution drafted by a Jew, inspiring the Nazis to refer to it as the '*Judenrepublik*' (the Jews Republic); and finally the Third Reich which aimed to overturn emancipation and go further with the 'Jewish Question' than in previous centuries. All is reflected in the Süss historiography, not always directly nor precisely, given time lags and inconsistencies and the usual disagreements between historians within any generation. Nevertheless, (and regardless of the fact that it was only after 1918 that the archives were fully opened) there are significant differences between what was written in the 1830s or after 1848 or after 1870, or during the 1920s or after 1933, and of course after 1945.

8

Lion Feuchtwanger's Jew Süss

In 1925, Lion Feuchtwanger's novel, *Jud Süss* (*Jew Süss*), was published, initially in a short print run.[1] It was the first novel he had written but his second to appear in print.[2] Earlier when *Jud Süss* had been rejected, he had been advised to write about a different historical figure. That book was published first in 1923.[3]

From late 1916 to late 1918, Feuchtwanger had been a leading figure in the Munich theatre world.[4] In the winter of 1923–1924 during rehearsal for a 'version' of Christopher Marlowe's *Edward II*, on which he and Bertolt Brecht were collaborating for the Munich *Kammertheater*, Adolf Hitler attempted his Beer Hall *putsch*.[5] That event, along with the fact that Berlin was fast becoming the cultural capital of the Weimar Republic persuaded him to move to Berlin where he remained until 1933.

Translated into over thirty languages including Finnish, Yiddish, Hebrew, Czech, Catalan, Icelandic, Polish, Russian and Japanese to name only a few, *Jew Süss* was a great success.[6] The first translation to be published was in English. It was by Willa and Edwin Muir, the latter better known as a poet, but the former, a linguist (and later novelist), was more likely to have been the main translator. Published first in the USA in October 1926 by Viking Press under the title, *Power* (the word 'Jew' being deemed unsuitable for an American readership), it appeared the following month in Britain with Martin Secker under the title *Jew Süss*.[7] Within a short time it went through many printings.

Reviewers were full of praise: Arnold Bennett found the novel 'remarkable' … a splendid story … [which] entertains … enthrals and simultaneously … teaches).[8] The anonymous reviewer for *The Times Literary Supplement* thought it had 'an unmistakable quality of greatness'.[9]

In late 1927 on a visit to Britain Feuchtwanger was hailed as 'the brilliant German novelist and dramatist, whose *Jew Süss* was the book of the year, both in Germany and England'.[10] Feuchtwanger would make more than one visit to Britain before he was forced to leave Germany.

Why this novel became a best seller is not altogether clear. The historic character was at least familiar to German readers but outside Germany its appeal can only be explained in terms of the telling – a vivid story presented in clear language, likened to a 'well drawn strip cartoon', with 'a series of scenes in which the background is ... clearly sketched, the foreground dominated by colourful characters, stylized for instant recognition' with 'blocks of dialogue or inner monologues superimposed'.[11] Apparently the author's skill and the novel's special qualities attracted the readers rather than the subject matter. This might also explain its appeal to non-Germans, although Germans too could enjoy the book without necessarily having to reassess the character of Süss. The publishers, who had initially turned down the novel, had underestimated Feuchtwanger's skill and failed to realize that a controversial subject could be made palatable, especially if the context was, to some extent, favourable, which it was in the middle years of the Weimar Republic. Süss could be presented not as a villain but as a tragic hero brought down by his own failings and not as the wrong man (a Jew), in the wrong place (Württemberg), at the wrong time (early eighteenth century).

This was not Feuchtwanger's first attempt to write on the subject. His play, also entitled *Jud Süss*, had opened during the First World War in October 1917 at the Munich *Schauspielhaus* but soon fell victim to the censor.[12] A five-act play on the subject by Fritz Runge, which had appeared in 1912, may have drawn him to the subject.[13] Feuchtwanger had several plays performed in Munich and elsewhere between 1917 and late 1918. *Jud Süss* also had productions eighteen months later in Vienna and Frankfurt.[14]

Once it was realized that the troops would not be home by Christmas 1914, and that it would not, in the words of the German Crown Prince, be a 'short and jolly war', antisemites found a ready audience for their claims that Jews were not volunteering in relation to their numbers. The War Ministry agreed to conduct a census (*Judenzählung*) and on discovering that the accusations were unfounded, decided not to publish the findings. Thus the rumours were not quashed and antisemitism continued to grow.[15] This may well have inspired Feuchtwanger to write a play about a controversial Jew and present him in a favourable light. Despite his claim to have first read Manfred Zimmermann's sympathetic account of Süss only much later (when planning to write the novel), he probably had read it earlier when preparing to write the play.[16] In 1929 when he said this he might well have been trying to cover his tracks since by this time his reputation as a novelist had outstripped that of playwright. On the last page of the published version of the play, he advised directors to consult the work of the Württemberg historian Christian Belschner though only for illustrative material. Otherwise he was not keen to reveal his sources.

Aside from a favourable review by Heinrich Mann in the liberal (Jewish-owned) *Berliner Tageblatt*, the others were poor.[17] The times were not favourable for a play on the topic of any Jew, least of all one so controversial. A Munich reviewer, sprinkling his comments with Yiddish terms, complained that 'recently it appears the theatre wants to present us with all the famous Hebrews of world history'.[18] Staged in Vienna eighteen months later, the play was dismissed by a critic for the Social Democratic paper as 'chocolate with garlic', garlic here being presumed to relate to Jewish cooking.[19] For another reviewer it was 'true cinema drama' (given that theatre critics at this time often looked down on cinema, should not be assumed to be favourable), adding that to 'non-Jewish eyes and ears' it appeared 'arrogant' and 'insolent'.[20] The role of Süss, Feuchtwanger later recalled, was always taken by a non-Jewish actor. In Frankfurt, it was Eugen Klöpfer who later took a leading role as the father in Veit Harlan's *Jud Süss* since by then he was too old to play Süss.[21] But much later Feuchtwanger mentioned a Jewish actor in the role in Vienna, namely Schildkraut (obviously, Rudolf, then in his fifties, rather than his son, Joseph, then only twenty-one).[22]

Born in Munich in 1884, Feuchtwanger was the eldest of nine children. His family were Orthodox Jews. His father had been born in Fürth as were his father, grandfather and great-grandfather before him.[23] During Süss' own lifetime Fürth already had a sizable Jewish community and even a Jewish publishing house which had been responsible for the publication of the Jews' defence of Süss.[24] As a child Feuchtwanger may well have heard a Jewish legend that the day after the execution Jews from Fürth had come to the gallows and taken down the body of Süss for burial, replacing it with another corpse. This is how he would close his novel, though not the play.[25]

As a university student in Munich, Feuchtwanger wrote his doctoral dissertation on Heinrich Heine's fragmentary novel, *Der Rabbi von Bacherach* (*The Rabbi of Bacherach*). The sceptical and worldly Heine, though a convert to Christianity, mainly as an entré to German society, had chosen a medieval setting for his tale about the persecution of the Jews. Like other German authors, he too was inspired by Sir Walter Scott, though his was to be a 'medieval historical novel with Jewish materials'.[26] It remained his sole effort to produce something in this genre, begun in 1824, but only published incomplete sixteen years later.[27] Feuchtwanger's choice of topic already reflected an interest in turning to the past to write about the present. At the outbreak of the First World War, Feuchtwanger had been living in Tunisia with his wife, Marta, and was interned by the French authorities. After being allowed to return to Germany, he served briefly in the army. Early in his marriage, he and his wife lost an infant daughter, whom they had named Tamar (they would have no more children); this was the name in the play which Feuchtwanger gave to the daughter of Süss but in the novel changed to Naemi.

There are, however, more significant differences between play and novel, in particular the ending. In the former after the lascivious Duke has caused the death of Tamar whose existence he has only just discovered, Süss turns against his master and betrays the latter's plan to make Württemberg Catholic. The coup is foiled, the Duke suffers a stroke but unlike in the novel, does not die. Instead, he becomes mentally and physically incapacitated. In both play and novel, however, Süss is still blamed, imprisoned and then executed. In both he makes no attempt to try and save himself by offering the information, only recently divulged to him, that his biological father is 'Baron Heydersdorff'.[28] He refuses to save himself. In the play (though not in the novel) he ignores the entreaties of the pious daughter of a member of the diet whom earlier he had procured for the Duke, despite being smitten with her and she with him.[29] Feuchtwanger put the subject aside. A few years later he began work on a novel inspired by Walter Rathenau, Germany's foreign minister appointed in 1922.[30] The wealthy, intellectual son of the founder of AEG, the large electrical concern, Rathenau had in 1897 anonymously published a notorious article calling on fellow German Jews to 'assimilate and cast off all vestiges of oriental customs and appearance'.[31] A member of the Democratic Party (the left liberals), he signed the Treaty of Rapallo with the Soviet Union, recognizing the territory Germany had ceded to Soviet Russia in the spring of 1918 in the Treaty of Brest-Litovsk. He served only a few months before being assassinated either because of this treaty or because he was Jewish or because of both.

Feuchtwanger completed the novel in September 1922, three months after Rathenau's death but had to wait until 1925 for publication. His aim, he later claimed in 1935, was to present a man who went 'from doing to not-doing from action to inaction, from a European to an Indian world outlook'.[32] Since this proved difficult with Rathenau as the subject he returned to Süss which presumably he thought could illustrate the conflict between action and inaction.[33] Over the next thirty years he would write seventeen novels, the majority historical – the exception was his trilogy about the rise of the Nazis.[34]

Alfred Döblin (1878–1957), the German novelist, six years Feuchtwanger's senior and now best known as the author of *Berlin Alexanderplatz* (1929), set in contemporary working class Berlin, had earlier written historical novels with more remote settings, namely China and South America. For his eighteenth-century China novel, *Wang-lun*, published in 1916, Feuchtwanger had nothing but praise: 'possibly the fulfilment of what Goethe had once dreamt of – Eastern feeling and thought in a completely Western art form', he wrote at the time.[35] That novel's 'Taoism' also exerted an influence on his play along with 'Middle Eastern' and cabbalist speculations combined with elements of Schopenhauer.[36] Years later, however, after the publication of *Berlin Alexanderplatz* and also after the arrival of the Nazis, Döblin voiced his low opinion of the historical novel which 'is firstly a novel', he wrote, 'and secondly not history'.[37] Though an apt description of Feuchtwanger's *Jew Süss*, it is not known whether he had that particular novel in mind.

Feuchtwanger may have read an account by an historian (Zimmermann) and probably also some of the eighteenth-century popular material, though he never mentioned the latter, but in any case such preparation did not inhibit his flight of fancy. His interest was not in understanding the historic Süss but in using the historic Süss for his own purposes. Several years after the novel was published he declared that his intention had been neither to 'rescue Joseph Süss nor to destroy an antisemitic legend'.[38] What cannot be denied, however, is that he chose to write both a play and a novel about Süss, at a time when antisemitism was on the increase. Yet his aim he professed was 'to show the path of a white man, the path [which went] beyond the narrow European teachings of power, to the Egyptian teachings of the will to immortality, and on to the Asian teachings of not-willing and not-doing [*sic*]'.[39]

Like many other German writers at this time, including Jewish, Feuchtwanger was influenced by Orientalism. This is evident in his novel about Süss. In addition to the more general embrace of the wisdom of the East, which also related to the notion of 'not doing', the novel reflects a specifically Jewish variant of Orientalism.

For a Jew to be described as 'Oriental' was a marker of difference. A vague and flexible term about the 'other', it suggested that Jews could not be European even though they had lived in Europe for over a millennium. In 1801, Johann Gottfried Herder had claimed that they belonged to a 'foreign Asiatic people'; somewhat later Arthur Schopenhauer had declared that they should be denied civil rights because they were a 'strange, oriental people';[40] while the term antisemitism had been coined in the 1870s to suggest that the Jews spoke a Semitic language, a language of the East (Hebrew), proof that they did not and could never belong in Germany.

Jews responded to anti-Jewish Orientalism either by rejecting it or by assimilating it, as in Zionism, or in romanticizing it,[41] in an attempt to transform a hostile view into something positive. In so doing, they could reclaim – rather than deny – their 'Oriental' roots. For philosopher Martin Buber (1878–1965), this ultimately led him to Zionism – Jews belonged in the Middle East rather than Europe. But he also claimed that German Jews were uniquely placed to establish cooperation between Asia (which he argued was in decline through Westernization) and Europe because of the German propensity for metaphysics.[42]

Since wisdom was to be found in the East, from which the Jews had originated they brought with them something special, according to Feuchtwanger in the section of the novel (Book Five) entitled 'The Others'. It begins with a description of 'the land of Canaan, infinitely small' where 'the Orient and the Occident meet'. 'From the Occident there beats a wild continuous wave upon the land of Canaan: a thirst for life and personality, a will for action, for happiness, for power … knowledge, possessions.' In contrast, 'in the south under the pointed pyramid lie dead kings embalmed in gold and spices, refusing majestically to give their bodies to destruction'. He then goes on to describe the wisdom of the East:

> from the east … comes a message of gentle wisdom: Sleep is better than waking, to be dead is better than to be alive. Non-resistance, surrender to annihilation, passivity, renunciation … These three waves flow over the tiny land and mingle … one clear and resounding of will and deed, one hot and glowing of majestic refusal to submit to death, one soft and dark of surrender and renunciation.[43]

Feuchtwanger had already expressed a similar idea in late 1917 when replying to a letter from an acquaintance regarding his play. He then wrote that he was not concerned with the 'problem of Jew and Christian' but rather

> wanted to present the development of a man of the deed and a man of power into a man of renunciation, a European man into an Indian. That I needed a half-Jew for this development, explains itself in the theory … that all practical philosophy culminates either in a will to deed or in resignation. Action is, crudely expressed, the result of European, renunciation, the result of asiatic philosophizing. The Jews appear to me now already for geographic reasons the obvious broker between both systems. From nature torn here and there between action and renunciation. From this idea I have positioned the people and events of the play.[44]

Thus the Jew has become a hybrid and it was precisely this that gave him the capacity for wisdom. In the play Süss sees 'the light' (his words) and regrets striving while in the novel he submits, having learned the wisdom of the East, which is about submission rather than doing.[45]

Almost two centuries after the Jews of Fürth presented their version of Süss as a martyr, Feuchtwanger created his own: the first during the First World War and the second in the defeat and its immediate aftermath. Politically on the left, he was witness to its post-war fragmentation, possibly another reason why inaction could seem an attractive option. During the war action was easily associated with militarism while afterwards with political failure.

Feuchtwanger's novel reflects little of what was then known about the historic Süss, about which he would have had some knowledge, at the very least through reading Zimmermann. Given the novel's final chapters, it is also evident that he had read some of the popular eighteenth-century accounts. Nevertheless, *Jew Süss* would fit Döblin's description as 'firstly a novel and secondly not history'.

The novel focuses on Süss' short time in Württemberg and his quest there for power (hence its American title). It strays, even further afield than Hauff, who born in Württemberg, had grown up with the legend and known individuals who when young had been present at the execution, which at least enabled him to capture something of the Württemberg mentality as, for example, in the character of the father. Feuchtwanger's link with Süss, on the other hand, is likely to have derived from Fürth and the legend of the Jews, especially their belief in his 'martyrdom'. The removal of the body on the day following the execution by Jews from Fürth may be part of their legend, which as a child he may have heard, rather than be purely his own invention.

The story begins with a description of the Duke of Württemberg, followed by the introduction of Süss to the Duke at the nearby spa through the machinations of Isaac Landauer. Süss now begins to serve the Duke. Up to this point, Feuchtwanger does not deviate from what the historians had written; after this, his imagination takes over. Clearly he has read some sources but nevertheless has chosen to ignore them, unless their information helped him tell the story in the way he wanted. He does mention by name a number of individuals referred to in the sources, although he usually assigns them different roles, since his concern is to tell a good story rather than follow the historical sources. For Feuchtwanger, facts were the rubble of the past to be gathered up and reassembled in a form best suited for story-telling while providing a semblance (but only a semblance) of authentic detail.

Space forbids a detailed summary of the plot but very briefly: Süss, who has enemies but also friends, discovers resting on a riverbank the beautiful and pious daughter of a member of the diet. Later, to her horror, he procures her for the Duke, an offer she is not in a position to refuse, though by that time it is Süss whom she loves and he her. This character has been given the name of the pietist poet Magdalena Sibylla Weissensee (1707–1786), the daughter of Philipp Heinrich Weissensee, a theologian and member of the *Landschaft* who was one of the few members friendly to Süss (he kept him informed of discussions in the Landschaft).[46] At the time of Süss' arrival in Württemberg she had been married eleven years to Emmanuel Rieger, the brother of Pastor Georg Conrad Rieger, who had preached against Süss, but who also praised him immediately after his execution for at the point of death having found God. She was unlikely to have had contact with Süss.[47]

Süss also has a daughter (replacing the sister in Hauff – the paternal rather than fraternal relationship being more credible, given the necessary age difference). The mother, Süss' wife, who gave birth to the daughter, dies after one year of marriage. Taking elements from the legend Feuchtwanger describes Süss' mother as an actress and his father a musician. But the uncle, the mother's brother, is made to be the prominent eighteenth-century rabbi, Jonathan (Johann) Eybeschütz (1690–1764), a rabbi in Prague during Süss' time in Württemberg, who had once been accused of dabbling in Cabbalism, and whom the historic Süss would have had no occasion to meet nor would he, a hard-headed businessman, have had an interest in Cabbalism. Süss fears the uncle who later brings the daughter to live with Süss and will later tell him that his natural father is Baron Heidersdorf. The daughter is kept hidden with her nurse in a hunting lodge. Süss visits his daughter from time to time.

Süss' conscience is pricked when he learns of a pogrom directed against a poor Jew falsely accused of the blood libel. But the novel's turning point is the loss of his daughter. On a hunting trip in the forest the Duke comes upon Süss' house, led there by Weissensee, bent on revenge for Süss' role in his own daughter's violation. To Süss' horror, the lascivious Duke discovers the existence of Naomi whose death, as in the play, he then causes through his amorous advances. He climbs a ladder to the daughter's bedroom window; she escapes to the roof, stumbles and falls to her death.[48]

The daughter's death causes the disillusioned Süss to turn against his master. He gives up his quest for power and betrays the Duke's plan for a coup against the Estates. The Duke is outraged on discovering this but dies suddenly in the presence of Süss – either as a direct result of the betrayal or because of the fatigue caused by the aphrodisiac or because of the excitement and his exertions. Süss has realized that one should not put one's trust in princes. The Duke's fellow conspirators fear exposure. Süss offers himself up: 'Arrest me; and then you are safe, whoever comes out on top'.[49] He would make a 'conspicuous scapegoat to intercept the first outbreak of wrath ... Yes, arrest the Jew! That will be our salvation! The Jew must hang!' He is promptly arrested, after which he is tried and convicted, and never mentions his noble ancestry which Feuchtwanger assumed (wrongly) would have saved him.[50] He goes nobly to his death, wearing the scarlet coat, as in the contemporary accounts, and with the 'solitaire gleaming on finger', as in Schiller, for the regent 'had forbidden him to be deprived of the ring'.[51]

Feuchtwanger has made use of the Jewish legend, insofar as Süss dies a martyr, though his route to martyrdom is circuitous. He also makes dramatic use of the non-Jewish legend in presenting Süss as the natural son of Heidersdorf. Since Jewish descent is matrilineal, Süss was a Jew, despite his mother's 'misbehaviour' which would have offended Jewish notions of virtue, certainly in 1698 if less so in the early twentieth century. He has also taken other elements from the non-Jewish legend, namely his womanizing and life of luxury. But in having this half-Jew 'freely' choose to die as a Jew, he is able to present him as a martyr to the faith, as in the Jewish legend, becoming almost Christ-like in making the supreme sacrifice because he has learned (late in the day) that power and wealth are not worth seeking and so redeems himself by choosing death. He thus reaches martyrdom by a slightly different route than that prescribed by Jewish custom and practice. Feuchtwanger has created his own story, doubtless in the belief that he has captured the man, Süss.[52] His Süss has learned the futility of seeking wealth and power, whereas the historic Süss may merely have thought that he had played his hand badly or experienced bad luck, given the timing of the Duke's death.

Feuchtwanger used the Heidersdorf legend to reinforce Süss' virtue, but in one respect he did not deviate from what is apparent in all the sources, namely that Süss, while in prison, did become a devout Jew. On the other hand, Feuchtwanger not only has him repent and abandon his quest for wealth and power but he also has him learn a wisdom which emanates from the East, namely that of 'not doing'. Thus his quest for power was doomed from the start and he now does die the wiser. His failure to achieve the success he sought could serve as a moral lesson for Jews and others.

In 1929, Ashley Dukes, a translator for the theatre mainly from German, adapted Feuchtwanger's novel for the London West End stage. It was at the request of the leading stage actor Matheson Lang who was to play the Duke.[53] Initially, Dukes had reservations about the subject matter and suggested that it would be more appropriate if the task went to a Jew, but Lang was persuasive (Dukes had already done one play for him). It is obvious that Dukes found Lang, a major stage actor with a deep bass voice, incongruous in the role: adding that Lang 'was not even a Jew himself but a cousin of the Archbishop of Canterbury [Cosmo Lang] with a Scots accent which became more noticeable when he made his nightly curtain speeches in the cities north of the Border'.[54]

Dukes also made himself familiar with Feuchtwanger's 1917 play but felt he should create something different for British audiences which, in his view, would have found some aspects alien. He was also grateful that the novel had little dialogue.[55] His preference was to prolong 'the drama up to and including the execution but': he wrote, 'Lang had different ideas … and more than one of my suggested closing scenes disappeared in the final version'.[56] In the middle of a lavish production with over forty actors and actresses on stage in 'elaborate fancy dress', Dukes' wife, dancer Marie Rambert, staged a ballet (with music by Constant Lambert). One critic found this a 'weakness' (a 'skipping rope dance') and remarked on the programme's reference to Dukes' marriage to 'a Mll. Rambert': it was 'very nice to make a family party of it' though the play required something better.[57]

Rehearsals for the play began in July 1929. It toured northern cities and opened in Blackpool and reached London's West End at the end of September 1929. The melodrama was a great success. A young Peggy Ashcroft played Süss' daughter in her first important role. Speaking her lines naturally, then unusual for ingénues, she received high praise but failed to obtain the role in the British film which went to the daughter of one of the film's producers Pamela Ostrau.[58]

Most of the reviews were favourable aside from the *Jewish Chronicle* which felt Jewish behaviour had been misrepresented because:

> no Jew would have left his daughter in the charge of a man while he was far away from her, even if a Rabbi', and any Jew upon discovering Naemi after she had thrown herself out of the window, would have instantly sent for a doctor. "Jew Süss', as Feuchtwanger has him, is a type which, as a matter of fact, is not yet by any means extinct. 'Jew Süss' as Mr. Ashley Dukes presents him, is nothing like any Jew that was or is, or humanly speaking, ever will be.[59]

The critic for the *Daily Express* commented on the number of Jews present in the audience: 'its Jewish subject' having led to 'a greater rush of Jewish playgoers to the theatre than I have seen for months. Indeed, the management estimates that out of 1,200 people in the theatre, probably 800 were Jews and Jewesses',[60] while the *Daily Express* mentioned the 'enormous interest in the play ... shown by the thirty-hour wait of the queue and the rapt attention with which every word was followed'.[61]

The novel's popularity and Lang's drawing power helped at the box office. But the run was cut short by the Wall Street crash which occurred five weeks after the West End opening. Audiences began to dry up and the play closed in early 1930. The following year in October 1931, it had another production in Dublin at the Gate Theatre, directed by Michael Mac Liámmoir and Hilton Edwards. The middle-aged Duke was played by the precocious sixteen-year old Orson Welles in his first stage role.[62]

Feuchtwanger's widow, Marta, mentioned conflict between Dukes and Feuchtwanger over copyright, after an unauthorized stage production appeared in Yiddish in a New York theatre.[63] In his memoir written nearer to the time, Dukes makes no mention of this, merely that his version had been performed in New York in Yiddish.[64] The Yiddish actor Maurice Schwartz (1890–1960) had apparently translated (and possibly also adapted) Feuchtwanger.[65] It opened in October 1929 but its appeal was limited and closed shortly thereafter; it then opened in another New York theatre in English and with some success.[66]

Feuchtwanger would seem to have been pleased with the adaptation, since he arranged for Dukes to translate it into German, under his supervision.[67] But one year after its London opening, the *Jud Süss* that appeared on the Berlin stage was not by Feuchtwanger but by the playwright and one-time dramaturge for Max Reinhardt at the Deutsches Theater in Berlin, Paul Kornfeld (1889–1942).

The director was Leopold Jessner, renowned for his expressionist productions, who from 1919 until early 1930 had headed Germany's most important theatre, the Prussian State Theatre in Berlin. His controversial avant-garde productions caused an outcry from conservatives and Catholics who accused him, among other things, of 'casting Jews in leading roles and judaizing' the state-subsidized theatre.[68] Kornfeld's choice of subject is likely to have resonated with Jessner since he had an interest in Jewish issues, but his preference was for Kornfeld's version of the Süss story not Feuchtwanger's.[69] Nevertheless, he was not adverse to a Feuchtwanger play and in April 1930 directed in Berlin an earlier play from 1923: *Wird Hill Amnestiert? (Will Hill be Amnestied?).*[70] It may have been, at this point, that Feuchtwanger learned of Jessner's plans, though he would still have the satisfaction of radio adaptations of the Duke's version broadcast from stations in Frankfurt, Cassel, Stuttgart and Freiburg.[71]

Kornfeld's play opened on 7 October 1930 at the Theater am Schiffbauerbaum (after World War II it became the home of the Berliner Ensemble). Several weeks earlier, during rehearsal, the Nazis had made their breakthrough in the Reichstag elections to become the second largest party. A revival of the Süss story had thus become all the more potent.

The abstract sets were by Caspar Neher who had often worked with Brecht (as well as Feuchtwanger on the 1923–1924 Munich production of the Brecht-Feuchtwanger *Edward II*). Süss was played by the distinguished stage and film actor, Ernst Deutsch, a Prague-born Jew and friend of Kornfeld since school days, the Regent by Hans-Heinrich von Twardowski (ten years earlier he had played Alan in *The Cabinet of Dr Caligari*). The large cast also included Lotte Lenya as the widow

Götz. These actors would soon go into exile. Other cast members would continue with their careers in the Third Reich such as Erich Ponto who played Remchingen (a villain in this version) and later Amschel Rothschild in *Die Rothschilds* (1940); Hilde Körber, then the wife of Veit Harlan in a minor role; comedian Theo Lingen, whose popularity later allowed him a special dispensation since his actress and opera singer wife was half-Jewish (Brecht's ex-wife Marianne Zoff) and Otto Wernicke who played the Duke whose wife was Jewish and who enjoyed a similar dispensation.[72]

Kornfeld had been interested in Süss since the publication of Feuchtwanger's novel, but also fascinated with the subject of Don Juan and his hope had been to combine some aspects of both in his portrayal of Süss.[73] Though Feuchtwanger's novel may have drawn his attention to the subject, he wrote a very different play: humorous in parts, even ironic, it reveals a crafty Jew whose intuition and insight into the people he encounters as he insinuates himself at court enables him to advance himself. He arrives as the poor Jew from the forest (a place of darkness and mystery), though prior to that from the 'Heidelberg ghetto [*sic*]'. He quickly metamorphoses from a haggling, wise-cracking peddler to a smart businessman who never misses a business opportunity, becoming both friend and adviser to the Duke. Adored by the Duchess and other women, he also appears the *gallant* – and this metamorphosis takes place within a mere twelve-month period. But he is feared and hated by the other ministers and by the people for the taxes he imposes to increase his master's wealth. This leads to his undoing. The ministers plot his demise but it is the Duke who by mistake drinks the poison. Kornfeld's Süss appears closer to Selma Stern's portrait – her biography appeared some fifteen months before the play's premiere, though whether Kornfeld read it or even had an interest in doing so is not known. His Süss is a credible portrait of a German Jew who having emerged from the ghetto and adapted easily, makes money and friends in high places but enemies as well and is ultimately betrayed by the careerists he has helped or displaced. Attractive to women, he helps the widowed Frau Götz and her daughter and son. The last mentioned will turn on him. (Süss did have an affair with a widowed Frau Götz whose husband had been a privy councillor and he also had contact with her daughter, while another Götz, doubtless a relative, was a privy councillor during his time in Württemberg.)[74] Kornfeld has Süss help the Götz son about whom there is a running joke concerning his swift advancement, but he turns on Süss at the end, doubtless an allusion to the character of Lanbek in the Wilhelm Hauff novella.

An important element is the friendship between the Duke and Süss. As the Duke is dying, he tells Süss to flee but the latter is too bereft to do so and is then arrested.[75] He is tried, expects only five years since, in his view there are no legal grounds for his conviction, and is therefore shocked to learn the verdict, based on a law not in use for 180 years, namely the ban on sexual relations between Jews and Christians. Despite legal objections raised by the distinguished professor of law, Hilprecht (sic), the regent upholds the verdict.[76] Absent is any allusion to religion except when told of the death sentence, Süss utters a few words from the important Hebrew prayer, the *Shema*. Usually ignored as a source, Kornfeld's play, rather than Feuchtwanger's novel, is likely to have been of more use to the scriptwriters of the 1940 film and traces can be found, especially in the earlier version of the script, in particular the description of Süss' arrival in Stuttgart as a poor Jew.

Jessner pruned the play considerably, especially the mass scenes before the execution which pilloried the antisemitism of the masses.[77] Whether this was done out of fear of incitement or because Kornfeld had a tendency to write at length is not known.[78] Though Neher's set created a 'sense of timelessness', the play was timely: the allusions to Hitler, according to one critic, could be discerned in the 'grand Hitler tone' of the Regent's speeches.[79] But given the date of writing, rather than of the rehearsal or of the performance, it has been suggested that Kornfeld had General Kurt von Schleicher in mind, an important figure who worked behind the scenes in the recently installed government of Heinrich Brüning and who, given his military background, also had links to the elderly President Paul von Hindenberg.[80] (He was later assassinated in the Night of the Long Knives in 1934.)

The play failed to get good reviews but did have productions elsewhere (Frankfurt, Kassel, Stuttgart, Freiburg and Berne).[81] Jessner left Germany in 1933 for Israel but then went to Vienna and after that the USA; Kornfeld left for Prague, his birthplace, in 1932 and died ten years later in the Lodz ghetto. Feuchtwanger's novel inspired one other stage adaptation. The novel's Hebrew translator, Avi Shaul, borrowed from Dukes and his version had performances in Tel Aviv in 1933.[82]

At the time of the Nazi takeover on 30 January 1933, Feuchtwanger was out of the country on a lecture tour in the USA. Several weeks later his Süss novel was burned. He went into exile in Sanary-sur-Mer in the south of France, where Aldous Huxley was then living, and where a number of German writers and artists – Heinrich and Thomas Mann, Stefan Zweig, Joseph Roth, to name but a few – would take up residence for a time. He remained there until the Germans invaded France in June 1940 after which he was interned. Thanks to the efforts of Mann, now in the USA (and no admirer of Feuchtwanger's work), who had helped set up a rescue committee for German refugees, especially writers and artists caught in France, Feuchtwanger was rescued from a camp near Nimes. His escape and arrival in New York received much press coverage in the USA and Britain – the *Daily Express* headline read: 'Jew Suss Flees in Woman's Dress', the disguise given him by his rescuer when he escaped the camp.[83] Shortly before boarding the liner taking him to the USA, Veit Harlan's *Jud Süss* had its Berlin première. Six months later in April 1941, Feuchtwanger published in the *Atlantic Monthly* an open letter to his 'Berlin friends' who had taken principal roles in *Jud Süss*:

> You have, Gentlemen, made from my novel a touch of *Tosca*, you have transformed my novel, possibly all seven of you, have acted in stage versions of it. In discussing specific points with me, you proved that you understood the book, and you talked about it in high terms.[84]

Neither Feuchtwanger nor his wife ever viewed the Harlan film, though this did not deter him from claiming ownership of the Süss story. Possibly this was done in the hope that, post war, this would encourage the West German authorities to keep the film out of circulation and continue with the ban on any screening in Germany (still in force today).[85] As a highly successful author he may also have felt that he owned the story – that it was his work which had inspired Harlan and his two co-scriptwriters. Feuchtwanger and his wife settled in Pacific Palisades, California from where he wrote more best-selling novels. After his death in 1958 his widow continued with his claim to ownership of the Süss story. But Harlan's script was as different from Feuchtwanger's novel as Feuchtwanger's had been from Hauff's novella or from that by any other writer on the subject. There is no ownership of the story of Süss. It has been retold in different ways and for different purposes by more than one writer.

9

The British film Jew Süss *(1934)*

In 1933, the year that Hitler was appointed German Chancellor, Britain's largest film company, Gaumont British, submitted three different scenarios to the British Board of Film Censors on the subject of the persecution of German Jews. The first, 'A German Tragedy' by Franz Schultz, submitted in May, was rejected as a 'pathetic' story which 'undoubtedly [came] …, under the heading of political propaganda' as well as undesirable 'at the present juncture', given 'recent agitation in Germany' against Jews. 'Feeling still runs very strongly in London on this subject', they added.[1] The day previous to the Board's rejection battles between Fascists and Jews had broken out near London's Leicester Square,[2] which gave rise to fears that further disturbances could be easily provoked. The second scenario was rejected in June. Though no author was mentioned 'City without Jews' was obviously based on Hugo Bettauer's eponymous novel, the subject of a 1924 Austrian silent film. (Bettauer had been assassinated the following year.)[3]

The British Board of Film Censors had no legal status. To pre-empt state control, twenty years earlier the film industry had approached the British government to approve their plan to set up their own body to classify, cut or reject feature films. This was financed by the industry. The rigorous censorship controls excluded films on a variety of topics, including unemployment a topic of particular interest during the 1930s.[4] In 1929 one-time Liberal Home Secretary Edward Shortt, (later Sir Edward), was appointed president of the Board. He admitted to not liking sound films and during his six years in office many were banned (in 1934 the number was twenty-three).[5] This of course did not apply only to British films but to any films intended for exhibition. The local authorities, which licensed the films for exhibition, took note of their classification.

Drawing attention to the plight of German Jews would have been construed as political propaganda. Such films, it was also believed, were likely to lose money and the British film industry was hardly unique in not wanting to take that risk. To gain approval, film-makers had to navigate strict censorship controls. The boycott of Jewish goods and premises promoted by the Nazis, which began on 1 April 1933, put the spotlight on the issue of Jewish persecution. The Board, however, saw no reason to make any allowances which partly explains the rejection of the first two scenarios.[6]

Later that year, however, on 2 November 1933 the Board relented when Gaumont British submitted its third scenario on the subject. *Jew Süss* met with their approval (though not without qualifications), doubtless helped by the fact that it had come in the guise of a costume drama as well as being based on a best-selling novel. Their only objection related to matters of taste. The novel was described as 'very powerful', its language and many scenes 'coarse and outspoken' but the scenario was considered 'somewhat milder'. Nevertheless, 'a good many modifications' were still required: the Duke's lecherousness was too explicit: 'the execution scenes … [also needed to] be considerably curtailed and softened. No struggles should be shown and no tightening of the rope. Laughter and hysterics should be omitted'.[7] The Board's approval was still required at a later stage: the completed film was presented on 14 June 1934, just two months after the Hollywood-made *The House of Rothschild*, another film about historic German antisemitism, had been approved subject to only a minor cut in dialogue.[8] *Jew Süss*, however, was passed for adult viewing with no deletions.[9]

During the silent era there had been plans to make a British film based on the Feuchtwanger novel: when in 1927 Feuchtwanger visited Britain the press reported him as having been paid £8,000 for film rights and the film critic C. A. Lejeune later recalled that he had been presented to the press.[10] At the same time his novel had also stimulated interest in a film on the subject in Germany, but it was to be based on Wilhelm Hauff's novella, then conveniently out of copyright.[11] Three years later, in 1930, the same year that Kornfeld's play, *Jud Süss*, appeared on the Berlin stage, plans to make a sound film based on Hauff were also announced: it was to be a Franco-German co-production, a 'Pathé-Natan-Superproduktion' in two versions, one in French and one in German, the latter to have been directed by Conrad Wiene, brother of Robert Wiene, the director of *The Cabinet of Dr Caligari* (1920), and starring the leading stage and film actor of Jewish origin Fritz Kortner.[12] Neither Hauff film project materialized. Instead it was in Britain that a film on the subject, based on Feuchtwanger, was made. In Germany interest in a film on the subject had disappeared by 1933. One based on Hauff, however, was conceivable but another six years passed before that was announced (for obvious reasons, aside from copyright, the story could no longer be based on Feuchtwanger). The film that came to be made was hardly based on Hauff but instead was a Veit Harlan version, tailor-made for the new conditions.

British film rights had initially been acquired in the 1920s for £6000 by Ludwig Blattner who later sold them to Gaumont British.[13] But these rights were 'silent rights'. With sound, the rights issue became more complicated. Dialogue had to be written and, when based on a novel, affected copyright. Words came with a price tag and the original contract with Feuchtwanger had to be renegotiated as well as with the English language stage adaptor, Dukes, and the London publisher, Martin Secker. All this put up costs. As early as August 1932, several months before the Nazis came to power, a synopsis had been prepared.[14] Apparently ten different 'treatments' (emphasizing the story's highlights) were ready by June 1934. They were in preparation for a script which was only ready just before shooting began.[15]

Berlin-born Lothar Mendes (1894–1874), who was also Jewish and a one-time Ufa director (though hardly an important one), was appointed director. According to a report in the British film press he took credit for getting Gaumont interested in the subject, declaring that 'For years

I have been carrying about with me the idea of Jew Süss. It seemed strange to me that I was never able to persuade my friends in Hollywood to make a film'.[16] (But whether he was in a position to persuade anyone is questionable. He had left Germany in 1926 for Hollywood where he directed a few films, including for Paramount and then also married and quickly divorced a British actress.) He declared that he had seen the possibilities of *Jew Süss* after seeing the play in New York, but could interest no one until he came to England 'on holiday'. His holiday is also likely to have involved a search for work since by then Germany had become off limits. He met with the Gaumont British executives, probably Michael Balcon, the chief executive, and possibly one or more of the owners, the three Ostrer brothers (Isidore, Maurice and Mark).[17] Balcon was determined to make the film.[18] All these men were Jewish, an observation hardly worth commenting upon since Jews, unable to make their way in other more established industries due to prejudice, were (given their numbers) over-represented in the new film industries in a number of countries.[19]

What might have worked in a novel or in the theatre might not on screen, especially given the need to attract larger audiences with broader tastes. Box office takings could not be ignored. Some thirty years later, Balcon reflected: 'Now that events can be seen in their historical perspective, one cannot escape the conclusion that in our own work, we could have been more profitably engaged. Hardly a single film of the period reflects the agony of those times'.[20] He failed to mention two reasons for this, though came close with the word 'profitably' – namely profits but also censorship.

After the arrival of sound in the late 1920s, film-making became much more costly and complicated since new and more sophisticated equipment was required. Silent films had had the potential to reach larger audiences: language hardly posed a problem, only new titling being required. Films were now limited by language – subtitling was not popular and dubbing was not that straightforward as well as increasing the costs. Theatres also had to be converted. The British film industry found it difficult to compete with Hollywood and had been particularly hard pressed since the arrival of sound. But it was just beginning to make headway with the costume drama: Alexander Korda's *The Private Life of Henry VIII* (1933) had done very well, especially in the USA.

Arthur Rawlinson and Dorothy Farnum wrote the *Jew Süss* script, assisted by German refugee Heinrich Fraenkel (also Fraenkl), a film journalist, then also reviewing German films for the US trade paper *Variety* as well as working on film scripts. Of particular interest is the fact that it was the second complete script of a British film to be published. Edited by Ernest Betts, a film critic who later became a scriptwriter, the publisher was Methuen. The first, also edited by Betts, *The Private Life of Henry VIII*, had been published by Methuen the previous year.[21] Even though publication occurred one year after the film's appearance, it contained a number of passages not to be found in the film. Betts decided to use the script which had originally been submitted rather than the actual shooting script or one which took into account the subsequent cuts. Tellingly, he even includes at one point 'dialogue to be written'.[22]

Also in the script is a nod to British audiences when Süss refers to the Duke as 'We Carl Alexander, Duke of Württemberg and Teck'.[23] This was not how Carl Alexander would have been referred to at the time. But 200 years later, one of his descendants was Queen Mary, then the wife of the reigning King George V, and her title had been Princess Mary of Teck. Her father, the nephew of the then reigning Württemberg king, had been made Duke of Teck four years after her birth.

According to Balcon, *Jew Süss* was Gaumont British's first film on an 'epic scale'. The costs would also be epic, reputed to be in the region of £100,000–125,000, not high by Hollywood standards though high by British.[24] The set designer was Alfred Junge, who had come to Britain in 1926. Influenced by Art Deco, he had come from a theatre design and applied arts background like other German designers. He transformed British art direction.[25] From 1932 to 1937 he was art director at Gaumont British and had considerable power, supervising all visual aspects of a production. His sets, opulent, elegant and striking, rarely distracted from the story. Always appropriate to each scene, they did not intrude, and sometimes were more convincing than what took place in front of them. In 1948 Junge would win an academy award for best art direction for Michael Powell's and Emeric Pressburger's *Black Narcissus* (1947). The costumes for *Jew Süss* were elegant and striking. Music, composed by Louis Levy who would have a long career composing for films, was not intrusive, though the motifs were repetitive – Baroque dances for the court and Jewish motifs for the Jews (either portentous Hebrew sacred music or popular East European Jewish music with Slavic overtones). Four stages were in simultaneous use with 214 technical and production personnel in continuous employment for five months.[26]

Conrad Veidt took the lead; apparently he had not been the first choice. That had been Emil Jannings, then considered to be Germany's leading actor, an Oscar winner whose lack of English with the arrival of sound had limited his opportunities in Hollywood. Apparently he had turned down the role.[27] Veidt was another prominent German film actor and probably more suited to the role. Though he had a strong German accent, surprisingly this did not diminish his appeal but rather increased it.[28] Elisabeth Bergner, another well-known German actor, now in exile in Britain, was also considered for another role but was contracted to another British company.[29] Veidt had officially emigrated from Germany in April 1933, shortly after marrying his third wife who was Jewish, but had already appeared in British films the previous year: *Rome Express* for Gaumont British and for Gaumont Twickenham, *The Eternal Jew*, about the persecution of the Jews during the Spanish Inquisition, a subject unlikely to endear him to Joseph Goebbels. Matters were then compounded with a part in the Gaumont British film, *I Was a Spy* (1933), set during the First World War in Belgium and directed by Victor Saville. His portrayal of a German officer drew protests from the German Embassy. According to Saville, while Veidt was working on that film, he was personally telephoned by Goebbels at his home in an attempt to persuade him to return to Germany.[30] Veidt did return to Germany but only briefly to complete some location shots for a film he had worked on just prior to his departure, *Wilhelm Tell*, with a script by Nazi writer Hanns Johst (1890–1978), and starring actress Emmy Sonnemann who two years later would marry Hermann Goering. Pressure was increased to persuade him to remain in Germany. Feeling unable to discuss anything by telephone relating to his next film, *Jew Süss*, he eventually did so when filming in Prague but later was confined to his Bavarian hotel near to where filming was taking place. Gaumont British was informed that he could not return to Britain for 'health reasons'. Balcon sent out a British doctor to conduct another medical examination and the Germans, unwilling to create a diplomatic incident, released Veidt to return to Britain.[31] He never went back to Germany where his daughter from his second marriage lived; he died of a heart attack in 1943, age fifty, the year after playing the German officer, Major Strasser, in *Casablanca* (1942).

The other major Jewish role, Landauer, the court Jew who introduces Süss to the Duke, was taken by another German émigré actor, Paul Graetz, a veteran of German film, cabaret and theatre. Three years later he would die in Hollywood. Prominent English actors took other roles: Frank Vosper played the Duke as a boor, Gerald du Maurier, who died shortly after filming and before the release of the film, played Weissensee and Cedric Hardwicke, the sombre Rabbi Gabriel. Benita Hume played the frivolous Duchess in an arch manner and the tiny Haideé Wright played his mother – incongruously in one scene Süss picks up her up like a child and sits her on his lap. Joan Maude, who on stage had the role of Magdalene Sybille, was the only stage actor to make the transfer to screen. Interestingly, in contrast to many other actors, she gave a subtle and sensitive performance. Despite her highly praised stage performance, Peggy Ashcroft, did not obtain the role of Naemi, though she did appear the following year in Alfred Hitchcock's *The 39 Steps*. Pamela Ostrer, the eighteen-year old daughter of one of the Ostrer brothers, played Naemi.

Veidt's portrayal of Süss, as a serious, sensitive, mild-mannered,

mournful gentleman, at times a tortured soul, hardly fitted even
Feuchtwanger's portrait of Süss, much less the historic Süss, though
anything about the latter would have been unknown to British audiences
and probably to Veidt. In an interview shortly before the film opened,
published in the film press, though it may have been ghost-written,
he only mentioned the word Jew once and that was when referring to
the title of the film. Whether this was tact or based on advice, since
he would have had difficulty in visiting Germany, is not known. He
declared that he had found within Süss 'still some spark of soul, of human
nature'.[32]

Veidt's tall, lean and graceful figure was always centre stage. He wore
his elegant clothes well and the camera never missed a chance to capture
the glittering solitaire diamond ring on his finger. His total identification
with the role imbued his performance with great dignity, especially when
facing death. Yet his acting style, not dissimilar to that in his earlier performances in what have been characterized as 'Expressionist' films, was often
at odds with that of the other actors, though no critic commented on
this nor did they refer to his heavy German accent since he was a star –
apparently at the time it was even deemed an asset although his voice was
also pleasant.[33] His face, in particular, was extremely expressive, as befits
someone who took a number of leading roles during the silent era. During
filming the writer Christopher Isherwood, who had written the screenplay
for a Gaumont British film, *Our Little Friend*, then in production, was at
the studio. Observing Veidt perform, he was suitably impressed:

> Veidt had to read a letter of bad news and, at a certain point, burst into tears. There
> were three successive takes and, in each one – despite the intermediate fussings of
> the technicians and the make-up man – Veidt wept right on cue, the great drops
> rolling down his cheeks as if released from a tap.[34]

He also described an incident, which occurred during the execution
scene. Something went wrong with the lights resulting in a five-minute
delay:[35]

Veidt sat in a cart, his hands manacled, on his way to death – a wealthy and powerful man ruined, alone … as … filming was about to begin, something went wrong with the lights … Veidt stayed in the cart … a stenographer came up to him and offered him a piece of candy. The gesture was perhaps deliberately saucy. Some stars would have been annoyed by it because they were trying to concentrate on their role and remain 'in character'. They would have ignored the stenographer. Others would have chatted and joked with her, welcoming this moment of relaxation. Veidt did neither. He remained Süss, and through the eyes of Süss he looked down from the cart upon this sweet Christian girl, the only human being in this cruel city who had the heart and the courage to show kindness to a condemned Jew. His eyes filled with tears. With his manacled hands he took the candy from her and tried to eat it – for her sake, to show his gratitude to her. But he couldn't. He was beyond hunger, too near death. And his emotion was too great. He began to sob. He turned his face away.[36]

The script stayed close to the novel, even if the actors played it differently, sometimes almost against type. The scriptwriters also introduced a few pertinent lines, relating to Jewish suffering, which for obvious reasons had been absent from the novel, given the date of writing – nor would the tone have then seemed right. Surprisingly, the British censor did not request a cut even if such sentiments could be taken to be 'political.'

The opening titles read: 'Württemberg in the eighteenth century – A time of brutal and universal intolerance and the Jews above all suffered oppression and boycott'. True, the Jews at that time were oppressed, but they did not suffer boycotts even though they were doing so at the time the script was being written. The titles continue:

At last there rose up a man who by sacrificing all to securing political power resolved to bring prestige to the state, break down once and for all the barriers of the ghetto. Joseph Süss Oppenheimer was a man of human frailty. His work remains unfinished, his story lives.

Before the actual story of Süss begins, we see Jewish boys at the Cheder (religious school) receiving religious instruction. One boy asks: 'Why can't we leave the ghetto?' and is told: 'Whether you live here in poverty or outside the wall, you will always pay the price of our heritage. Perhaps some day the wall will crumble like the walls of Jericho and all the world will be one people', after which there is a cut to a ghetto scene with men in rags carrying huge sacks. This last sentence also reappears at the very end of the film, though it is not to be found in the published script, one of several discrepancies between the shooting script and published version. (The schoolboys were fourteen-year olds, taken from the London-based Jewish Free School and paid a pound a day.)[37]

At the beginning of the film when Süss scoffs at fears of Jewish persecution, Landauer, a court Jew dressed in traditional caftan, unlike Süss in elegant eighteenth-century dress, warns him: 'They did it in 1430, they can do it in 1730, they can do it in 1830, they can do it in 1930. Who is going to stop them?' Surprisingly the censor passed this line, emphasizing the story's contemporary relevance.

Persecution, though only one of several themes in the novel, is prominent in the film. Moreover, casting Veidt in the lead offers a very different impression of Süss. Lines in the script which made him sound more opportunistic have been cut, though he is allowed to say: 'I want position – luxury – respect' which is then qualified by 'not for my sake only but for the sake of us all. I want power', the last mentioned an allusion to the American title of the film and novel.[38] The published script even has him saying 'In spite of being a Jew, I want beautiful women to treat me as an equal. I want to sit down to table with Dukes and Prince' though that has been cut.[39] His womanizing here made palatable as a quest for equality when he also says: 'I want to sit down to table with Dukes and Princes. Not for my sake only, but for the sake of all of us.' Yet despite his interest in Magdalene Sybille he does not protect her from the Duke, whose mistress she unwillingly becomes. Yet she helps him in the end by warning him that his name appears on the Duke's list of men to be arrested in the planned coup.

In the final cut, the film was 108 minutes, reduced from thirteen to just over ten reels. Nevertheless, it still had its longeurs, as noted by some critics, especially the American ones. Despite skilful editing, appropriate and not too intrusive music, beautiful sets and costumes and some good acting, the film unravels two-thirds in after the daughter's death. The pace slows down as the writers attempt to tell the full story. Indeed, one might say that it is the script which is at fault or rather the British scriptwriters Farnum and Rawlinson. And it is also worth emphasizing that the lead in this British film based on a German novel was a German, the director was German, the sets were designed by a German and presumably the editor was German given that his name was Otto Ludwig (he edited a number of films during this period).

The execution scene is quite powerful, not only because of Veidt's dignified and restrained performance, though he appears merely a bit rumpled rather than emaciated and in rags, but also because the mode of execution is made very clear. Feuchtwanger's own description had been very brief perhaps because he took it for granted that the reader was familiar with the details, especially the height of the gallows from which the cage is hoisted on high.[40] The published script includes a sketch by Junge of the specially constructed viewing platforms which are not visible in the film but indicate that he had looked at the contemporary illustrations.

Snow is falling which Süss first notices from his cell window. Snow will also appear in Veit Harlan's 1940 film. In the 1934 film Jews gather at the base of the scaffold to pray both in Hebrew and in English; like Old Testament Hebrews', they recite the holy prayer, the *Shema*, first in English ('Here O Israel, the Lord our God') and then in Hebrew after which he repeats the prayer in Hebrew – his last words. In the 1940 film, it will be German dignitaries at the base of the scaffold.

There was a gala London premiere for *Jew Süss* on 4 October 1934 at the Tivoli Theatre on the Strand. In aid of the Lord Mayor's Colliery Disaster Fund, it was timed to be simultaneous with its New York opening. Gaumont British had so orchestrated it that when Prince George (later the Duke of Kent) entered the Tivoli theatre, his photograph was flashed on the screen in New York. Apparently, the Duke was keen to see the

newsreel, which was part of the programme, because it included film
of the arrival of his brother, the Duke of Windsor, in India only a few
hours previously. In the Duke's party were other royalty, namely Queen
Marie of Romania (Queen Victoria's granddaughter whose son, Carol
II, was then the king of Romania). Also present in the audience were
Veidt, Feuchtwanger and the latter's neighbour from his new residence
in Sanary-sur-Mer, Aldous Huxley.[41]

Jew Süss was the second most successful British film at the British box
office for 1934 (after Alexander Korda's *Catherine the Great*) and the sixth
most popular film at the British box office, once the non-British films
were included.[42] The most popular film was *The House of Rothschild*,
produced by Darryl Zanuck, the only prominent non-Jewish Hollywood
producer and then head of Twentieth Century Pictures, which he had
helped found the previous year, and which the following year would
be merged with Fox to become Twentieth Century Fox. Like *Jew Süss*,
The House of Rothschild also emphasized the Jew's desire to make his
fortune to escape persecution. But it had been intended as a vehicle
for British actor George Arliss who had been in Hollywood for many
years and had brought with him the script by accomplished scriptwriter
Nunnally Johnson, after having played Disraeli first in a silent film in
1919 and then again in sound. Almost twenty minutes shorter than
Jew Süss, it portrayed a love story between a Rothschild daughter and a
British officer and included a Technicolor sequence at the very end – full
colour films came later in the decade. Nevertheless, the film fed a Jewish
stereotype – wily Jews, clever with money who outwit the authorities.
Fritz Hippler felt able to incorporate a sequence in his egregious antisemitic documentary, *Der ewige Jude* (1940), to illustrate how international
Jewry had obtained its worldwide financial stranglehold.

Glowing reviews for *Jew Süss* appeared in a number of British
papers.[43] Not all, however, were positive: *The Times* found it slow and
the *Spectator* 'disjointed'.[44] Documentary film-maker and critic Paul
Rotha thought it 'overdone', lacking 'taste' and questioned the need for
an historic film ('When shall we realize that the camera belongs to the

present?'). It so happened that he preferred the accompanying newsreel to the feature film, namely the extraordinary footage of the assassination of King Alexander I of Yugoslavia on a visit to Marseilles, seated beside the French Prime Minister, Jean Louis Barthou. The former died on the spot while the latter subsequently from his wounds. 'What chance had the mere hundred thousand odd pounds of Süss against reality?' Rotha asked.[45]

The *Observer* film critic, C. A. Lejeune, thought the film had 'class' … [it was] impressive, well written, richly set, photographed handsomely … without fuss' but questioned whether £125,000 should have been spent on a film unlikely to be 'entertainment for the masses'. The money, she declared, could have been better spent on documentaries on 'English farming and the epic story of unemployment' (her husband, a journalist, worked at this time for John Grierson's Documentary Film Unit at the Empire Marketing Board) but she commended Gaumont British for 'devoting the proceeds of the … premiere to the fund for the distressed miners'. Nevertheless, she hoped that they would think harder and devote a film on the subject of British industry, agriculture or mining with 'the same care and money they spent so generously on a film about a little German municipality of 200 years ago':[46]

> Presumably … Jew Süss must be regarded as a plea for sympathy with an oppressed people, but even if you discount the fact that most of the Jews in this picture are just what the less tolerant Gentiles have always imagined them to be, you may feel, as I do that *The House of Rothschild* has already argued the case against pogroms reasonable well. With all the sympathy in the world for the oppressed Jew, I fancy that there are other problems worthy of being tackled at some expense by our native film industry.[47]

A few reviewers alluded to the political situation in Germany: 'Jews are news, as the Fleet Street shibboleth runs and in that respect *Jew Süss* is unlikely to fail because Jews were never so much news as they are today'.[48] 'But for Hitlerism, this film would perhaps never have been made') wrote another: 'Its motive force [is] … a desire to protest … against injustice to Jews'. It also alluded to the possible motives of the film's producers: 'In an industry so rich in Jewish talent as the film industry this desire is natural' and that may have 'encouraged Gaumont to risk … a sum stated to be not less than £125,000'.⁴⁹

Film critic James Agate complained about the 'Wandering Jews, Rothschilds and Süsses', preferring the 'utterly delightful *Peculiar Penguins*, the short which accompanied the film. Describing himself as an 'anti-anti-Semite', such films, he wrote, preached to the converted. His particular dislike of the 'recent orgy of Jew-baiting in Germany' was that it would 'lead to a great many more films extolling that people at unbearable length'.⁵⁰ On an altogether different note, *Punch*, rarely free of antisemitism, joked that the Tivoli, the cinema screening the film, 'must begin to Aryanise itself or will be too much thought of as the abode of Hebraic eminence and idiosyncrasy', since it had already screened Veidt in *The Wandering Jew* and Arliss in *The House of Rothschild*, adding 'A little Gentile leaven in the Tivoli pograms – I mean programme – would not be unwelcome'.⁵¹

Nevertheless, the majority of British reviewers were well disposed to the film for several reasons: either they had liked the novel (though one pointed out the novel's 'neutrality'),⁵² liked costume dramas, or liked the British film industry aiming for a 'prestige picture, the sort of picture which will increase the demand for British pictures abroad'.⁵³

The film, however, fared less well abroad. In the USA it failed to follow in the footsteps of Korda's film and in Vienna it led to an outright ban. Feuchtwanger's latest novel, *The Oppermanns*, which was not an historical novel but about the impact of the rise of the Nazis on a German Jewish family had been published that spring in the USA, where it had become a bestseller. Balcon engaged a public relations man, A. P. Waxman, to promote Gaumont British films, beginning with *Chu-Chin-Chow* which opened at the same time as *Jew Süss*. The latter opened at Radio City Music Hall, then the largest cinema in the world, seating 6200, with long queues at the box office. The publicity emphasized the record takings in the first few days, apparently outstripping those for *The House of Rothschild*.[54] Preceding the screening were lavish production numbers including Footlight Flashes, devised by Vincent Minelli. The film's soundtrack was turned down for the final seven minutes while the Radio City Music Hall orchestra accompanied a choir singing backstage 'a Hebraic chant', a decided improvement to the film, commented one critic sardonically, to be denied to audiences outside New York.[55]

The subject lacked 'mass appeal' was the view of the trade journals.[56] One warned that the theme, 'the ancient hatred of the Jews' will 'require some 'smart show-selling' outside New York, not too difficult for the cities, but harder for the smaller towns. His advice was to 'sell away from the foreign-made angle and play up Veidt as one of the ranking stars'. And 'where the community warrants such treatment, sell the Jew-angle strongly'. Otherwise, he suggested, 'avoid the racial slants altogether'. 'If you buy this picture', he warned, 'you must give it a campaign' that will match the strong drama of the picture itself'.[57] It should be noted that in the USA at this time Jews and Jewish life had disappeared from the screen. Since the introduction of restrictions on immigration in the early 1920s, the emphasis was on integration. Film audiences could also now be found outside the larger cities (with its large immigrant population) and in small towns. It has even been suggested that Hollywood did not want to endanger the German market after 1933 and that Jewish subjects embarrassed the Hollywood moguls.[58]

Most critics did not miss the film's message but criticized the script. It lacked 'the clarity and the subtlety of Lion Feuchtwanger's famed novel', and was 'two reels too many ... [with] a wandering scenario and lethargic pace' though, according to *Time* magazine, 'the opulent settings and confident style are further evidence that in the last two years British studios have become a serious menace'.[59] Another critic commented that the faltering narrative indicated that the British still have 'to learn a few of the glib, American cinema virtues of pace and suave story-telling to be completely satisfying'.[60] *The New York Times* criticized the 'muddled narrative', 'obscure' motivation and the 'well-bred Oxonian accents of the bearded, patriarchal Israelites' amidst 'handsome historical settings'.[61] 'Power cost money and it looks it – a further twenty-five minutes cut would have achieved wonders', advised *Variety*.[62]

The film did well in New York, given its large Jewish population, but not elsewhere, not only because of its subject matter but also because of the film's weaknesses. It also aroused controversy within the Jewish community. The eloquent New York Reform Jewish rabbi, Dr Stephen Wise, delivered a sermon at Carnegie Hall, where the congregation of his so-called Free Synagogue met on Sunday mornings. An early, outspoken critic of the Nazis, he had not kept a low profile but had led mass demonstrations and had called for the boycott of German goods, though he failed to gain the support of the wealthy New York German Jewish community, sometimes disparagingly referred to by other Jews as 'court Jews' who were in contact with wealthy Jews in Germany to whom they were often related. Keeping one's head down, they believed was the safer option.[63] An eloquent speaker, Wise made Süss the subject of his sermon. If Jews seek worldly success or high office, he declared, they can only expect to come to grief; they should instead concentrate on spiritual matters:[64]

> Let me rid your minds of that silly notion which too many Jews have that if only we can have Jews in public office, it will go well with us. I do not mean that the Jew should not aim at public service, but do not imagine that Cabinet members or governors or judges can save the Jewish people here or anywhere else if the hour of crisis arrives. The power of one Jew over other Jews cannot save the people in time of stress. Is it necessary to point to Germany? No Jews in the world ever attained the dignity, the eminence or the power of the Jews in Germany up until 1933.[65]

Ironically, this might appear to be a quietist message, not dissimilar to that prevalent in eighteenth-century Württemberg, but it was not, since Wise was outspoken about the plight of German Jews. On the other hand, he would soon be in and out of the White House, pleading with Franklin Roosevelt the cause of German Jews, though a decade later he would be accused of being too close to the White House and as a consequence fearful of speaking out when the Holocaust was underway.[66]

On 23 November 1934, six weeks after the simultaneous London and New York premieres the film opened in Paris at the Elysée-Gaumont to mixed reviews, depending on the political persuasion of the reviewer. Jewish and anti-Nazi reviewers mentioned the number of German exiles working on the film while François Vinneuil in the rightwing paper, *Action Français*, aside from mentioning the longueurs, also declared that though he had been expecting 'semitic propaganda' in a film based on a novel by Feuchtwanger, things instead appeared to be 'more complex'. Absent were the 'jeremiads and messianic abuse to which Jewish theatre and film always resort,' the scriptwriters, it seems, having been 'afraid to give too pronounced a colouring to their portrayals, have evaded the issue, initially with some skill, then less cleverly'. The film is, he wrote:

> grist to all mills, providing evidence for antisemites and for defenders of Israel'
> ... [which] despite its obscurities and its evasive character ... is a work that holds
> the interest almost to the end ... in contrast to the extreme frivolity of cinematic
> production.[67]

Several weeks earlier however, just twelve days after the London-New York premiere, the film had opened in Vienna. There too critics divided according to political persuasion. But there it ran into immediate trouble and was withdrawn after only six days. In February of that year the Christian Social-dominated government had destroyed the Social Democratic opposition outlawing all political parties not allied to those in the government. This led to resistance in 'red' Vienna and a bombardment of those holding out in the new Socialist-built housing estates. 'Red Vienna' was red no more. But having destroyed the enemy on the left, the government still had an enemy further to their right, the Austrian Nazis, now subsidized by Hitler and growing fast, attracting the unemployed and a disaffected younger generation not inclined to the left.

Engelbert Dollfuss, chancellor since 1932, feared a takeover from a resurgent Germany under Hitler. *Anschluss* had been forbidden by the Paris Peace Treaties but stripped of her territories Austria was barely viable economically, its problems compounded by the impact of the depression. Lurching from economic crisis to crisis, Austria was always dependent on foreign help and credits. The Christian Social party, the political arm of the Austrian Catholic Church, was clerical, authoritarian, deeply conservative and anti-liberal, against among other things economic liberalism, secularism and individualism and of course also antisemitic since liberalism was associated with the Jews. Their unruly partner in the coalition was the fascist (pro-Mussolini) *Heimwehr*. (Other smaller parties were also antisemitic.) Thus Jews, at this time, given the decline of the Liberal parties had little choice but to vote Social Democratic as the only party which was not antisemitic (the Communists were weak in Austria), though some longed for the return of the Kaiser and the good old days.[68]

Still, antisemitism alone was insufficient to turn Nazis and Christian Socials into allies. The former desired *Anschluss*; the latter did not, fearing a Protestant-dominated, resurgent Germany. In July 1934, the Nazis continued their terror campaign, aimed at absorbing Austria into the Third Reich: in July 1934 Chancellor Dollfuss was assassinated, but Mussolini, unwilling at that time to see the Third Reich reach his north-western frontier, thwarted the coup by sending troops to the frontier. By 1938, however, he would negotiate a treaty of friendship with the Reich, enabling Hitler to achieve his goal of *Anschluss*.

From 1933 onwards, many Jewish artists fled Germany, some went to nearby Austria where they were not always welcome. The year following the ill-fated Viennese screening of *Jew Süss*, the Austrians signed an agreement with the Germans to purge artists of Jewish origin from cultural life. That included the film industry. It was also claimed that year that 120 of the 166 Viennese cinemas were in Jewish hands.[69]

The first Austrian Republic was a federal state with Vienna, the largest city, a state as well as the capital. As in the USA, *Jew Süss* was more likely to attract a metropolitan audience – especially one with Jewish inhabitants. In some respects Vienna was similar to New York, though other factors were less propitious. As in the USA, the Catholic Church also campaigned for tighter censorship controls. But Austria also had to contend with the recent changes in her near neighbour, Germany, where Nazi control had eliminated both Jewish subjects and artists from cultural life. Such actions were endorsed by the Film Committee of the Catholic Church of Austria because 'the spirit of new German pictures' instilled a belief in morals and 'love for home and country', a somewhat surprising comment given the difficulties then facing the German Catholic Church.[70]

Jew Süss opened in four Viennese cinemas. On the day of the premiere, large advertisements appeared in several newspapers, mainly democratic or liberal in persuasion. Such papers also gave the film good reviews. Indeed, by reading the review it is possible to identify the newspaper's political position, the response to the film being a litmus test: favourable reviews came from the liberal or democratic newspapers, usually with Jews on the staff, negative from papers supporting the Christian Social Party. In the latter there had been no advance publicity, the exhibitors being loath to waste their money, though a paper linked to the *Heimwehr*, a member of the government coalition, did run advertisements.[71]

Reviews in papers close to the government were uniformly hostile but in others were either mixed or favourable.[72] One Christian Social paper had initially (and probably inadvertently) publicized the film and its 'success' in London, Paris and New York, but a critical review appeared the following day: Feuchtwanger, described as 'the Jewish writer', had endowed Süss with some noble qualities, nevertheless history had forced him to show the 'dark side'. Though the novel did not belong to great literature, the tendentious element was more apparent in the film in which the Jewish appears good and the non-Jewish bad. The review closed with the warning that 'films of this tendency are crowding Vienna as of late ... they go against the feelings of native Austrians ... [and] possess a polemical character', raising the question: 'for whose political use are they intended?', warning the producers that they were 'likely to achieve the opposite of their intentions'.[73]

The official (government-owned) newspaper, the *Wiener Zeitung*, suggested that there would have been no objections had the film been based on Hauff, but Feuchtwanger was well known for his views that 'Christians are inferior and that which is Jewish appears worthy of praise'. The film 'offends every Viennese', especially the scene 'which will outrage any Christian, in which the Duke seduced a girl in front of a cross'.[74] Such a sequence no longer appears in the extant copy and will have been cut from the film. Another paper supporting the Christian Social party, indeed the Chancellor Schuschnigg had written for it before he took up office, did not review the film immediately but two days after the opening reported several disturbances having taken place in a cinema. It was the only paper to do so. Under the headline 'The Film *Jew Süss* a Provocation to Catholics' it attributed the disturbances to the fact that several non-Jewish characters appear as 'morally inferior' and 'degenerate'. The high point of the 'anti-Christian propaganda', 'directed by a Polish Jew who had emigrated to England', was the blasphemous use of the cross in front of which the Duke seduced a girl and warned 'It is only understandable that the well-intentioned Catholic public of Vienna may give vent when viewing such a scene. We are merely waiting to see what position the authorities will take on this propaganda concoction.'[75]

Four days later, another article appeared in the same paper under the heading, 'Will the film, *Jew Süss*, not be banned?' and mentioned that Catholic circles were apparently 'still justifiably outraged … at this 'Jewish *tendenzfilm*, which grossly insults the feelings of Catholic people.' Removing the worst scenes from this 'shoddy piece of work' was not enough since the film would not lose its 'tendentiousness'. There was 'no compelling need' for a screening in Vienna and the authorities should 'reconsider and proceed with a ban'.[76] But they had singled out for praise Veidt's performance. Given the heavy press censorship already in place, this call for a ban is likely to have had government approval, or at the very least from some individuals in the government.

Another scene which caused offence related to the false accusation of ritual murder. There had in fact been twelve ritual murder trials within Germany and Austro-Hungary between the years 1867 and 1914 (eleven had collapsed while the twelfth resulted in a murder conviction, though not for ritual murder).[77] And the year after *Jew Süss* opened in Vienna the government intervened to force a priest to tone down his play which referred to a ritual murder which was then being performed in a rural area.[78] Thus a sequence which may have seemed remote to a British or American audience was not to an Austrian one.

Film screenings had become contentious. They provided a suitable arena for public protest, enabling protesters to disrupt and make their case. Goebbels pioneered the tactic in throwing smoke bombs during a Berlin screening of the Hollywood-made *All Quiet on the Western Front* in 1930, which had led to the film's withdrawal in Germany on grounds of public order.[79]

With *Jew Süss*, however, there were no witnesses to the disruptions. The British First Secretary, W. H. Hadow, had his doubts about whether the film was a 'masterpiece', as described by Edgar Granville, Liberal MP and parliamentary private secretary to the Foreign Secretary Sir John Simon, who was concerned about the ban.[80] 'The public remonstrances alleged to have taken place … could not be proved', he wrote, but merely press claims that the film *could* lead to disruptions.[81] The Austrians, in their reply made clear their concern that the 'performance of such a realistic play [*sic*] must undoubtedly lead to friction and possibly to brawls between opposing factions' which they hoped to avoid.[82] That, plus affidavits from the directors of the four cinemas screening the film,[83] suggests that no demonstrations had actually taken place but rather that the government feared demonstrations from Nazi hotheads as in the reference to 'brawls between opposing factions'.[84] The disturbances, first reported in one pro-Christian Social newspaper on 19 October,[85] two days after the opening, had been reported in the German press on the same day. This suggests that a film, which papers sympathetic to the government had declined to review, had not gone unnoticed. The tactic of ignoring the film, however, had not kept the enemy at bay. Thus the ban may have been introduced to prevent Nazi hotheads from seizing the initiative.

The ban quickly came into operation. It was introduced by the federal police authorities on the grounds that the film had 'aroused strong opposition from cinema-goers' which had led to 'disturbances' and that in order to prevent 'further demonstrations and … physical injury' as well as to maintain peace and order, the film was to be withdrawn for screening in Vienna.[86] A brief notice announcing the ban appeared in those papers whose readers were likely to view the film. The details, dated 22 October 1934, had been circulated to government departments the previous day. Several points already made in the press were mentioned, namely that 'all people of the Jewish faith [are shown] as morally virtuous men while those … of the Christian faith are frequently … bad and corrupt arousing hostility in wide circles of the Viennese public [as] expressed in many unfavourable criticisms in the Viennese daily press'. But only one theatre was mentioned, the Fliegerkino in the ninth district, where 'it has even come to demonstrations'. Despite the film's distributors having removed 'three especially disagreeable scenes', the ban was deemed necessary, based on a recent clause added to the Federal constitution (19 June 1934). Failure to comply would incur a fine of 10,000 Austrian schillings or three months jail. The ban was described as having been at the instigation of the Vice Chancellor, Prince Starhemberg, the leader of the *Heimwehr*.[87] It is worth noting that a *Heimwehr* newspaper had not initially criticized the film.[88]

The Austrian distributors for Gaumont British were informed of the ban but their lawyers requested a temporary reprieve in order to consider additional cuts.[89] The British Minister (equivalent to ambassador since the embassy had been downgraded to legation on the fall of the Habsburg empire) raised the issue with the Secretary-General at the Ministry of Foreign Affairs concerning 'the unfortunate effect of this prohibition of a film produced by a British firm of such standing as the Gaumont British Corporation', but to no avail.[90] The Austrian Film

Industry's Association also protested, pointing out the damage done to the Austrian distributor.[91] The British Legation also sent a written protest to the Department of Foreign Affairs.[92] The Commercial Councillor personally presented a *Note Verbale* to the economic-political section of the Foreign ministry, 'adding privately that the local firm was inclined to suspect that the ban had been inspired by their competitors' and that after the distributors had 'noticed that the press – *not the audiences* – took exception to a certain scene in the film, on the grounds that it was derogatory to the Christian religion' had, 'of their own accord, cut this scene out of the film in all four cinemas on the third day'.[93] (This scene no longer appears in the film.) The British denied the disturbances, pointing out that the distributors had 'obtained a legal affidavit from the directors of the four cinemas in which the film was shown', and that during the six-day run 'there was not a single disturbance on the part of the public … in direct contradiction to the statement attributed to the police which appeared in the newspapers'.[94]

The British were worried for commercial reasons, fearing that the ban would affect the distribution of other Gaumont British films as well as have repercussions on the planned screening for Hungary and Poland where negotiations had just been broken off. They requested 'an early report on this case in order that British film producers may be warned, and thus avoid a similar unfortunate experience in future'.[95]

Three days after the ban came into operation, the film was reviewed in the weekly journal of the Austrian Institut für Filmkultur, a body which had only recently been set up, the purpose of which was to promote good films and to prohibit bad ones 'through special controls and expert opinion'.[96] Its creation indicated that the government was keen on introducing strict controls. Its head was Ignaz Köck, a reviewer for Catholic Action. Only three days prior to the ban coming into force, he had written about the need for good Catholic films and a 'strict, centralized film censorship applicable to all of Austria, empowered to ban anything hostile to the state, anti-Christian and disrespectful of the Austrian people and its customs' and to promote 'good' films through premiums and reductions in the entertainment tax, a system not dissimilar to that which had recently been introduced in Germany.[97]

Köck now reviewed the film. He mentioned the ban, introduced because of the film's 'offensiveness'. *Jew Süss* was a 'propaganda film ... a nationalist Jewish film ... to be decidedly rejected as a monstrous revilement of all non-Jews'. He singled out the ritual murder scene as 'a monstrous Jewish impertinence and an insult to all Christian peoples'.[98] The timing of the campaign to ban *Jew Süss*, it is clear, was part of a move to tighten control over film screenings and to censor any film deemed to be 'anti-Christian'.

This particular review was picked up in Germany the following week. The recently founded film paper, *Deutsche Filmzeitung*,[99] mentioned both the disturbances and the ban as having already been reported in the German press.[100] Though no love was lost between the Catholic critics of the film and the Nazis, this spat was too good for the latter to ignore. After all Feuchtwanger was a banned writer. But the Nazis had little interest in insults to Christianity. For them the Jew was pitted against the German rather than the Christian (antisemitism rather than anti-Judaism).

Jew Süss may have aroused criticism in the USA and to a lesser extent in Britain either because of its length (or longeurs) or because it was a film with a message. In France, however, it was the actual message which divided the critics, mainly according to their political beliefs. In Austria, the film also divided the critics, again according to their political beliefs, though their hostile critics enjoyed the backing of the state.

In Germany, obviously, there was no possibility of a screening and thus no possibility of dividing the critics, though the film did merit an entry in the Reichsfilmarchiv for 1934: 'The film, which is based on the book by the Jew Lion Feuchtwanger and distorts the historical facts, is under Jewish direction and is in part turned into a glorification of "Jew Süss" by German emigrés.'[101] The Ministry of Propaganda was well aware of the British film, but at this point in time their interest was not in making their own version of the story but in getting its lead, Veidt, to return to

Germany to appear in German films. Though they failed in their attempt, doubtless they experienced *Schadenfreude* when the film in which he starred was denied a screening in a country on which they had designs and which four years later they would make a part of Greater Germany.

3. Süss (Conrad Veidt) pays the Duchess (Benita Hume) a visit while she is in her
bath, bringing her jewels for her to select. *Jew Süss*, 1934. This still was used to
advertise the film and appeared above the marquee greatly enlarged to the height of
the building at the Tivoli cinema on the Strand where it had its British premiere. *Jew
Süss* (1934).
British Film Institute.

4. Süss (Conrad Veidt) catches sight of the cage in which he is to be executed.
Jew Süss (1934). British Film Institute.

5. Süss (Conrad Veidt) as he is locked in the cage.
Jew Süss (1934). British Film Institute.

6. Süss (Ferdinand Marian), arrives at the palace with a box of jewels, hoping for business.
Jud Süss (1940). British Film Institute.

7. A crucial moment: Süss (Ferdinand Marian), the courtier, approaches Dorothea (Kristina Söderbaum) at Carnival. Her fiancé, Faber (Malte Jaeger) protects her, her father (Eugen Klöpfer) watches, Süss is rebuffed.
Jud Süss (1940). British Film Institute.

8. Barefoot, dishevelled, his once elegant attire in tatters, an undignified Süss
(Ferdinand Marian) pleads for his life.
Jud Süss (1940). British Film Institute.

10

Veit Harlan's Jud Süss: *in production (1939–1940)*

Sometime in October or November 1938 – either just before or just after Kristallnacht – an order went out from the Propaganda Ministry to German film companies to produce antisemitic films. Such an order has never actually been found but after the war more than one individual working in the industry testified at the trial of Veit Harlan that such an order had been issued at this time for each film company to produce a film with antisemitic content.[1] Four years had passed since the film industry had been purged of Jews. Work was only available to those admitted to membership of the Film Chamber (*Reichsfilmkammer*), part of the Reich Chamber of Culture (*Reichkulturkammer*), and denied to those of 'non-Aryan' descent. The occasional quarter-Jew slipped through the net, such as director Erich Engel, who had once worked with Bertolt Brecht and who had also been friendly with Veit Harlan from whom he would distance himself.[2]

Film content had also been cleansed of Jews.[3] Aside from a few exceptions, it had become *Judenfrei* (Jew-free), in contrast to films produced during the Weimar era.[4] There were exceptions. Three films made in 1933 and one in early 1934 did include Jewish characters – negative of course: *SA Mann Brandt*; *Hans Westmar* about the Nazi martyr Horst Wessel (also a Sturmabteilung man) but retitled given that aspects of Wessel's life (his relationship with a prostitute) made him an unsuitable Nazi role model; and Ufa's contribution to the new order: *Hitlerjunge Quex* (*Hitler Youth Quex*) about the martyrdom of a Hitler youth.[5] In early 1934 another film fits this category, produced by a film company associated with the party which focused on the precursors of the Nazis, the *Freikorps* (Free Corps), directed by an ardent Nazi and former member of the *Freikorps* as well as author of a book which had greatly pleased Adolf Hitler.[6] In these films Jewish characters appeared only in minor roles, their purpose being to remind audiences who the villains were, namely those who had supported the Weimar Republic, that is the Jews and their associates, directly responsible for Germany's humiliating decline. Jews also made the occasional fleeting appearance in a few other films between 1933 and 1939, but so fleeting as to have often gone unnoticed.[7]

The film industry knew what was *not* wanted. Yet films with a political message were surprisingly rare, and then more often nationalist than Nazi. Not only were Jewish actors purged from the screen and all Jewish professionals from every aspect of film production but subject matter was too. Alhough Jews as negative characters were acceptable, they were surprisingly rare in films up to 1939, nor was every negative character Jewish. When the Nuremberg Laws were announced in the autumn of 1935 the film industry was unable to offer anything to reinforce the message, nor was anything in the pipeline. At this point in time the Germans had to make do with a Swedish import, a comedy about a Jewish immigrant to Sweden, *Petterson und Bendel*.[8]

Once the Olympics were over it was a return to business as usual. The first stage in the persecution of German Jews had been the anti-Jewish boycotts of 1933; the second was the Nuremberg Laws two years later; and three years after that (after the Olympic interlude) in early 1938 the Aryanization of Jewish property. By the end of that year *Kristallnacht* forced a majority of German Jews to make efforts to emigrate. At that stage, however, it was still Nazi policy to encourage Jews, deprived of a livelihood, to emigrate. Though many Jews, mainly male, died as a result of *Kristallnacht*, extermination was, so to speak, a by-product of the violence.

Two feature films in which Jewish characters were more than just marginal were planned in 1938: *Robert und Bertram* (made by Tobis) entered production in late 1938 and opened in July 1939 and *Leinen aus Irland* (*Irish Linen*) made by Wien-Film (Austria), a company newly formed after *Anschluss*, which opened in October 1939 just after the outbreak of war. Both films were supposedly comedies, though this description fits the former rather than the latter. Given that they went into production at the time of Aryanization rather than later in the year after *Kristallnacht* and that both had Jewish characters who were not quite centre stage, it is more likely that a specific order came later in November 1938 or shortly thereafter.

In response to this order, three films were produced which opened in late 1940: two feature films, one about Süss (*Jud Süss*) and one about the Rothschilds, *Die Rothschilds* (*The Rothschilds*), the former produced by Terra and the latter by Ufa. The third film about Jews was not a feature film but a documentary made by the Propaganda Ministry which opened two months after *Jud Süss*: Fritz Hippler's notorious *Der ewige Jude* (1940) (*The Eternal Jew*). It is possible that a fourth film about Karl Lueger, the fin de siècle antisemitic Mayor of Vienna, produced by Wien-Film (Vienna), was also made in response to this order but *Wien 1910* (*Vienna 1910*), due to numerous complications did not open until 1943.[9] Thus three of the four major film companies then in existence (Ufa, Wien-Film and Terra) were at this time involved in making a specifically antisemitic feature film. The odd one out was Tobis. That was where Veit Harlan had been working until seconded to Terra, once Goebbels had become dissatisfied with the Terra director then working on the film. *Die Rothschilds* opened on 17 July 1940, *Jud Süss* on 24 September 1940 and *Der ewige Jude* on 28 November 1940.

Contrary to what has often been assumed, Goebbels did not decide on this film as a riposte to the British-made film of 1934, *Jew Süss*, despite his attempt to detain Conrad Veidt when on his visit to Germany to complete work on another film and thereby prevent him starring in the British film, and despite the Nazi press later welcoming the ban on the film in Vienna, and despite the film's negative description in the Reichsfilmarchiv. No one in the industry had attempted to make a version until the order had been issued in late 1938. Nor do we have any evidence that Goebbels himself had ever viewed the British film before

1940, indeed his comment on the film which he recorded in his diary appears in June 1940 just as production on the Harlan film was ending which suggests that this was his first viewing. He writes:

> This evening I viewed the *Judenfilm* (the Jews' film) in Lanke' [Lanke was the Berlin suburb where he lived] with Conrad Veidt. Here the Jews have made a saint out of a financial hyena. But they can swindle us no more.[10]

Nevertheless, Harlan recalled that earlier he and others had viewed the British film (along with the Yiddish film, *The Dybbuk*, made in 1937).[11]

The film's first director had not been Harlan. The idea for the film had come from the first scriptwriter, Ludwig Metzger (1898–1948), occasionally described as a Nazi from Württemberg, but who had come from nearby Baden (Karlsruhe). He had not been a Nazi Party member, and at one point employed as his secretary a *Mischling*, a half-Jew, Karena Niehoff.[12] But Metzger's mother had been 'Swabian' and doubtless he grew up hearing about Süss, the bogeyman. Metzger claimed to have written a script about Süss, based on Wilhelm Hauff, for a silent film as early as 1922, which conveniently antedates the publication of Lion Feuchtwanger's novel. From 1934 he had been producing mainly musical features for German radio and after 1936 worked in film – his name appeared on an approved list of scriptwriters.[13] At the time the directive was issued Metzger was a scriptwriter at Terra. He claimed to have first learned of it in January 1939 when Terra's dramaturge, Alf Teichs, mentioned it in the presence of his co-scriptwriter, actor Berthold Ebbecke, towards the end of a discussion about a script the two men had just delivered *Zentrale Rio (Central Rio)*.[14] Teichs, however, was lukewarm about the suggestion on the grounds that it had already been done in Britain but agreed to take the suggestion higher.[15] He had apparently divorced his *Mischling* wife to comply with the Nuremberg Laws but allegedly still lived in secret with her, which might explain his lack of enthusiasm.[16] Nevertheless, Goebbels later found that Teichs 'made an intelligent impression' and was keen to make him Head of Production.[17]

Teichs was soon moved to a better job at Ufa and, after the war, quickly received Allied approval to work in the greatly reduced German film industry.[18] Metzger, described as 'a loud, ambitious and tough man', detected Teichs' lack of enthusiasm and took his proposal direct to the Propaganda Ministry where, according to his co-scriptwriter, Ebbecke, it 'went off like a bomb'. As a consequence, their collaboration on the frothy *Zentrale Rio* came to an end.[19]

At this time the film industry was undergoing further reorganization. Terra's production chief, Alfred Greven, was replaced. He was moved to Ufa in February 1939, where he was responsible for the Rothschild film, and then in the autumn of 1940 to France, where he headed the newly formed company, Continental, to produce, sell and distribute films in Occupied France. Though after the war he maintained that he had objected to the *Jud Süss* proposal, others disagreed.[20] According to Peter Paul Brauer, who took over from him in February 1939, the film was already state-commissioned; moreover, Greven had pointed out that the film was '*staatswichtig*' (important to the state).[21] Of the many people involved in the *Jud Süss* project, especially in getting it off the ground, Greven was the only one to have been a Nazi Party member.[22]

A contract for a film treatment was signed with Metzger on 18 February 1939 and a further contract for 'world rights' was dated 21 July 1939. [23] He and a dramaturge at Terra visited the Stuttgart archives to examine the documents relating to the trial of Süss. It was a flying visit, lasting at most two days in late March 1939. It has been suggested that when they caught sight of the vast collection of trial documents, they undertook no research.[24] On the other hand, the archivist may have selected documents suitable for a scriptwriter, namely those containing the salacious bits since some first names and details of the encounters appear in the film: for example, the mother who is keen to send her daughter to the Duke's masked ball against her husband's wishes and the name of the heroine, Dorothea, which was the name of one of the women that Süss forced himself on.[25]

A first version of the script was ready by July 1939. Brauer, Terra's then

Head of Production, with no experience of directing a film, appointed himself director.[26] Wolfgang Zeller was made responsible for the music: his credits included composing music for Carl Dreyer's classic horror film, *Vampyr* (*Vampire*) (1932), many of Emil Jannings' films as well and the 1936 Nazi documentary *Ewiger Wald* (*Eternal Forest*).

Sets were built during the summer of 1939. Both set-builders had previously worked on classic Weimar films. Karl Vollbrecht had built sets for several Fritz Lang films: *Die Nibelungen* (1922–1923); *Metropolis* (1925–1926); *M* (1931). He had also worked on the anti-war *Kameradshaft* (1931). The other set-builder was Otto Hunte who also worked on *Die Nibelungen* and *Metropolis* as well as on G. W. Pabst's *Die Liebe der Jeanne Ney* (*The Love of Jeanne Ney*) and in 1930 Josef von Sternberg's, *Der blaue Engel* (*The Blue Angel*) with Marlene Dietrich, as well as later that same year the musical comedy about unemployment: *Die Drei von der Tankstelle* (*The Three at the Filling/Petrol Station*). After the war he did the sets for the first post-war German film, *Die Mörder Sind Unter Uns* (*The Murderers Are Among Us*) (1946), directed by Wolfgang Staudte, who himself had had a small part in *Jud Süss*. Both set designers, along with the composer would be retained when Harlan took over.

The Terra catalogue, which featured forthcoming films for 1939–1940, gave pride of place to the film. Billed as 'a major film' (*ein Grossfilm*), it was described as being after Wilhelm Hauff's 'well-known story and on factual reports in the Stuttgart archives':

> it tells the dramatic story of the famous Jew Süss who came to Württemberg a man without means, who in a short time became the most powerful man in the state until swept away by an uprising. The story of the uprising against this bloodsucker gives the tension and intensity right up to the moment of the arrest of the Jewish minister in the midst of a revolutionary crowd. A first class cast will secure for this film the significance it deserves.[27]

Other films mentioned in the catalogue included a new Helmut Käutner film, *Kitty und die Weltkonferenz* (*Kitty and the World Conference*) and a thriller which was to star Ingrid Bergman, *Tatort Westbahnhof* (*Scene of the Crime, West Railway Station*), to be made in Vienna by Terra's sister company. Two photographs showed Brauer in the act of directing and another of a rear view of a plump blonde on a balcony overlooking the Stuttgart square where Süss had been executed, suggesting that the story was so familiar that little more need be said.[28]

Despite the claim that the synopsis provided by Metzger was based on Hauff, it was very different. The hero has become Georg von Lanbeck as opposed to Hauff's Gustav Lanbek. He also has no sisters. But when at the end Lanbeck arrests Süss, he delivers a line straight from Hauff: 'Now your Reich (empire) has come to an end' (though in the novella these words had not been spoken by Lanbek), after which according to the catalogue 'Süss whimpered for mercy but the hangman led him away. He paid for his crimes on the gallows'.[29]

An even greater emphasis on the message appeared in the headline: 'The First Major Film on the Jewish Danger'. Süss, 'the incarnation of criminality,' 'ensnares' the Duke who bestows on him the highest office. This enables him to bring his 'racial compatriots' into Württemberg who bring ruin.[30] Two years previously on 8 November 1937 a touring exhibition entitled *Der ewige Jude* (*The Eternal Jew*) had been opened by Julius Streicher. On 18 July 1938 the censors had approved a film whose purpose was to unmask the Jew in disguise – the assimilated Jew. The story of Süss illustrated that theme. Indeed, publicity for the Süss film mentioned that Süss was to be 'unmasked before the camera',[31] or that it would be 'a film without a mask',[32] or that Süss was a 'typical example of the Jew who poses real danger to his host country not through the external characters of his race but because he conceals his Jewishness through assimilation'.[33]

Goebbels, however, was not satisfied with Metzger's script. After the war Metzger claimed to have only written a treatment rather than a script, confirmed by Wolfgang von Gordon, his then partner in a post-war publishing venture, hardly therefore the most reliable source. Gordon had been brought in to Terra to share the post of dramaturg with

Teichs. There was certainly sufficient time for Metzger to have written a script and for Goebbels and others to be displeased with the result. The contract for the script was dated six months after the contract for the treatment.[34] And in 1942 when Metzger was in dispute with Harlan over credit for his treatment for the film *Der Grosse König* (*The Great King*) and even threatened legal proceedings, he described himself then as the author of the script for *Jud Süss*.[35] Hippler refers to two scripts being worked into one when the second scriptwriter was brought in.[36] It is therefore more likely that the Propaganda Ministry did not like the script, which would have been delivered on the eve of the war. With the outbreak of war Goebbels was also back in Hitler's good graces, his affair with Czech actress Lida Baarova having come to an end, and he now returned to his work with a vengeance.

The script that survives is the second script on which Metzger was forced to work with Eberhard Wolfgang Möller (1906–1972), the latter a party member since 1932, poet, playwright, novelist and author of numerous works for the Hitler Youth, including an exemplary life of Hitler: *Der Führer*. He also had written a play about the Rothschilds – *Rothschild siegt bei Waterloo* (*Rothschild Triumphs at Waterloo*), broadcast and performed in 1934 and published in 1939, but he would not be involved in the Rothschild film.[37] He also acted as a consultant on theatre for the Propaganda Ministry and was brought in to work on the script by the State Secretary in the Propaganda Ministry, Leopold Gutterer. Möller, a state prize winner for literature (1935), had never worked on a film script before, but had worked on 'the Jewish Question' (the Panama Scandal and the Rothschilds) though until now, it was stated he had stayed away from the 'newest art'.[38] And ultimately he would stay away, which meant that after the war, when as a member of the SS he was incarcerated for a time in Hohenasperg where Süss two centuries earlier had also been held, he would escape being summoned to testify at Harlan' trial.[39] He kept such a low profile that Harlan had thought he was dead.[40]

Metzger complained that Möller had been put in over him, that he had 'no clue about film scripts and wrote impossible dialogue'. Moreover, he was forced to visit Möller in Thuringia for ten weeks to work on the script.[41] According to one witness, Möller had not been keen on the choice of subject on the grounds that it showed the culpability of an 'Aryan' Duke, which could be 'compared to a leading figure in the Third Reich'.[42] At the time Möller described Metzger as an experienced scriptwriter.[43] Nevertheless, despite apparently being sidelined, Metzger was still paid generously, if payment can be related to contribution and actually received more than Möller (RM 12,000 as opposed to RM 8,000 or 10,000), while Harlan received 20,000 for his contribution to the script.[44] And when the film became a huge success Metzger received an additional payment.[45] Of course Harlan also received payment as the director.

By November 1939, however, Brauer had even stopped referring to Metzger as one of the scriptwriters, though that did not stop him from referring to the film as based on Hauff.[46] The surviving script on which Möller and Metzger collaborated is clearly the work of Möller.[47] It is completely unsuited to the screen. Hauff has been jettisoned as unsuitable (as Möller made clear in an interview). This was because he lived at a time which wanted to 'liberate' Jews and Poles (with regard to the latter, the Second World War had just begun with the invasion of Poland) and thus could not avoid 'a certain sentimentality in the ending'.[48] He also mentioned Albert Dulk's dramatization which 'attempted to confer nobility on Süss' but dismissed all this as 'harmless nineteenth-century liberalism'. From there, he declared, there is a 'great leap' to the 'political and moral obscenities' of Feuchtwanger and Kornfeld.[49]

Significant is the reference to Kornfeld because traces of his work can be found in this script. It begins with a page of a chronicle being turned and the words: 'How Jew Süss came into the country. Since olden times all Jews were banned from entering the land of Württemberg under the heaviest penalty'. In the first scene Süss attempts to gain entry to the gates by bribing with jewellery. When rejected, he utters Yiddish curses. The second scene shows Süss with other poor Jews gathered around a campfire, plotting their entry into Württemberg. Here one can detect the borrowings from Kornfeld who himself was trying to turn around a familiar antisemitic view about how the Jew arrives poor on forbidden German territory, though his purpose had been to turn this to comic advantage as Süss' outsmarts the natives, a situation which surfaces in the Harlan film when his secretary Levi makes fun of a gatekeeper. In Möller's script, however, the legend has been returned to its more familiar (and negative) origins.

Harlan would eliminate these scenes along with an antisemitic ballad, obviously a Möller creation, in the form of a *Bänkellied*, a genre which told of cataclysmic events in song and pictures:

Dear friends and kinsmen
Hear the song of the great vampire
Evil are wolves, rats and vipers,
Yet the most evil predator is
The Jew, the Jew, the Jew.
Leads the regiment into the land
Sucks us dry
Takes our home and hearth
Chase the Jew to the devil
Storm, fire, pestilence are abominable
Hateful also are war and unrest
But mild in comparison
To the person who takes profit from everything
Refrain:
Like the Jew, the Jew, the Jew.[50]

Möller declared himself 'happy to be in such an important artistic and political position, helping in the creation of the first German antisemitic film, at a time when the Jew again fully lives up to his reputation as the ferment of political subversion.'[51] But he was soon replaced. On 9 November, shortly after a flying visit to Poland, Goebbels recorded in his diary that he had read the script: 'The SS model becomes excellent: the first truly antisemitic [feature] film'.[52] But he had been appalled at what he had witnessed in Poland and now felt 'tackling the Jewish disease' had become urgent.[53]

It was not the script, however, which Goebbels objected to but the director, Brauer, who had not been making progress with the production, especially with casting.[54] He swiftly replaced him with Harlan, who was then working at Tobis, cutting 800 metres from his latest film, *Pedro soll hängen (Pedro Should Hang)*, at Goebbels' request given its 'religious elements'.[55] It would not open until 1941.[56] Goebbels instructed Brauer himself to inform Harlan about his new appointment. Harlan claims to have protested that he was working at Tobis but to no avail.[57] He was not quite in Goebbels' good graces. The latter had been displeased with the triangular relationship depicted in his most recent film, *Die Reise nach Tilsit (The Journey to Tilsit),* based on the Hermann Sudermann story, which had inspired Friedrich Wilhelm Murnau's Hollywood-production of *Sunrise* (1927). Goebbels recorded in his diary that Harlan was putting his own marital problems on the screen. Doubtless Goebbels felt some discomfort since he himself had been acting similarly.[58]

Harlan was given fourteen days to make the changes, an indication that he had mainly been expected to direct. He immediately set to work and did a rewrite. The previous script had had literary pretensions with a hard-edged theatricality in the dialogue, also at times stilted. This Harlan jettisoned, replacing it with well-paced dialogue, introducing racy elements while also enlarging the part of Dorothea, now to be played by his new, Swedish born wife, Kristina Söderbaum. But some scenes and characters were retained. Goebbels was pleased with the script – 'a splendid reworking'.[59]

Born in 1899, Harlan was the son of playwright Walter Harlan, considered in the early 1920s by an antisemitic *völkisch* publication to be a 'friend of Jews'.[60] He had been an actor mainly for the stage and for a time with Leopold Jessner at the Prussian State Theatre.[61] He had been briefly married to a Jewish actress, Dora Gerson, from whom he was divorced and then to another actress, Hilde Körber, with whom he had three children and from whom he had just been divorced shortly before being appointed to direct *Jud Süss*. He had been on social terms with Goebbels, ultimately providing cover for him while the latter conducted his affair with Czech actress Lida Baarova: it was at Harlan's house that Goebbels, Baarova, Körber and Harlan heard together the announcement on the radio of the news about *Anschluss*.[62] But after Goebbels' wife sent an emissary to Hitler, Baarova was despatched to Czechoslovakia, despite a failed attempt by Körber to intervene on her friend's behalf.[63] Goebbels was soon back in favour with Hitler. Once war broke out he would play an important role.

Harlan had appeared on stage after 1933 in important plays, such as one partly written by Mussolini, *Hunderte Tage (Hundred Days)*, which had been about Napoleon's 100 days for which Hitler attended the Berlin opening. He also appeared in Hanns Johst's play, *Schlageter*, about the Nazi martyr, Albert Schlageter, executed in 1923 by the French for sabotage in the Occupied Rhineland, though there is some doubt that Schlageter should be categorized as a Nazi even if the Nazis were keen to count him as one of their own.[64] In that play it was Harlan who delivered the oft-quoted line incorrectly attributed to Hermann Goering: 'When I hear the word culture, I want to reach for my gun'. In April 1933 he gave an interview to the party newspaper, *Völkischer Beobachter*, which appeared under the title 'How I Became a National Socialist' in which he made clear his support for the new regime and attacked Jewish actor Fritz Kortner and Jewish writer Hans Rehfisch, the latter having once written a play about Dreyfus. (After 1945 he would deny that these words were his.) He directed his first film, a comedy, *Krach im Hinternhaus* (*Trouble Back Stairs*), two years later.

In 1937 Harlan directed *Der Herrscher (The Master)*, a film based on Gerhart Hauptmann's *Vor Sonnenuntergang (Before Sunset)*, a play which had been performed in London's West End with Peggy Ashcroft as the young wife and Werner Krauss, as the elderly widower marrying for a second time against the wishes of his children. (Krauss would later take several roles in *Jud Süss*.) There had been audience protests on the opening night in September 1933 about Krauss' appearance – a few months earlier in March he had been appointed vice-chairman of the theatre section of the Reich Culture Chamber. Ashcroft went on stage to try to calm things.[65] Though the play had originally been about the personal happiness of a man in the sunset years of his life (hence the German title), the script by the well-paid Thea von Harbou (*Metropolis*, 1926–1927) and former wife of director Fritz Lang who was now in the USA, had undergone a transformation as well as a change in the title to *Der Herrscher* (*The Ruler*). The father, played by Jannings was an authority figure, an industrialist, to whom his children and employees should have submitted and submit in the end they do. But Harlan also made his contribution, filming it in such a way as to make its message about leadership clear with the silhouette of the figure of the father looming above his factory and the people below. Goebbels was pleased: 'Modern and National Socialist just as I want films to be'.[66]

After this, Harlan's star rose fast. Casting for *Jud Süss* had already begun before Harlan took over on what would be a state-commissioned film (*Staatsauftrag*). Ferdinand Marian had not been Brauer's first choice. That had been Gustav Gründgens, then *Generalintendant* at the Prussian State Theatre who was protected by Hermann Goering who controlled Prussia and its state theatre. Other actors who had screen-tests included René Deltgen, Richard Häusler, Rudolf Fernau, Paul Dahlke and Siegfried Breuer all of whom, according to Marian, tried to outdo each other with appalling performances so as to avoid the role.[67]

Once appointed director, Harlan had more cachet than Brauer: he was able to attract a number of good actors for the major roles. Though Krauss was under consideration, he ultimately took four roles, but after the war claimed that this had been a ruse to avoid the film altogether since Goebbels did not like actors trying to show their tricks. But he was foiled.[68] Heinrich George, another important stage and film actor took the role of the Duke, though he was not keen to play an unsympathetic character.[69] A former communist who had worked with Brecht, he had also played the foreman *in Metropolis* (1925/1926) and the lead in *Berlin-Alexanderplatz* (1931). Other actors had had film careers extending back to the silent era such as Albert Florath who plays Röder and Theodor Loos who plays Remchingen, the latter's film career dating to 1913. In 1941 Lion Feuchtwanger wrote that at least seven of the actors had once appeared in his own play about Süss but did not mention any by name – we know that Eugen Klöpfer who plays the father did play Süss in Frankfurt.[70]

Of course there was the issue of Jewish physiognomy. If it was so readily identifiable, how could non-Jewish actors take the roles? Krauss had made it a point of pride that he could rely on his acting skills alone to create a Jewish character and refused to wear a false nose.[71] Nearer to the opening Goebbels was forced to issue a disclaimer, namely that none of the actors were tainted with Jewish blood.[72] Several actors, however, had close links to Jews: for example, one of Krauss' sisters was married to a Jew. But it was Marian who was in the most difficult situation: his wife had been married and divorced from a Jewish actor, Julius Gellner, who would soon be working in Britain for the BBC German Service.[73] Their *Mischling* (first-degree) daughter lived with her mother and Marian.[74] The press had been instructed not to refer to the film as antisemitic, since it was an 'objective representation of the Jews'.[75]

Harlan was also keen on authenticity. Whether that had been his own idea or whether it had come from elsewhere is not known, though Goebbels too had been interested in capturing Jewish life before its demise and had sent cameramen to Poland for this purpose in October 1939. Such material appeared in newsreels and most importantly in the Hippler documentary, *Der ewige Jude*, which opened two months after Harlan's film. Had Harlan been more aware of the implications of his film, he might not have made the effort to obtain Jewish extras to lend the note of authenticity. The script he inherited specified that the Jews would be celebrating Purim, doubtless because it was thought that they would appear unruly and thus in a poor light. In Harlan's script however, Purim is not mentioned but the camera directions state: 'the face of Süss dissolves into the face of the rabbi, who utters a prayer of revenge; and in whose eyes burn "an uncanny demonic fire". The camera then turns on 'fifty caftan Jews' who in Hebrew repeat the rabbi's verses.[76]

Harlan visited Lublin in January 1940. It is not, however, clear whether this was to observe Jewish customs or to 'consult with a rabbi' or to find extras since he could not find such Jews in Germany, where they had been assimilated for generations. Accompanying him were his two assistants, Alfred Braun, former Social Democrat and head of Berlin radio during the late Weimar period, who after being interned for six months in 1933 left Germany but returned on the outbreak of war and Conny Carstennsen (real name Friedrich Wirth), his production manager and a nominal Nazi Party member – Carstennsen had worked for the Soviet-subsidized Prometheus (which among other things had funded Brecht's *Kuhle Wampe*).[77] No filming was done on this trip. But Harlan did tell an official, obviously someone from the SS, that he needed Jews to perform 'happily' after the official had offered to 'round some up'.[78] He heard them sing. Conditions were 'frightful', he later recalled. There were transports, he claimed. He told the rabbi that he needed Jewish actors to perform in a film, and that arrangements would be made to transport them.[79] They sang for him and presented Harlan with a Torah scroll.[80]

This plan to bring Jews into the Reich at a time when the expulsion of Jews was planned had government approval. On 17 January 1940 instructions to the press stipulated that that 'under no circumstances' should it be reported that these extras were being brought in 'from a Polish ghetto' to appear in Harlan's film.[81] Nine days later a similar comment was published about the imminent arrival of 120 Jews from the ghetto.[82] These extras did not arrive. Though Harlan declared this was because Goebbels was against the idea, this seems implausible, given the press directives. Carstenssen stated that they failed to arrive due to the outbreak of typhus.[83]

Harlan had to find his extras elsewhere. He found them in Prague where the sequences were filmed at the Barrandov studios in mid-March. Deportations from the Protectorate to Poland had already begun, but had been suspended by Goering in February 1940. That same month Jews were forbidden to use certain streets, and the previous month had been forced to sell all valuables. Their food coupons were also drastically cut. Aryanization had led to increasing pauperization. Most Jews were unemployed. In March they had to register with the Jewish Religious Congregation of Prague. That was when the extras were found.

According to Otto Lehmann, the film's producer, he had made enquiries in Berlin with the SS-run Central Office for Jewish Emigration (Zentralstelle für Jüdische Emigration) who directed him to the Prague Office where SS officials put him in touch with Prague's Chief rabbi, 'someone with a doctor's title', whom he referred to as Dr Rössler, a name no one else referred to and which after the war, the Jewish community did not recognize. Yet Harlan insisted he had been advised on Jewish religious ritual by someone at the Alt-Neu Schul (the Old-New Synagogue) which then had no rabbi – at the time apparently there were only two rabbis in the city, neither with this name.[84]

Harlan was keen post-war to implicate the Jews in the making of his film.[85] The extras were engaged not only for the synagogue sequences but also for the arrival and expulsion of the Jews from Stuttgart but not for the Frankfurt ghetto sequence. They had been sought not so much for their physiognomy, though that could have been a factor, but for their music and knowledge of religious ritual. Yet the Jews of Prague were on the western side of the divide within European Jewry and were unlikely to have been Chasidic, Harlan's preferred sect. Thus they required instruction from Harlan in order to produce the 'demonic effect' which he thought so desirable.

The extras were bussed to the studio daily, paid a small amount (though there is dispute about how much) and given a meal at noon.[86] Another German director, Boleslaw Barlog, who had worked on *Jud Süss* when Brauer was directing, was in Prague at the same time, making his own film. He visited the Old-New Synagogue), the oldest in Europe, and befriended one of the extras. After the war he recalled asking him why they were working in a film with 'anti-Jewish tendencies' to which he got the reply: 'We live so poorly here that these days are an event for us'.[87]

The widow of a singer, originally a Dresden *Kammersinger*, declared after the war at a meeting in Berlin as well as writing to Harlan that her husband had said that he had treated the extras well.[88] Another witness, who did not appear in the film, did testify against Harlan. Then a young Czech Zionist, he described how he and other young Zionists had been approached at their meeting place in Prague by some of Harlan's people. He questioned them about the film and was told that it would be 'historical' and would have no 'antisemitic tendencies'. [89] They were not taken in. Aware of the implications, they refused.[90]

One of the Czech extras, Michael Chasin, survived, probably the only one to do so. Describing himself as the leader of the choir, he told of Harlan's efforts to elicit particular performances from the extras. He was especially keen that those praying should perform with 'rocking movements', which Chasin claimed made a serious religious service appear 'ridiculous'.[91] When the extras also protested that this had nothing to do with praying and moreover, could only be found in the East, that is on the eastern side of the divide within European Jewry, their protestations were ignored. Chasin then made the unlikely claim that Harlan later brought in 200 non-Jews to perform in the way he wanted.[92] That number of extras cannot be seen in the film. Nevertheless, Harlan seems to have been pleased with the result: in the unedited version of his memoirs he described the scene as producing a 'demonic effect',[93] a description excised by the editor of his posthumously published memoirs. Goebbels too was pleased, recording in his diary on 18 August 1940: 'an antisemitic film, we could only wish for'.[94]

11

Veit Harlan's Jud Süss: *on screen*

Veit Harlan's film about Jew Süss declares in its opening titles that it is based on historical fact, a not uncommon claim for films made during the Third Reich and certainly not for one in which Joseph Goebbels had been so closely involved. An interest in history may even account for the scriptwriter's flying visit to the Stuttgart archives in a quest for new material. Nevertheless, only a few of the more obvious facts about Süss survive in the film, namely that there was a court Jew, Joseph Süss Oppenheimer, who served Duke Carl Alexander, who devised unpopular economic policies, who appeared to be a man of wealth and enjoyed luxury, kept a mistress and upon the death of the Duke was tried and executed in a cage. That much in the film accords with what is known about Süss. All else is invention.

As told by Harlan, the story of Süss takes the form of an eighteenth-century German bourgeois tragedy – the disruption of social harmony and its impact on a bourgeois family, through courtly intrigue.[1] In this film, however, it is the Jew, as the agent of the court, who destroys the family. The character, as played by Ferdinand Marian, can for a female viewer, at times, elicit sympathy. The film's purpose, however, was to take a popular genre and give it a National Socialist twist, making the Jew the agent of disruption. The last, incidentally, was also the role assigned to Süss in the Hauff novella, though there it was more tentative but did accord with the legend.

Few traces of Hauff had survived in the script which Harlan inherited. There is a Carnival sequence. The female who drowns is now 'Aryan', unlike in the novella when she was the sister of Süss. Played by Harlan's wife, Kristina Söderbaum, she drowns herself in shame for having been raped by Süss, whereas in Hauff, she is bereft without the protection of her brother. Other sequences taken from Hauff include Süss playing cards during the masked ball and being challenged by three masked men who escape with the call 'freedom of the mask'. Another sequence taken from Hauff is greatly transformed: whereas in the novella it is the two Lanbek sisters who eavesdrop on the plotters (their father, brother and other conspirators), in Harlan's script it is Süss and his secretary, Levi, who do the eavesdropping – in a high angle shot in dimly lit stairs, they peer through a narrow Gothic-like opening in a stone wall at the plotters below. And there is also an important line taken from Hauff, which easily fits Nazi teachings, namely when the father declares that he will have no '*Judenkinder*' (Jewish children.)

The film also differs considerably from the British film, based on Lion Feuchtwanger's novel. The only influence that can be detected is in the final execution sequence with the snow falling. Nevertheless, Feuchtwanger would maintain, without ever having viewed the film, that Harlan had made a travesty of his story, accusing Harlan in 1941 of having taken it and adding a bit of *Tosca*.[2] This refers to the torture scene at the end of the film when Süss, playing Scarpia to Dorothea's Tosca, agrees to stop the torture of her fiancé in exchange for sexual favours. This, however, was already in the Moeller-Metzger script that Harlan inherited. Though much of that script he jettisoned, this was the one scene which he retained since it will have held an obvious appeal for him – in his films, the female character, played by his wife, often comes to an unfortunate end. Aside from wanting to cast his new wife in this important role, she also fit a Nazi ideal not only because she was blonde and blue-eyed with a small sweet voice but also because she appeared childlike, even infantilized – she was not a knowing female. Harlan also had a sadistic streak, apparent in many of his films. And the innocent Söderbaum played a suitable victim.

Harlan made numerous changes. Indeed, he completely rewrote the script. And given that ultimately Goebbels was the producer, and that it was he who had appointed Harlan to do the job, the latter had a good idea what was required, though occasionally he miscalculated and drew Goebbels' wrath. Moreover, as a seasoned film director, he also knew what would work on screen. And he would make clever use of the dissolve, establishing links between sequences for emphasis as when the face of the ghetto Jew dissolves to that of the Jewish courtier or reverts again when on trial at the end, or when the gold coins dissolve to the ballet dancers paid for by the gold, or when the Württemberg coat of arms at the outset dissolves to the nameplate of Süss.[3]

Harlan's post-war assertion that the Moeller-Metzger script he had inherited was '*Stürmer*-like', after Julius Streicher's virulently antisemitic weekly, may to some extent have been true, though not to the extent that he hoped would be believed.[4] He jettisoned much of the script but retained the rape and the drowning of the childlike Dorothea. He also added a new sequence which intensified the antisemitism. This concerns the smith Bogner, a character which was not to be found in the earlier script. Süss has devised a new property tax which results in Bogner having to pay an exorbitant sum on that part of his home and workplace that abuts the road. The smith refuses, rightly considering the scheme to be diabolical. His wife comes to Süss to beg for mercy, bringing her small child with her, but Süss is hard and shows no pity. We later see him seated in his elegant carriage, his beautiful mistress at his side. They have come to enjoy the spectacle: the demolition of half of the smith's house. The mistress, thrilled to see the house split in two, likens the 'sweet house' (with a play on Süss' name, German *süss* meaning 'sweet') to a doll's house. Catching sight of Süss, Bogner lunges at his coach and smashes in the side with his anvil. For this he will be executed. In the very next sequence the drums roll, the wife screams, Bogner is hanged and the crowd shout 'Jew, your turn will be next'. The elegantly attired Süss shows fear, for he is a coward, which accords with an antisemite's view of the Jew. This event also anticipates his own execution. Harlan may have added this sequence for dramatic effect and to explain the increasing hostility of the people but ultimately this makes the execution of Süss appear as a just outcome. It also undermines Harlan's post-war position that he had toned down the antisemitism in the script he had inherited.

It is not only the script or the dissolves which contribute to the film's antisemitism. Music was extremely important in driving home the point that the Jew was not German. Whether the composer Wolfgang Zeller was given free rein or whether Harlan gave him detailed instructions, is not known. But at key points it is often the music rather than the image which conveys the message. This is already apparent in the opening titles which are accompanied by portentous and sinister music obviously composed by Zeller. For a few seconds no image appears and then we see a Jewish star above an eight-branched candelabra with the candles lit. A tenor is singing a Hebrew prayer: this music is not composed by Zeller but is taken from a recording of Jewish religious music with the voice possibly that of a Hungarian cantor.[5] The words 'Jud Süss' now appear in a typography simulating Hebrew typography, followed by the announcement that this is: 'A film by Veit Harlan', and that the script is also by Harlan as well as by the two other scriptwriters, Eberhard Wolfgang Möller and Ludwig Metzger, in that order. In the lower right-hand corner a short, dark-haired man with a thick, flattened nose appears: we are intended to link the voice on the soundtrack with this troll-like figure, likely to have been one of the Prague extras, who appears to be singing from a prayer book. We will see him again in the synagogue sequence when the men participate in wild dancing and in the sequence when the Jews enter Stuttgart. The portentous music returns but when the cast list comes on screen different music is heard – a German folksong, 'All mein Gedanke' ('All my Thoughts'), later set by Brahms, which will soon shift to a minor key, for the story to be told will be sad.

Originally 97 minutes long or 2663 metres, the film begins in 1733 with the coronation of Carl Alexander as Duke of Württemberg. A map of Württemberg appears with the word Stuttgart and the date, 1733, superimposed. This image fades to a portrait of the recently deceased Duke, after which the camera travels down to the portly new Duke standing beneath. He is taking his oath of office, administered by the leader of the diet, Sturm, played by Eugen Klöpfer, who some twenty years earlier had played Süss in Feuchtwanger's play. The Duke swears to look after his subjects with 'paternal concern'. In this he will fail because his love of luxury will cause him to bring a Jew into the country. It is the man swearing him in who will be the real father for it is he who will exhibit 'paternal concern' for his country, rather than the hereditary ruler. This accords with Nazi beliefs. An exception was made for one hereditary ruler: Frederick the Great, who was also militarily successful and who had extended the borders of Prussia. He would always be depicted as a hero in many films and in Harlan's next film, *Der Grosse König* (*The Great King*), two years later. In contrast, Carl Alexander is associated with giving a Jew considerable power. Hence his story made him a suitable subject for a Nazi antisemitic film, added to which his enormous sexual appetite also provided entertainment.

In the next sequence, the chaste and lovely Dorothea, played by Söderbaum, appears with her fiancé, Faber, her father's legal assistant, at the harpsichord. Together they are singing (she in her sweet little girl voice and he in his tenor) the song 'All my Thoughts', its opening line being 'All my thoughts are with you'. This will become her musical motif. Demurely attired, though displaying some décolleté, she is innocent, too innocent for her own good and will require male protection, even control, for it is she who helps smooth the entry of the Jew into Stuttgart. The couple embrace, but are interrupted by the father who orders Dorothea into the kitchen to prepare the dinner. Conveniently, she has no mother, no mature female presence, only the occasional appearance of a maid in a very minor role. The father places his hand on Faber's shoulder, a sign of his approval. Faber has dedicated Dorothea's new notebook to his 'dear fiancée on the day our dear Duke has taken his oath of office, signed in love and faith, Hail to Württemberg'. Private happiness has thus been linked to public good. But there will be disappointment, not only because of the Duke's behaviour but also because of Dorothea's. Childlike, she is unable to sense danger. Moreover, in the very next sequence she will reveal her ignorance when at the table her father asks her: 'To whom shall we drink?' and she suggests her fiancé to which her father declares that Faber is not important, nor are they, and asks her again. This time she gives the correct answer: 'To our Duke'.

From this modest home the film cuts to the coronation celebrations at the palace, in a skilfully choreographed sequence, obviously adding to the costs of the film – lavish sets and many extras in elegant costumes. The Duchess enters. We see her with her back to the camera as the Duke strides in. The women curtsy. He comes straight to his wife to tell her that her present will come later since he reminds her, in this sumptuous setting, that he is poor. Outside the troops march to martial music; behind them jubilant crowds celebrate. The Duke and Duchess step onto the balcony. The Duke proclaims: 'My people! My Country'. At his side, Sturm replies that 'Württemberg is the most blessed land under the German sky'.

The Württemberg coat of arms dissolves to a nameplate with Hebrew lettering. The music has become eerie. To the side of a door we see three letters in the Roman alphabet: 'JSO'. The Duke has sent an emissary to the Frankfurt ghetto, a world of narrow dark streets with strange, unattractive, unkempt people living in close proximity. His coach departs. People gather out of curiosity. The emissary, Remchingen (Theodor Loos), lifts the knocker. The door is opened by Süss' secretary, Levi (Werner Krauss), and he enters. Outside a coarse and repellent butcher (also played by Krauss) converses with a bearded, old man at the window (again played by Krauss) as to what such a person should want from Süss, at which point the man at the window suddenly notices that his daughter's dress has slipped too low over her shoulder and he orders her inside. She is called Rebecca and leaves with a knowing smile. Jewish women, unlike German women, especially unlike Dorothea, are not chaste.

The emissary enters a dark interior. Dressed in black and wearing sidelocks, Süss is a demonic figure. His elfin secretary, Levi, is excited. Süss, with a knowing look, tempts the emissary: he opens his cupboard to display his treasure – sparkling diamonds and many crowns, an indication of his clientele. As in a fairy tale the stranger is tempted but it is not the witch but the Jew who is doing the tempting. The emissary is overwhelmed by the display. But these jewels are available only on condition, namely that Süss be allowed entry to Württemberg where, as the emissary tries to explain, no Jews are allowed. This of course Süss already knows. That is his price. He drives a hard bargain; his eyes narrow. Marian's performance is a tour de force. The deal is struck. The emissary is off. Levi is astounded at this development, declaring in a Yiddish intonation that no Jews are allowed there. Süss' eyes narrow as he tells him: 'I open the door for you all. You will go about in satin and silk. It can be tomorrow, it can be the day after tomorrow, but it will be!'

The scene dissolves from the darkened room to a sunny landscape. A carriage hurtles across the countryside, so fast that it overturns. An elegant gentleman in eighteenth-century dress emerges from the overturned carriage. It is Süss, now without his sidelocks. Brushing himself off, he exclaims, 'You call this a road?' The lovely Dorothea is also travelling at this time. She offers him a ride. Together they will pass through the city gate. Süss has entered Stuttgart, the city forbidden to Jews, enabled by the unknowing female.

As in a fairy tale, Süss has the ability to mutate. On their journey he impresses Dorothea with talk of his travels. Not only does she lack a racial awareness since she is unable to detect a Jew but she even expresses a desire to visit Paris like Süss, for he is worldly. She is impressed but does wonder if he has a *Heimat* (home), here alluding to the antisemitic view of the Jew as rootless. However, she has already put her foot wrong, since a virtuous German female would only wish to stay at home where she can be protected. She requires male control.

Missing no chance for good contacts (and a pretty face), Süss later pays Dorothea a visit at home but meets with instant hostility from her fiancé, Faber, the proto-Nazi in the film. (He has been given the name of one of the judges who acted against the historic Süss.)[6] His antennae are sharp: he knows instantly that Süss is a Jew and suggests that he seek lodgings at an inn which caters to Jews. Crestfallen, Süss lowers his eyes, in a revealing piece of acting which at this moment runs counter to the film's message. Later he will appear as the cruel minister and more in character as the cowardly Jew, but at this particular moment he elicits sympathy. Nevertheless, now less elegantly attired, he has not been able to disguise the fact to the discerning, that he is a Jew. Visibly shocked, Dorothea realizes her mistake.

Marian will portray Süss in a number of roles: the ghetto Jew; the Jew as peddler or salesman; the elegant eighteenth-century gentleman and cavalier; the cruel powerful minister. But in this sequence he is the sensitive, gentle stranger offering his thanks. In much of the film he is the Jew as perpetrator, but in this particular sequence he is the Jew as victim, someone who has been humiliated when advised to seek lodging at an inn specifically for Jews. Soon Süss will become the ingratiating salesman, peddling his wares, in this case jewels, to the easily tempted Duke. Later he will pander to the Duke and then become the powerful and cruel 'minister', before reverting to type as the grovelling, cowardly Jew, on trial for his life. The Jew, endowed with a 'protean nature', nevertheless will still retain the 'essence of his nature'.[7] Despite this first encounter in Stuttgart, Süss manages to insinuate his way into court, as in Kornfeld's version of the story, and from there he obtains an appointment, eventually becoming a minister. He is actually referred to as 'Herr Minister', with a certain degree of sarcasm. Embarking on a policy to fill the Duke's coffers, he increases taxation, causing outrage – this is not so far removed from the actions of the historical Süss. Unrest grows. Süss manipulates the Duke. He panders for him at the masked ball. Parents are outraged as their daughters are enticed. Again this was alluded to in Hauff and indeed had formed part of the investigation when the case against the historic Süss was being prepared. At Carnival Süss will also try to win over Dorothea but her fiancé comes to her rescue. Both father and fiancé protect her, as the minister is rebuffed.

Süss also now enables Jews to enter Württemberg. Like a plague of locusts, they arrive, poor, dishevelled, filthy, physically repellent. They even sing songs with an alien tonality. In fact the song sung by the Jewish extras was a Zionist song, recently composed by European-born

Yedidya (Gideon) Admon-Gorochov (1897–1982), a fervent Zionist who emigrated to Palestine from Ukraine, and who was keen to throw off European influences. The melody is influenced by Bedouin music, and the words are about a camel. The Czech extras are unlikely to have known this song 'Shir Hagamal', better known as 'Gamal, Gemali' (The Song of the Camel Driver), which in the film, apparently, is sung in an uncharacteristically sombre manner.[8] The song is likely to have been found in a book of Jewish songs published in Berlin in 1935.[9]

Süss engages the services of a rabbi/astrologer, also played by Krauss, who reads the stars for the Duke in order to trick him. Coughing incessantly, he too suggests that the Jew brings disease from the ghetto. He tells the Duke that the stars are aligned in his favour and thus the coup, planned by Süss on the Duke's behalf to seize power from the diet, can proceed. This will involve the arrest of members of the diet, including Sturm and his assistant Faber, but funds will be needed. Thus Süss seeks out fellow Jews to finance the coup from which they will benefit. He finds them in the synagogue where business deals are struck, as in a sequence in *Der ewige Jude*.

It is this synagogue sequence, carefully orchestrated by Harlan, which he believed produced a 'diabolical effect'. The Jews perform their rites in an unruly manner, rocking and jumping up and down. The short, dark-haired man with the flattened nose, who appeared when the titles rolled as well as when the Jews entered Stuttgart, runs up onto the platform. He too jumps up and down as the music reaches a crescendo. The Jews are alien. One critic described this as the 'Asiatic effect'.[10] For Nazis, 'Orientalism' or in this case, the pejorative '*Asiatentum*', indicates something not German and thus to be feared.

Members of the diet, however, are alert that something is afoot and have made their own plans, backed by members of the guilds, as in the legend. Dorothea's father and fiancé conspire. Süss had made an offer of marriage to Dorothea through her father who declares that he will have no Jewish children the same line as in Hauff, though there it had referred to the son marrying a Jew, rather than the Jew (Süss) seeking the daughter's hand. Fearing the power of Süss, as it now touches his own family, the father permits his daughter to marry Faber in a secret ceremony, but before the marriage can be consummated Faber is arrested as a conspirator. Dorothea seeks out Süss to plead for her husband. He is being tortured nearby and as the screws are tightened she will hear his scream and recognize his voice. This is the 'touch of Tosca' that Feuchtwanger had referred to.

Unlike Tosca, Dorothea is childlike and also timorous when she enters the apartments of the Jew. Dressed in a silk dressing gown, his manner with her is cloyingly ingratiating but soon become threatening. We catch sight of his huge baroque bed in the next room but he quickly shuts the door. The innocent Dorothea, wide-eyed and demure, at the open window suddenly hears the cries of her husband. Süss, the seducer, tries very hard to persuade the virginal bride. She is fearful but trapped. This scene is likely to have been influenced by the testimony taken from the eighteenth-century Christina Dorothea Hettler. However, she came to see Süss on more than one occasion.[11] When thwarted, Süss becomes aggressive and insistent. There is a tussle and from a high angle shot we see him fall upon the frightened Dorothea on his bed.

The rape sequence was already in the script which Harlan inherited. If the woman is the man's property – and National Socialists' views on women were not progressive, then rape is theft, for the rapist has stolen the property of the rightful owner. It is not surprising that a member of the SS included a rape sequence in his script for it is through the woman that the race is to be preserved. If defiled, she is not only spoiled goods and no longer suitable for another man, as has been the case in many societies, but for the Nazi her racial purity has also been lost. Preserving the German race is paramount. *Rassenschande* (race defilement) is the name of the crime which has been committed. A shamed Dorothea escapes Süss. We see her running through the countryside. She will drown herself in the River Neckar. Though jokes were made that Söderbaum in Harlan's films had become the Reich's floating corpse (*Reichswasserleiche*), there was, from the Nazi perspective, a good reason for her to drown in this film, though she also drowns again in *Die goldene Stadt* (*The Golden City*) (1942) for a similar reason – having been made pregnant out of wedlock by a racially inferior Czech. In Hauff, however, it is the sister of Süss who drowns not from shame, for she has remained pure, but because after the death of her brother she is alone and unprotected and abandoned by the man she has loved, who has acted as her brother's prosecutor, unable to break with custom and defy his father. Hauff himself was not unaware that custom was beginning to break down elsewhere. The drowning in the Harlan film is different. This female has been defiled, racially defiled. She has no value and she knows this. The point has already been emphasized earlier in the film, when Dorothea's father, approached by Süss for her hand in marriage, tells him that he wants no '*Judenkinder*', words which Hauff has the father utter to his son. Like Lea in Hauff's novella, Dorothea drowns herself but does so out of shame. In a night-time sequence similar to one in an earlier Harlan film, *Die Reise nach Tilsit*, there is a play of light from the hand-held torches, as boats search the river to find Dorothea. Her body, quickly found, is carried to shore by her husband. He carries it through the town, followed by the crowd, to place it before the door of Süss. Inside, Levy, the cowardly Jew, is terrified.

At a ball at the palace, the Duke collapse and dies. Süss is instantly arrested and reverts in another dissolve to the poor Jew in rags, on trial for his life. Even his language reverts, now speaking German with a Yiddish intonation. A coward, he begs for mercy for he is, he states, only a poor Jew. Dorothea's father, the figure of authority, pronounces judgement. 'After months of detailed examination we have found the accusations justified … extortion, profiteering, trade in offices, sexual misconduct, procuring and high treason' and concludes, 'Should a Jew have carnal relations with a Christian, he is to be hanged'. He then announces the reintroduction of the ban on Jews in Württemberg. Süss declares that everything he has done has been at the command of his sovereign. As the cage travels upwards whimpers: 'I have been nothing but a servant of my sovereign.' And then even calls the Duke a traitor and offers his houses and money: 'I am only a poor Jew and want to live.' He dies without dignity. After the war Harlan insisted that as the cage was hoisted, Süss (following his script) had uttered Biblical curses, a sequence which Goebbels had cut.[12] But the shooting script does not contain these curses.[13]

Standing below the cage Faber remains unmoved. As in the British film, the snowflakes fall. And as in the British film, the gallows have been done away with. In both films Süss enters the cage at ground level. The Jews leave Württemberg for the father of the dead Dorothea (as well as the father of his country) has announced their expulsion while also reminding his audience of the ancient law forbidding sexual contact between Jews and non-Jews. Both these lines suggest that this film's purpose was to reinforce the Nuremberg Laws and the forced emigration of Jews from German territory (expulsion), rather the actual extermination of a people. This is the ending which the Reichsfilmdramaturg, Fritz Hippler, would describe in 1942 as a 'happy end'.[14]

12

Veit Harlan's Jud Süss: reception (1940–1945)

By late summer 1940, Veit Harlan's *Jud Süss* was ready. It passed the censor (obviously a perfunctory exercise) on 6 September but the previous day, three weeks before its Berlin premiere, it was screened at the Venice Film Festival – which since the outbreak of war only showed films from Axis countries or Axis-friendly countries. It did not win the prize in the foreign film category. That went to another entry from Italy's German ally: Gustav Ucicky's *Der Postmeister* (*The Postmaster*), based on a Pushkin short story. An illegitimate son of Gustav Klimt, Ucicky had been making films far longer than Harlan – since the 1920s. However, two years later Harlan would win the foreign film prize for *Der Grosse König* (*The Great King*). Nevertheless, *Jud Süss* still received high praise from the festival critics. The twenty-eight year old Michelangelo Antonioni, a critic before turning his hand to directing, wrote:

> We have no hesitation in saying that if this is propaganda, then we welcome propaganda. It is a powerful, incisive, extremely effective film … There isn't a single moment when the film slows, not one episode in disharmony with another: it is a film of complete unity and balance … The episode in which Süss violates the young girl is done with astonishing skill.[1]

Later that month in the official fascist film journal, *Cinema*, edited by Mussolini's son, Vittorio, he took a more critical stance with a comment about the 'unconvincing cruelty' of Süss.[2]

On 24 September 1940, *Jud Süss* opened in Berlin at Germany's largest cinema, the Ufa-Palast am Zoo, which fourteen years earlier Siegfried Kracauer had enthusiastically described as a 'palace of distraction', a 'shrine to the cultivation of pleasure', an 'optical fairyland', with its 'hallmark elegant surface splendour'.[3] Goebbels was very pleased with the premiere, recording in his diary: 'A very large audience with almost the entire Reich Cabinet in attendance. The film was an incredible success. You hear nothing but praise. People rave. This is what I wanted.'[4]

Hitler was not in attendance, having foresworn cinema-going for the duration of the war; for him the line between entertainment and propaganda was distinct. For Goebbels it was not: as he told the Reichsfilmkammer in late March 1933, 'the best propaganda works so-to-speak invisibly … without the public having any knowledge that it is at the initiative of the propaganda [ministry]'.[5] Thus what came in the guise of entertainment was most effective. It is this which partly complicates any attempt to assess the film's effectiveness.

Other leading figures in the Nazi hierarchy seemed to have concurred with Goebbels. Heinrich Himmler, the head of the SS, which also ran the concentration camps, as well as chief of the German police which included the Gestapo (secret state police), the security services (Sicherheitsdienst or SD) and the order police (Ordnungspolizei), was present at the gala evening which began not with the film but with live music – the Berlin opera house orchestra performing the bombastic Liszt tone poem 'Les Préludes' which also happened to suggest the German wartime newsreel signature tune.[6] One week after the Berlin screening Himmler made the film compulsory viewing for all members of the SS and the Police who were expected to see it 'during the course of the winter'.[7] Those members of the Order Police and Security police who had not yet viewed the film could attend special screenings but would be expected to pay the reduced price demanded by the cinema-owners. Members of other services, on the other hand, could attend the special screenings only if there were empty seats – this also applied to family members.[8] Himmler, it is clear, thought the film did the job.

There was a clamour for tickets for the Berlin opening. Some members of the SS expressed disappointment on learning that they could not be accommodated, despite the services they had rendered in procuring the 'racially pure Jewish extras'. An exchange of letters within the Propaganda Ministry between the Head of Personnel, Hans Hinkel, on behalf of his SS comrades and the State Secretary, Leopold Gutterer, makes this clear. Despite offering assurances that no women would be given tickets and that full SS dress would be worn, the SS could not be accommodated: no extra tickets were to be had.[9]

Separating the film's propaganda value from its entertainment value is not necessarily straightforward as illustrated by the clamour for tickets by members of the SS. They did not want to be excluded from a gala occasion but were also seeking an appropriate reward for their efforts, keen to view a film which entertained as well as confirmed their belief that the Jews posed a serious danger to Germany.

A similar enthusiastic response to a highly publicized film can be found among others committed to the Nazi cause, or from those who were not necessarily Nazi but were antisemitic. The film served to reinforce their prejudices about Jews. But a word of caution is in order. Any assessment of the film's reception also depends on other factors, apart from the particular make-up of an audience. Context was also important. Political conditions, especially outside Germany, were subject to change. And the military situation was far from static. When *Jud Süss* first opened in Berlin, the Germans were militarily triumphant. By 1941 this had begun to be less apparent.

Jud Süss received the highest distinctions (*Prädikate*) which included 'Staatspolitisch' (of political value to the state) and *künstlerisch besonders Wertvoll* (of special artistic value). It was also deemed valuable for youth (*Jugendwert*), though this resulted in complaints from some parents and teachers about the film's suitability, given that it included a rape sequence.[10] A book of the film was also published – a lengthy 200-page novel by J. R. George, the pseudonym for Hans Hömberg, the film critic for the *Völkischer Beobachter*, which contained numerous details not to be found in the film.[11] A shorter published version of the actual script was also available.[12]

An anti-smoking campaign in 1941 also used the film. The Germans, especially during the Nazi period, were keen on health and hygiene and were the first (by many years) to embark on such an initiative. The Jewish danger was equated with that of tobacco, both designated as *Volksfeinde* (enemies of the people). An image of a dissolute and dishevelled Süss in a dressing gown (a still taken from the sequence shortly before he rapes Dorothea), his bejewelled hand resting on her pristine neck, appeared below the caption: 'The Jew has his victim by the neck'.[13] In another poster, a grinning devil offers a suave chain-smoker a cigarette with the caption: 'May I offer you a Jud Süss?'[14]

Reviews were extremely favourable, not unexpected given that film criticism had been abolished in 1936. Journalists had been carefully vetted – Jews, philosemites and political undesirables having been purged. Thus a negative review was highly unlikely, though one carefully nuanced review did appear. That was by Carl Linfert in the *Frankfurter Zeitung* which before 1933 had been a liberal democratic paper (Kracauer had been on the staff). What was significant was not only his careful choice of words but also what he did not say: he avoided using the word Jew, aside from the occasional (and unavoidable) mention of the film's title and subject. 'The kernel of the film,' Linfert wrote, was not Süss' machinations but rather the coup that had been planned against the Estates,[15] an interpretation unlikely to have found favour either with Harlan, the other two scriptwriters or Goebbels. According to Linfert, the problem was not of the Jew's making but rather that of the Duke's, as indicated in his opening sentence: 'The history of Jud Süss … belongs to the history of court Jewry, those Jews who during the mercantilist period were so happily used by the princes in order to finance their court' (note the passive voice). Goebbels shut down the *Frankfurter Zeitung* in 1943; not surprisingly Linfert, also an art historian who covered art as well as film for the paper, quickly found work after 1945 with the Berlin paper *Kurier*.[16]

More typical, however, were comments from other critics: 'with the name Jud Süss, a dark chapter in German history';[17] 'an historical example of how Jewry knew to worm its way in';[18] or 'to thunderous applause' [the film left] 'a powerful impression'.[19] The party newspaper, *Völkischer Beobachter*, characterized the script as 'sober, simple and without hatred', capturing in the 'figure of Jud Süss the complete character of a race, as it has appeared in all times'.[20]

The film grossed RM 6.2 million and was one of the Third Reich's box office successes. Of the thirty most successful films screened during the period 1940–1942, it ranked sixth at the box office, and of those films especially commissioned by the state (*Staatsauftrag*), it ranked third (after *Wunschkonzert* from the same year and *Die Grosse Liebe* two years later).[21] In 1944, one year after Stalingrad, as part of a renewed antisemitic and anti-Bolshevik propaganda campaign, it was re-released in Germany and in the occupied countries.[22] It should come as no surprise that the film's success served Harlan well with Goebbels. His salary rose considerably and on the twenty-fifth Ufa celebrations, in 1943 he was made a 'professor'.[23]

Between the years 1940 and 1943 20.3 million people saw *Jud Süss*.[24] In Vienna where it opened at the Apollo Cinema, the venue for many premieres, it broke records, attracting 20,000 people in four days.[25] The German press continued to provide box office reports until 1943. Not only was the film widely screened in Greater Germany (Austria, the Czech Protectorate and parts of Poland), but also in allied countries such as Hungary, or in neutral countries sympathetic to Germany such as Romania and Spain.

The Nazis' Security Service (Sicherheitsdienst or SD) had been monitoring public opinion since the late Weimar period. Now a part of Himmler's empire, after the outbreak of the war it also began to cover cinema audiences. Not all the reports were necessarily accurate reflections of opinion.[26] Individuals leaving a cinema, one would assume, would be guarded in expressing too loud a disapproval of a film with an antisemitic message and also one which had been so heavily promoted. Nevertheless, some individuals did feel free to vent their dissatisfaction with Fritz Hippler's antisemitic documentary *Der ewige Jude* (*The Eternal Jew*), when screened two months after *Jud Süss*. There were complaints that the film had brought nothing new to the subject. The report also indicated that the documentary was viewed mainly by 'the politically active part of the population'.[27] These two films catered to different audiences. Moreover, the latter was also an unsuccessful film and in a different genre – documentaries fared less well. The crudely made *Der ewige Jude* about 'the Jewish bacillus' with its narrator's hectoring voice did not fill the cinemas.[28] Even Leni Riefenstahl's *Triumph of the Will* (1934), it should be pointed out, was less successful than her subsequent cinematic reputation might suggest.[29]

Monitoring the responses of individual members of an audience who chose to express an opinion is hardly representative of opinion.[30] Moreover, the reports were not always accurate. Some Security Service observers tried to please their masters by talking up the information.[31] For example, a local member of the Security Service in Luxembourg sent a report to Berlin on the audience's response to *Jud Süss*. Dated 5 November 1940, it read as follows:

> The screening of *Jud Süss* is a success … widely viewed by all groups. During the screening comments were repeatedly made against Jews. The film is much discussed by the public, whereby it has been emphasised that the clear treatment has made this especially easy to understand.[32]

Despite the film's apparent success with the Luxembourg public (Luxembourg was then under German control but two years later would be annexed), it did not lead to an extended run.[33] And when the final report was ready for internal circulation within National Socialist circles an important sentence had been reworked to read: '*Jud Süss* attracts great attention, the screening of which has led to demonstrations against Jews' – 'comments against Jewry' having become 'demonstrations'.[34] Clearly, that is what it was believed Goebbels wanted to hear.

Jud Süss did well in other territories under German control. According to the German film press, when the film first opened in Copenhagen in February 1941, it was sold out.[35] In Prague the Metro cinema had 35,000 visitors in three weeks; there were screenings in Brünn (Brno) and Ostrau (Ostrava).[36] Favourable reports also came in from Slovakia.[37] In Amsterdam it appeared at three Ufa theatres.[38] In Brussels it had a gala premiere at the prestigious Palace of Fine Arts (Palais des Beaux-Arts).[39] There were screenings in Norway and in Athens (apparently) the film enjoyed commercial success.[40] There were screenings in Riga in August 1941 and in Kiev in November 1941.[41] In August 1943, *Film-Kurier*, a German trade paper, was still reporting on *Jud Süss'* box office success in Ukraine where, dubbed into both Russian and Ukrainian, it had been one of five successful German films shown in the previous half year – the two from 1941 were *Quax der Bruchpilot* (*Quax, the Crash Pilot*) with the popular comic actor Heinz Rühmann and the euthanasia melodrama *Ich klage An* (*I Accuse*) and from 1942 *Die grosse Liebe* (*The Great Love*) with Swedish star Zarah Leander.[42]

In Poland, according to Holocaust survivors, *Jud Süss* was often screened prior to the deportations or dissolutions of the ghettos to prepare the non-Jewish inhabitants.[43] During the Auschwitz trial in 1961, according to *SS-Rottenführer* (corporal) Stefan Baretzki, one of the camp guards then on trial, films like *Jud Süss* were screened to those running the camps: '*Hetzfilme* [incitement films] like *Jud Süss* [were shown] and what consequences they had for the prisoners! The films were screened to the teams and you should have seen what the prisoners looked like the following day!'[44] Nevertheless, this particular statement was an interjection from Baretzki, an ethnic German from Czernowitz, (once located in Austria, then Romania and now Ukraine). The lowest ranking guard on trial, he had been arrested several times before for petty crime and his comment may have been an attempt to get him a reduced penalty. He could blame their actions on the film.

Jud Süss was also screened in some neutral countries though not in Switzerland.[45] In Finland, some twenty German films were refused a license, including *Jud Süss*.[46] In Sweden it was also banned.[47] In Spain, a special premiere took place in Madrid but thereafter the censor only permitted special screenings, i.e. at closed gatherings.[48] In Italy, in the year following the Venice Film Festival, the film opened in Rome, but ran for only fourteen days though had screenings in other towns.[49] Bulgaria, which joined the Axis on 1 March 1941, also showed the film.[50] In Romania, characterized in the German film press as a country with conditions similar to Hungary, namely 'in which the Jewish element was dominant and especially influenced the film market', it also had screenings.[51] King Michael and his prime minister Ion Antonescu attended the premiere.[52]

A member of the Axis since 1940, the Hungarian government of Admiral Horthy pursued antisemitic policies while the Fascist Arrow Cross, not yet in government, was extremely antisemitic. Synchronized into Hungarian, *Jud Süss* opened in Budapest's leading (Ufa) cinema, the Urania in late January 1941, running there until April, then reappearing again in August. In the first four weeks more than 100,000 people viewed the film, with the 100,000th viewer, an Armenian from Transylvania, being presented with a gift by the management.[53] Screenings took place elsewhere in Hungary, including in the new territories annexed from Romania (Transylvania) and from Czechoslovakia. According to one Hungarian film journal, 75,000 tickets had been sold in twenty-five days –the takings producing a sum sufficient to have financed one Hungarian feature film.[54] Goebbels' deputy in the Propaganda Ministry reported to Hitler that as of March 1941 Budapest's cinemas had been sold out for five straight weeks with tickets being ordered four or five days in advance.[55] During the premiere frequent applause was heard, which increased during the execution scene. And when Sturm announced the expulsion of the Jews loud shouts of 'Out with you! were heard.'[56] Militant Hungarian students also demanded that the film reach wider audiences by being shown in the provinces as well as in smaller theatres.[57]

Goebbels, not surprisingly, was delighted with the film's Budapest reception. His diary entry for 8 March 1941 mentioned demonstrations following a screening which offered proof that films which 'give our point of view can have an impact as well as inspire.'[58] The following year in February 1942 he told an audience of film people in Berlin that the screening of *Jud Süss* in Dutch cities had led to 'large demonstrations and pogroms against Jews, which resulted in a good half dozen Jews being hanged for trying to murder Germans'.[59] But no such incident was reported and Goebbels may have confused this with a stage-managed pogrom elsewhere in the Low Countries: in Belgium, in Antwerp, German newsreel cameramen had been on hand to film members of the Flemish Black Brigade and the Flemish SS, on the occasion of the premiere of *Der ewige Jude*, who marched through the Jewish quarter and set alight two synagogues.[60] If such demonstrations did occur in Budapest they are likely to have been the work of an antisemitic student group, the Turul Society, which specialized in street protests and had protested against other films featuring Jews, though it is not known for certain if they were behind these particular Budapest demonstrations.[61] In any case, the audience response is unlikely to have been spontaneous. Nevertheless, a satisfied Goebbels wanted this particular report to go direct to Hitler.[62]

Hungary provided particularly favourable conditions for a film with an antisemitic message. Indeed, antisemitism was then so pervasive that a pro-Nazi chief of staff of the Hungarian Army, Heinrich Werth banned screenings of the film to soldiers on the grounds that it was 'unsuitable for the cultivation of patriotism'.[63] Some of his officers had been requiring their men to view the film, even offering them reduced price tickets. But fearing that this could incite the soldiers to set off spontaneous pogroms, Werth decided the film was 'unsuitable', though the German ambassador protested against his decision. In January of the following year, however, the Germans were given permission to distribute 16-mm prints to small villages. By that time, Hungarians were feeling less well disposed to the Germans. After the German invasion of Hungary in the spring of 1944, *Jud Süss* was back in circulation.[64] But the context had changed: the Germans were the conquerors and only Hungarian collaborators and Arrow Cross members welcomed them.

It was in France that protests did not please the authorities. There were important differences between the north, the Occupied Zone, under direct German military control and the unoccupied south with its capital at Vichy, so-called 'independent' Vichy. *Le Juif Süss* opened in Paris (in the Occupied Zone) in a subtitled version on 14 February 1941 at Le Colisée on the Champs–Élysées, where two months before the outbreak of war Jean Renoir's *La Régle de jeu* had had its premiere. It ran there for eight weeks.

It also appeared the following month in a dubbed version in another prestigious cinema, the ultra-modern and very new Le Français (on one of the grand boulevards in the ninth arrondissement which had only opened shortly before the fall of France.) Jewish-owned, it was 'aryanized' a few months before the screening though bought by people close to the original owners.[65] The film ran there for five weeks.[66] Dialogue for this dubbed version has been described as more antisemitic than the original German though less misogynist.[67]

France of course had its own tradition of antisemitism, especially virulent from 1934 onwards after the Stavisky crisis (the confidence man Alexandre Stavisky had been a Jew) and again with the Popular Front (1936–1938), headed by Socialist premier Léon Blum who was also a Jew. Indeed, one of the Collaborationist critics, François Vinneuil (who also wrote under his own name Lucien Rebatet) likened Süss to Stavisky as well as to Bernard Natan (1886–1942), the Franco-Romanian Jew who had bought Pathé in late 1929, renamed Pathé-Natan, and who in 1935 had been convicted of fraud. Natan died in Auschwitz in 1942.[68] (In 1930 the film to have been based on Wilhelm Hauff's Süss novella, had been advertised as a 'Pathé-Natan-Super-Produktion'.)[69] However, in 1934, when Stavisky had only been dead ten months, the antisemitic Vinneuil-Rebatet, conceded in *Action Française* (the title also of the movement's paper) that the British film did have some good qualities.[70]

Maurice Bardèche and Robert Brasillach in the second edition of their co-authored *Historie du Cinéma* (1943) – the first edition, sometimes described as the first 'critical' general history of the medium by a French author(s) had appeared in 1935 – described *Jud Süss* thus:

an admirable antisemitic film ... the subject already having been treated twice [*sic*] by Jews ... The execution of the Jew, the vengeful frenzy of the crowd animates the end of the work in a crescendo almost joyous ... comparable to the crescendo of the better American films.[71]

Brasillach was later executed – controversially for 'intellectual crimes'. The third edition, which appeared in 1948, three years after his death, included only one change to the description of the film: the adjective 'admirable' as in 'admirable antisemitic film' was dropped. While in prison, Brasillach had been working on this new edition. Whether it was he who decided on the omission or whether it was his co-author, his brother-in-law, Bardèche, is not known. Critics in the Occupied Zone were enthusiastic about the film but then critics likely to have been opposed to the German conquest were unlikely to be writing, or if they were, knew to be circumspect.

Though no precise figures are available, it is thought that by 1941 *Le Juif Süss* had been viewed by a total of 1 million in both zones.[72] Film critics like Brasillach and Vinneuil-Rebatet used the film to blame the Jews for France's defeat and demand their exclusion.[73] Though it did well in the Occupied Zone, enthusiasm soon dissipated not because the French were concerned with the plight of French Jews or because antisemitism was on the wane but because from August 1940 and for the next seven months American and British films had been banned, along with those French films released after 1937 (the time of the Popular Front). Desperate cinema-goers had to make do with what was on offer. *Jud Süss* opened towards the end of the seven-month period. The German occupiers had a captive audience, so-to-speak. Yet a Marcel Pagnol film – Pagnol was living in Unoccupied France – earned 24 per cent more in the same first-run Paris cinema, the Colisée, than had *Le Juif Süss* two months earlier.[74] Nevertheless, by May 1941, the German occupiers felt confident that French audiences were now ready for newsreels with some antisemitic content.[75] Though initially audiences had whistled and coughed, eventually they began to fall silent.[76]

In June 1941 the organization Centrale catholique française in Paris, a branch of the Centrale catholique du Cinéma et de la Radio, which from time to time published classifications pinned to the church doors, placed *Le Juif Süss* in Classification 4. This stipulated that despite some 'bad' sequences, the film would be harmless if preceded by a warning which, according to a German report, could 'hardly have been a worse classification for a film of German provenance'.[77]

Vichy administrators had been intent on trying to create an illusion of independence and succeeded in resisting German pressure to standardize film distribution in both zones. The protests which took place during the screenings of *Le Juif Süss* differed from those in Hungary since they were on behalf of oppressed Jews. In Paris in the early months of the Occupation there had been audience protests in response to the German newsreels reporting the German victories. This led to preventive measures being taken, such as not dimming the lights during screenings.[78] Initially, however, in the Occupied Zone there were no demonstrations against *Le Juif Süss*. This only occurred later (between 1942 and 1944) when some bombs (planted by the Resistance) went off at the special screenings for committed audiences.[79]

In the Unoccupied Zone, in contrast, not only were there some negative reviews but there were also some protests. In the spring of 1941 however, Vichy's collaboration with the German conqueror was still in its infancy. Their help in delivering Jews to Auschwitz was still in the future. Thus criticism of the film at this stage related to the exclusion (though not yet extermination) of French Jews. A Lyon critic denounced the film as 'anti-Christian and not very French'.[80] That journal was then suspended for four weeks.[81] Another found it 'contrary to the French spirit'. That too was banned in August 1940 and the following year its editor was arrested for having contacts with the Resistance.[82] In May 1941 some Lyon university students protested at the screening of *Jud Süss*.[83] Mainly Catholic, they included Henri Bartoli, later a co-founder of *Le Monde*, who claimed to have lobbed home-made tear gas bombs in a cinema. He also distributed *Témoinage Chrétien* (*Christian Witness*).[84] In April and May 1941 members of the clergy (both Protestant and Catholic) petitioned the government to ban the film.[85] In June 1941 Socialist students in Toulouse interrupted screenings, singing the Marseillaise and chanting 'Down with Hitler'.[86] Indeed, it has been suggested that the screening of this film shifted opinion in the south away from Vichy and towards the first organized movements of resistance.[87] It also proved a useful target for clandestine newspapers associated with the Resistance. In one article, which appeared under the heading 'Why we do not want the film *Le Juif Süss*', the film was described as a 'call hatred':

> the goal of this insidious film is to make us forget that the Nazis are the true enemies of our country and of Europe ... When you are shown the Jew Oppenheimer unleashing a war in order to consolidate his power, think instead of Hitler trans-forming Europe into a bloodbath. Everything that the Nazis accuse the Jews of doing they have done themselves a hundred times over. Never forget that ... Long live France! Long live truth! Long live liberty![88]

Vichy officials ignored the petitions, arrested demonstrators and temporarily shut down newspapers which published negative reviews. By September police reports began to suggest that the film was a liability. In December 1941 Vichy banned *Le Juif Süss* in French-controlled North Africa. Many Jews lived there but the concern of the authorities was not to be seen to be too close to the Germans.[89] By the summer of 1942, when the deportations of French Jews began, the film had begun to function as Nazi counter-propaganda. For the next two years it was taken out of commercial distribution in both zones though was still screened to fascist groups.[90] It was not that the French had rejected antisemitism, but rather that antisemitism had become too closely associated with the German occupier – not that dissimilar to the film's fate in Hungary after the German invasion, though in both cases by then the film's novelty had also worn off and the Germans were no longer seen as victors. Aside from the fact that by this time the film was no longer new, the extensive publicity, high production values, and the popularity of costume drama were not in themselves sufficient to sustain the film's popularity once the context had changed.

Separating the message from the medium is not always easy since the medium has a tendency to make the message palatable. Context also influences a film's reception. In many cases it was German conquest. In Germany, however, it was obviously different. Germans themselves had been well prepared for the removal of the Jews: the Nazis, in power for over seven years, had quickly taken control of all forms of media, purging undesirable personnel and introducing strict censorship at every level. Their attack on the Jews had been relentless, from exclusion in the first years, to emigration from 1938 onwards, and finally a policy of full-scale extermination from 1942 (if we exclude the many deaths between 1939 and 1941). On more than one occasion Hitler had emphasized that were war to come it would be the fault of the Jews. In his speech of 30 January 1939, on the seventh anniversary of his accession to power, he had prophesied 'the destruction of international Jewry from the face of the earth'.[91] This appeared in a newsreel, as well as in the documentary *Der ewige Jude* (1940).[92] Of course one could decide not to go to the movies, but there was no escaping the message which was also ever-present in the political wall posters, 'The Word of the Week', which appeared weekly between 1937 and 1943.[93] Germans had been well prepared for a solution of the 'Jewish problem'.[94]

In the absence of any public dissent or the expression of opinion critical of the Nazis, audiences had become conditioned to see the Jew as the enemy. *Jud Süss*, a lavish feature film delivered the message in a highly palatable form, unlike *Der ewige Jude*. It was, after all, still entertainment – a box office hit, though one which also pleased the Nazi hierarchy.

There is no consensus about the impact of this film on audiences. In the early post-war period claims were made about its negative impact, reflecting the then dominant view that the spectator was a passive rather than active recipient. Such an evaluation also conflates the film's impact with the film-makers' intentions. That it pleased Goebbels or that the SS clamoured for tickets or that leading Nazi figures attended the premiere or that there were screenings on the eve of deportations suggest that at the time many believed the film *would* have an influence. Yet that still only tells us what some *assumed* would be the film's impact. The conservative political and legal theorist Carl Schmitt expressed his doubts after the gala Berlin premiere. In a letter to writer Ernst Jünger, then an army officer serving in Occupied Paris, he strongly recommended that he see the film, but also concluded without elaborating that: 'It is overall in many respects revealing, if also perhaps not as its author intended.'[95]

A costume drama which was a box office success, which had been heavily advertised, with a premiere that was a much-publicized gala occasion could also, to some extent, 'distract'. Was it part of that 'cult of distraction' to use Kracauer's term when writing about an earlier period of cinema-going? If the message itself came in a highly palatable form, could it, on occasion, get lost? Or did it build on a particular disposition, or a mentality through audio-visual means, that is 'non-verbalised means'.[96]

It is also worth considering the audience. Obviously, Goebbels, Himmler and the SS, along with committed Nazi Party members, saw one thing. But what about those not necessarily well disposed to the Nazis? And were there differences between Catholic viewers and Protestant, male from female, young from old, middle class from working class, urban dwellers from those living in small towns? Class, gender, religion, age, geography, political disposition as well as the conditions of viewing are aspects not to be overlooked when evaluating film reception, and although admittedly such information is often not available, there were some comments from women, who found the execution sequence gruesome.[97] Nor should we ignore the stage of the war when most Germans viewed this film, that is an early stage when Germany was triumphant, much of Western Europe having been conquered and the Battle of Britain only having just begun. Though the RAF bombed Germany, and Berlin even late on the night of the premiere, nevertheless damage was minimal compared to the fire-bombing which came later.

We do not have such evidence for this film, nor do we for most films. What we do have is often anecdotal, the response of individuals recalling the film post-war or occasional references in diaries and the monitoring of audience response by the Security Service during the war.[98]

We know rather more, however, about the intentions of the film-makers, the role of the Ministry of Propaganda, the manner in which the film was publicized, the conditions of viewing and how audiences were primed to respond. It has been argued that the film merely confirmed antisemites in their beliefs, rather than made new converts,[99] that Nazi propaganda did not create new beliefs, but built on commonly held ones such as hostility to the left, to the Weimar Republic or to the Versailles Settlement while also confirming a preference for heroic leadership. Prejudice against Jews had a long history though many Germans had no contact with Jews – the Jews, constituting less than 1 per cent of the population in 1933, lived mainly in urban areas. For centuries there had been a tradition of hostility to Jews on religious grounds, more recently replaced by one based on 'racial'. As a consequence of Nazi propaganda, Jews had become depersonalized and Germans desensitized to their plight.[100] This is the context in which the film was screened in 1940. It should neither be viewed in isolation, nor 'in a cineaste's safe haven outside time and beyond history'.[101]

In his own defence Harlan later claimed that Ferdinand Marian (Süss) had received fan mail, though such letters were never produced.[102] It may well be that Marian did receive fan mail which of course could be proof that the letter-writer missed the point and was either responding to Marian's performance or to his 'star persona'. That, however, is insufficient grounds for claiming that the film is harmless. Certainly, the authorities maintained the opposite: they hoped the film would persuade audiences that the Jews did not belong in Germany. That explains Goebbels' enthusiasm; that is why he brought in Harlan to make the message palatable; and that is why he was so delighted with the result. Post-war, Harlan tried to play down his success in delivering what Goebbels wanted. If Marian had managed to make the villainous Jew appear attractive (to some females), then he (Harlan) will not have helped deliver what was required. Yet in his diaries Goebbels never expressed any dissatisfaction with Harlan's work on this film; quite the contrary, there was only enthusiasm.

If opinions about Jews did change, this is more likely to have occurred either during the previous seven years or in the context of war and far less likely as the consequence of viewing one particular film. Yet that is not to conclude that the film is 'harmless' – which is why to this day it remains banned in Germany – but merely that it is difficult to assess its precise impact on audiences. Antisemites may have had their convictions strengthened by viewing this film. We know how Nazi officials received the film, how carefully vetted critics assessed the film and that people flocked to see it. We also know that it was part of a propaganda campaign directed against Jews, and that it was intended to prepare non-Jews to accept their elimination as the solution to the 'Jewish Question'. Given that the film project was conceived before extermination policies were being fully implemented, the film may not have been intended to suggest the actual physical elimination of the Jews, but merely their removal (emigration) from German territory, as the Jews in the film are forced to leave Stuttgart. Yet the film ended with the execution of Süss which might suggest a later and final stage in the Nazi persecution of the Jews.

13

Veit Harlan on trial (1945–1950)

As the Second World War entered its final phase, Veit Harlan was working on the Third Reich's most expensive film, *Kolberg*. In colour, with a cast of thousands, it exhorted Germans to follow the example of the inhabitants of Kolberg, the East Prussian town on the Baltic, who during the Napoleonic Wars were willing to fight to the bitter end. Again Joseph Goebbels was closely involved. It opened on the twelfth anniversary of the Nazi takeover (30 January 1945), by which time few cinemas were still in existence, including the Ufa-Palast am Zoo, the Berlin cinema (once Germany's largest) where *Jud Süss* had had its premiere.[1]

Harlan left Berlin for Hamburg, his Berlin-Gruenewald home having been destroyed in December 1944 though he continued to give Berlin-Tannenbergallee as his official address.[2] Hamburg had been fire-bombed by the British in the summer of 1943. Much of the city had been destroyed, but it was geographically nearer to Sweden, his wife's birthplace, where their son had been sent with his nanny. Kristina Söderbaum was refused permission to accompany him but had managed in October 1944 to get back her Swedish citizenship, an indication that the couple were preparing for the German defeat.[3]

Though the Allies were closing in, Harlan had not completely given up. He was still working on future film projects, including a script for *The Merchant of Venice*. An obvious choice perhaps but he had to overcome objections in using a stage classic which he adapted so freely that little of the original remained. Its purpose, according to Harlan, was to show that 350 years earlier a genius like Shakespeare and British was antisemitic.[4] The British entered Hamburg on 3 May 1945, five days before VE Day; in the Allied division of Germany it became part of the British zone. It was in this zone that Harlan attempted to gain clearance in order to be able to seek work post-war, as a film-maker.

Harlan quickly became aware that his name would be high on an American and British 'blacklist'.[5] Realizing that retribution was now at hand, he began to prepare his defence. One month after the German defeat he circulated a thirty-two-page typescript account, dated 6 June 1945, and entitled: 'My Attitude to National Socialism' – in both a German and English version.[6] Aware that he had a difficult case to prove, he accused 'my Jewish colleagues after emigrating to foreign countries' for placing him on a blacklist, along with his wife and others and was especially keen to challenge his description as the 'Number One Nazi-Film Producer' as put about in many foreign newspapers, especially in his wife's native Sweden.[7] He went on to provide details of his trials and tribulations under Goebbels, in particular how he had been 'forced' to make *Jud Süss*.

In defence, Harlan also pointed to the help that he had given many individuals in the film industry who were married to Jews or to half-Jews, which had enabled them to retain their membership in the Reich Film Chamber, (without which they could not find work) and noted that later, during the war, he had helped those under threat of being conscripted into the 'dangerous Todt [labour] Organisation'.[8] This may well have been true, but because of his important position in the film industry and his support from the Propaganda Ministry, he was running less of a risk in trying to help others than those less well-placed. In the last year of the war he was in the fortunate position of being able to commandeer materials, equipment and technicians, prompting Leni Riefenstahl to complain about his monopoly of resources and in particular the services of one particular sound engineer whom she needed for her film with music, *Tiefland* (*Lowlands*), then already four and a half years in the making.[9]

In the summer of 1945 Harlan completed his first questionnaire (*Fragebogen*), essential if he were to find work. It was part of what became the process of denazification, intended to remove individuals from positions of influence if in any way they had been compromised. Harlan could present a technically clean record since he had never belonged to an 'unacceptable organization' – he had never been a Nazi Party member. (Nor had Riefenstahl, for that matter.) But he had 'profited' from the Third Reich – of that there could be little doubt, for he had only turned his hand to directing in 1935 after the exodus of directorial talent. He was asked by the British officer handling his case, a Captain Phillips, to provide further details about how he had helped Jews. This information he duly gave as early as 17 July 1945.[10] Aware that rehabilitation would not be easy, Harlan now engaged a lawyer, Otto Zippel, who would act on his behalf until his final acquittal in 1950.

In November 1945 Erich Kästner launched an attack on Harlan. Author of the popular *Emil and the Detectives* and its sequels, he had eventually been allowed, even encouraged by Fritz Hippler, then *Reichsfilmintendant*, to work (under the pseudonym of Berthold Burger) on the script for *Münchhausen* (1943), which had its premiere during the twenty-fifth anniversary celebrations of the recently defunct Ufa, Germany's large film conglomerate.[11] The attack appeared in the recently founded and aptly entitled *Neue Zeitung* (*New Newspaper*) and had been in response to an interview which Harlan had given to a Swedish journalist, subsequently reprinted in a Zurich newspaper in which he had cited his 'religious' outlook [*sic*] as his motive for trying to avoid making propaganda films. This was too much for Kästner, who called him a '*Gesinnungsakrobat*', a term of derision which he had invented to describe Harlan's 'acrobatic' ability to adjust his convictions to the new context.[12] Kästner's article was widely circulated. The battle lines were being drawn between those who had remained in Germany and advanced their careers against those who had remained but chose not to, or who felt forced to emigrate or had links with Jews or were on the left.

During January 1946 Harlan completed a second (now revised) questionnaire (*Meldebogen*). Negotiations had begun with the German *Länder* to take on the task of what was proving to be a bureaucratically complex task. Thirteen million adults in the British zone were required to complete the questionnaire, each to be vetted by newly appointed officials in newly created political ministries but under British supervision. Appeals against the initial categorization were to be heard within the local community in denazification tribunals whose members were described as 'local democrats and anti-Nazis', who themselves had already been 'denazified'.

In the view of many Germans, the opportunists were more dangerous than the so-called 'idealists', i.e. those who had joined earlier. Like Riefenstahl, Harlan had never felt the need to join the party to advance his career. Harlan was a big fish and not that easy to catch, despite every effort to do so. His denazification went at a snail's pace: he was not immediately summoned to appear before a tribunal. He wanted work as well as to clear his name (the two of course being inextricably linked) but until he was cleared he was unemployed. In the summer of 1946 his lawyer, now granted power of attorney, put in a request that Harlan be allowed to pursue his profession. In early January 1947 Harlan was informed that if he wanted to appeal against his pending categorization he would have to do so in Berlin, not Hamburg, where those in the arts ultimately could be dealt with.[13] The purpose was to prevent people like Harlan slipping through the net.

In the summer of 1947 Harlan was invited to attend a hearing in Hamburg. The main accusation was that he had made *Jud Süss*. He was therefore more than just someone who had profited during the Third Reich, but rather someone from the film industry who had been closely associated with Joseph Goebbels and whose name was already being linked to the Holocaust. Unlike Hippler, who made the documentary *Der ewige Jude* at the same time, Harlan had not been a Nazi. Unlike the director, Erich Waschneck, who had also made an antisemitic feature film in 1940, *Die Rothschilds* (*The Rothschilds*), his film was hugely successful.

On 25 November 1947 the panel viewed the film after which Harlan pleaded that the 'vague antisemitism' of his film should be judged in terms of what was then known and not in terms of the 'horrors' which occurred subsequently.[14] The director Wolfgang Liebeneiner and head of Ufa from

1942–1945, was summoned to appear as a witness, but declined on the grounds of 'short notice'.[15] Harlan had friends. But he had enemies too. The director Helmut Käutner wrote to the panel that Harlan had not been an 'ideological Nazi', but an 'unrestrained opportunist' and 'beneficiary' (Nutzniesser) and had used all his energy to advance his career but also a similar energy to rescue many endangered colleagues'.[16]

The 'Central' Committee in Hamburg created a special subcommittee to deal with Harlan's case. They held a meeting after the screening of *Jud Süss* at which it was mentioned that Wolfgang Schmidt, a fierce anti-Nazi and leftwing Social Democrat who was secretary of the denazification panel for cultural affairs in Berlin where the files of the former Reichskulturkammer were held, was shortly coming to Hamburg bringing with him his incriminating file on Harlan. One panel member proposed that Harlan's case should be handed over to the State Prosecutor, given his involvement in 'propaganda for the persecution of the Jews'. The proposal was rejected on the grounds that it was not within their power to do so though it was within their power to hand over his case to the 'Jewish Committee' which could then put the case before the State Prosecutor. This decision was accepted unanimously. Another meeting was called for the following week by which time Schmidt would have arrived from Berlin bringing the evidence.[17]

The day following this subcommittee meeting the Central Committee 'unexpectedly' held another meeting to which no members of the 'subcommittee' had been invited but to which both Söderbaum and Liebeneiner were, the last mentioned now having managed to find the time. This meeting Harlan's opponents described as a 'secret meeting'. Its function seems to have been to head off the move to hand over Harlan's case to the prosecutor and, most importantly, to do this *before* the arrival of incriminating material from Berlin. This committee decided to place Harlan in Category V (Exonerated) – the other categories ranged from Category I (Major Offenders), II (Offenders), III (Lesser Offenders), IV (Followers). Only this category would enable him to resume film-making.[18]

Some members, presumably perceived as unfriendly to Harlan, had not even been aware that a decision was due to take place and were thus either not present or had left the meeting before its adjournment.[19] Harlan later telephoned the chairman to be told the good news and that he could expect to receive the result in writing. This result probably came as a surprise to him because, on that very same day (12 December 1947), he had written an open letter to Lion Feuchtwanger, then in California. This had been in response to Feuchtwanger's earlier 'Open Letter', published in the *Atlantic Monthly* in 1941 and several months prior to that in the exile German language publication, *Aufbau*, which had been reprinted in the recently founded weekly, *Die Weltbühne*, in September 1947.[20] In 1940 Feuchtwanger had barely mentioned Harlan by name since his attack then had been directed at those actors who had appeared either in his 1917 play or in the later Ashley Dukes' adaptation translated into German. Nevertheless, in so doing he gave publicity to the Harlan film, which he described as a travesty of his work, a 'vile antisemitic movie'.[21] In so doing he was claiming ownership of a story that Harlan had stolen. Paul Kornfeld's name went unmentioned nor would it surface in the subsequent debate nor during Harlan's trial. Harlan's enemies pitted Feuchtwanger against him.

Harlan now found it prudent to respond, though the 1940 letter had not been addressed to him even if his name had been mentioned. It reveals that he still did not quite get the point:

> You wrote your famous novel and a play, *Jew Süss*, which was filmed in England. The enormous popularity of this literary work which successfully undertook to exculpate a criminal who was a Jew, it goes without saying, only because he was a Jew ... Goebbels would not have been Goebbels had he let this propaganda pass, which so-to-speak fell into his lap. For it must be said, that your book was also propaganda [these last words underlined for emphasis] which attempted to exculpate only because he was a Jew. Even if your attempt stemmed from noble motives and that from Goebbels from base, still an untruth remains an untruth – and so what followed from *Jud Süss* [the Harlan film] took a course for which German artists were in no way responsible.[22]

In Harlan's view, it was Feuchtwanger who could be blamed for the revival of interest in the case of Süss. No mention here of Kornfeld, in whose play Harlan's then wife, Körber, had a small part. (She was now a Berlin City Councillor representing the newly formed Christian Democratic Party and during his trial publicly gave Harlan her support, emphasizing that their three children bore his name).[23] Thus Feuchtwanger's attempt to present a virtuous Süss had made a Goebbels' retaliation likely. What this reveals is an unrepentant, but probably also desperate, Harlan since from 1935 to 1945 he had been a director and for most of that time a very important one with a commensurate salary. Like many other Germans he had now fallen on hard times, but he had fallen very far. Unemployed, he would remain so until he could obtain his clearance to work in a greatly reduced German film industry.

The media quickly learned of the result. A campaign began against the decision. Those now fortunate to have found new positions in the post-war film industry were keen to be seen to be on the 'right' side: Hungarian-born Josef von Baky, who in 1943 had directed the Ufa anniversary colour film, *Münchhausen*, was now a co-head of the Association of Film Producers in the American zone and cabled his protest.[24]

Such decisions only became legally binding once confirmed by the British Control Commission since the Regional Commissioner had the power to 'revise'.[25] Immediately upon learning the result, Major Kaye Sely (born Kurt Seltz in Munich who previously had served in the refugee-staffed Pioneer Corps),[26] now Head of Licensing Control, (Intelligence Section) in Berlin, wrote on 22 December 1947, ten days after the decision had been made, to his British superior in Hamburg Intelligence:

> You are no doubt aware that Veit Harlan, the infamous film director, has been placed in category V by the Hamburg Central Committee (Zentral Ausschuss) and I presume you agree with me that one can describe this decision as monstrous. The repercussions will be considerable.

He also mentioned the protests of the Film Producers Association in Hamburg, the American Licenses Film producers to the US Information Control, as well as 'the Berlin press [which is] ... up in arms', adding that he had 'seldom seen the German Cultural Affairs people so united over any subject'. He then went on to point out that since 'only the Regional Commissioner is empowered to revise this decision, we shall submit the whole case to him, with all the material we hold ... and we shall also perhaps suggest he sees the film *Jud Süss*.' Such material had been offered to the panel but they had declined to wait for its arrival before reaching a decision.[27]

A few days prior to this letter another refugee German Jew serving on the British Control Commission, Henry Ormond, had written Sely about information he had obtained from one of the panel members, obviously someone friendly to the occupiers, informing him about how they had reached the decision which Sely was now keen to reverse.[28] Refugees played an active role in trying to prevent Harlan's clearance. Though by no means the only people intent on preventing Harlan from resuming his career, they were often in a strong position to do so but had to work behind the scenes.

The fledgling press, often staffed by returning refugees, greeted the clearance with outrage. On 4 January 1948 the prominent journalist Peter de Mendelssohn, who before 1933 had worked on the liberal *Berliner Tageblatt* and from 1944 with the Allies' Psychological Warfare Division, had helped to found on his return to Germany the Berlin paper *Der Tagesspiegel* in which he now wrote: 'From the film *Jud Süss*, the way leads straight to the gas chambers.'[29] An attempt by Harlan to defend himself on radio – he had arranged this with the executives of the newly established Nordwestdeutsche Rundfunk – was scuppered after Hugh Carleton Greene, later Director-General of the BBC, intervened and Harlan did not broadcast. He lodged a complaint to no avail.[30]

In January 1948 the denazification committee reassembled, now composed of a new membership, consisting of four Social Democrats, one Christian Democrat, two Free Democrats, one Communist and two trade unionists though it was unclear about its role since the State Prosecutor was now involved in preparing a case against Harlan at the instigation of two organisations – one representing the victims of the Nuremberg Laws and the other of those persecuted by the Nazi regime. They did not know whether they should await the end of Harlan's trial before proceeding. These were uncharted waters and there was some confusion as to whether denazification proceedings and court proceedings could run in tandem and even whether members of the committee could attend the trial to hear the evidence against Harlan.[31] In March it was decided that the panel could not proceed since all the documents were now with the prosecutor, pending his decision on whether to charge Harlan. In the event they never needed to consider the question. The judiciary took over.

The Hamburg State Prosecutor began collecting evidence. Numerous witnesses, including the interned Fritz Hippler, then in the American sector, and many who had worked on the film were interrogated.[32] So too was the lone Jewish extra from Prague who had survived.[33] These witnesses tell us much about the film's production history.

On 15 July 1948 the prosecutor announced that Harlan was to be charged with crimes against humanity. His trial began the following year in March. Two months later the newly constituted denazification panel was inclined to place him in Category 4 (Fellow Traveller) but the process was suspended one day prior to the new German Basic Law (constitution) coming into force.[34]

A number of individuals testified on Harlan's behalf. They included Ferdinand Marian's widow – Marian had died in 1946 in a car crash – but she herself soon died in mysterious circumstances during the trial, drowning in a Hamburg canal.[35] Others who testified on Harlan's behalf included those who had worked with him on the film, including his close collaborator and assistant Alfred Braun, who before 1933 had worked on radio, been imprisoned in 1933 in Oranienberg concentration camp, had left Germany but returned in 1939 after which he worked closely with Harlan, including on *Jud Süss*.[36] Another was Conni

Carstenssen, (real name Friedrich Werth), his production manager, who before 1933 had worked for the Communist-funded film production company, Prometheus.[37] Individuals he had helped also gave their support, especially some in the *Mischling* category or who had been married to Jews or *Mischlinge*. Hans Meyer-Hanno, who had a small part in *Jud Süss*, had been married to a Jewish actress, Irene Sager. Harlan had written the Minister of Education when their *Mischling* son was to be expelled from school and intervened again when Meyer-Hanno was arrested for belonging to a resistance group by writing to the court where he was being tried. Meyer-Hanno was killed in prison, a few days before the capitulation.[38] Harlan also wrote letters in support of other *Mischlinge*.[39]

There is no reason to doubt that Harlan did make interventions. There is no reason to doubt his professions of *not* being antisemitic. His first wife, to whom he had been briefly married, had been Jewish and he was not the only film director to have made an antisemitic film who had once been married to a Jew: Hans-Heinz Zerlett, who directed *Robert und Bertram* (1939), was another example.[40] But he did make an antisemitic film, one which Goebbels was keen should be made at a time which had become extremely dangerous for Jews.

Harlan knew what was required both in the script and in the filming. He may have offered some resistance but that had more to do with inter-ference from outside by people who did not know how to make films. *Jud Süss* was too good an offer to turn down, despite his protestations to the contrary after the event and after the war – in his memoirs and in those of his wife.[41] It may even have been true that he would have chosen a different lavishly funded subject on which to work. But by that time, the opening months of the war, he should have been aware of what kind of film project might be on offer and that he might be called on to make such a film. Most importantly, he had positioned himself so that he would be asked.

Harlan was not the only person associated with the film who experi-enced difficulties. Heinrich George (the Duke) was arrested and died in

Oranienberg concentration camp in the Soviet Sector in 1946.[42] Werner Krauss experienced difficulties in his denazification and wrote to George Bernard Shaw, pointing out that he had acted in many of his plays in Germany, as well as on the London stage, and had even had the pleasure of being his guest when performing in London and asked him whether he thought it justified that the authorities had banned him for 'any further activity in connection with my professional calling as an actor', to which the ninety-one year old Shaw replied on 9 December 1947:

> All civilizations are kept in existence by the masses who collaborate with whatever government is for the moment established in their country, native or foreign. To treat such collaboration as a crime after every change of government is a vindictive stupidity which cannot be justified on any ground.[43]

Harlan, however, was also accused of distorting the Süss story, a curious offence, given that this had been true of his predecessors though, in his case, it was also at Goebbels' behest and therein lies the offence. A seventy-page book, hostile to Harlan, written by authors with links to the Jewish community in the area, pointed to the distortions in Harlan's script, as though this had not been true of his predecessors.[44] Some had championed the cause of Süss, endowing him with the heroic qualities (Dulk, Lehmann, Kohn, Feuchtwanger and Kornfield) while Hauff and later Harlan, had given negative qualities. But in the immediate post-war context, the Feuchtwanger version began to take on the status of the received version. Kornfield's work, along with that of others, was forgotten.

Historians played no role at this time: the opinion of Selma Stern, working in the Cincinnati archive, was not sought. Heinrich Schnee's first volume on the court Jew was still work in progress: it would appear three years after Harlan's acquittal. At the same time that Harlan was experiencing difficulty, he too was unable to obtain clearance and thus find employment but this did provide him with time to spend in the archives.[45]

In early post-war Germany the problem of coming to terms with the Nazi past was made more difficult in the absence of legal precedents. Harlan told the court: 'I am no politician. I am a director. My party is art. If convicted I could not return to my profession. My life would be at an end'.[46] He was acquitted on the grounds that it was difficult to determine the precise impact of the film and that in effect the Holocaust would have occurred with or without this film. The Prosecutor appealed and in 1950 the higher court in Cologne, clearly dissatisfied with the reasons given for the decision, referred the case back to the lower court in Hamburg for reconsideration. Harlan was then acquitted for a second time though on different grounds, namely that had he refused the commission he would have faced personal danger. (The judge on both occasions, it was later revealed, had himself been compromised during the Third Reich.)[47]

After a five-year break from film-making Harlan was able to resume his career. He still, however, faced one more hurdle. Eric Lüth, the Press Officer for the Hamburg Senate, called on German film distributors and cinema-owners to boycott any new film made by him. A court, however, found the boycott to be illegal.[48] Harlan went on to make another ten films before his death in 1964.

Conclusion

During his own lifetime Joseph Süss Oppenheimer had become legendary, though at the time of his death the occasional commentator was keen to appear neutral and attribute his fall to being the wrong man in the wrong place at the wrong time. Court Jews were not unique but Süss was a unique court Jew both in the power he acquired, in the life he led and in the manner of his death. Had he not been Jewish, it is doubtful that his life would have inspired such interest among writers, film-makers and the Third Reich's Minister of Propaganda. Told over and over, his story usually obscured the historic Joseph Süss Oppenheimer.

The timing of the retelling was also significant – often at important moments in Germany's history – post-Napoleonic Württemberg; Prussia on the eve of 1848; post-unification Germany when Jewish authors became drawn to the subject and again during the Weimar Republic. There was even a British response – a film conceived after Hitler's appointment as Reich Chancellor in response to the boycott in Germany of Jewish shops. And finally again in Germany, shortly after Kristallnacht, when another film was planned on the subject which had its first screening at a time of German military triumph. Frequent screenings continued during the war in occupied countries and as deportations began to take place. Thus yet another story about Süss, a villainous Süss, became associated not only with the expulsion but also with the destruction of European Jewry and the name of Süss became inextricably linked with the Holocaust. For Goebbels, Süss was the villain he had been looking for, yet he had not come up with the idea himself. Nor had the British film induced him to promote an alternative

German (Nazi) version. Yet when in early 1939 it was presented to him, he seized on it. But this was not the only version of the life of the Jewish upstart, nor was Feuchtwanger's the only other. The life of Süss, has lent itself to multiple retellings.

Notes

Notes to Chapter 1: Joseph Süss Oppenheimer: origins and early career (1698–1732)

1 Haasis, *Joseph Süss Oppenheimers Rache*, p. 106.
2 Haasis, *Joseph Süss Oppenheimer, genannt Jud Süss*, p. 10.
3 Ibid., p. 13; Stern, *Jud Süss: ein Beitrag zur deutschen und zur Jüdischen Geschichte*, p. 303.
4 Davis, *Women on the Margins: three seventeenth-century lives*, p. 9.
5 Stern, *Jud Süss*, pp. 16–7.
6 Ibid., p. 9; Haasis, *Joseph Süss Oppenheimer*, p. 20.
7 Jersch-Wenzel, 'Jewish economic activity in early modern times', p. 95.
8 Stern, *Jud Süss*, p. 9.
9 Ibid.
10 Haasis, *Joseph Süss Oppenheimer*, p. 33.
11 Ibid., p. 14.
12 Ibid.; Stern, *Jud Süss*, pp. 8 and 9 cite an interrogation from 4 June 1739.
13 Haasis, *Joseph Süss Oppenheimer*, p. 14.
14 Stern, *Jud Süss*, p. 9; Schnee, *Die Hoffinanz und der moderne Staat, Geschichte und System der Hoffaktoren an deutschen Fürstenhöfen im Zeitalter des Absolutismus*, iv, p. 112.
15 Haasis, *Joseph Süss Oppenheimer*, pp. 14–16; Stern, *Jud Süss*, p. 9. Stern describes the third brother Daniel as a full brother while Haasis (p. 16) describes him as a half-brother, claiming that Süss made a 'careless mistake', when on 4 June 1737 under interrogation, he mentioned only one sister and two older half-siblings. Adverse to accepting Daniel as a full brother, Haasis maintains that Süss' father married three times, rather than two, that Daniel came from the second marriage and Süss from the third, thus making Daniel the elder and that each of Süss' two elder Oppenheimer half-brothers came from a different marriage while a third half-brother, along with two sisters, came from his mother's second marriage. Stern, based on Süss' own testimony, states that Süss had two older half-brothers, one brother and one sister. There were of course half-siblings from Süss' mother's second marriage although, aside from Haasis, they have gone unnoticed, possibly because they were on the maternal side and

thus not Oppenheimers, added to which Süss had little contact with them. Stern (pp. 187–8) provides an early legal document, dated 17 November 1718, which relates to Süss and Daniel in which Süss refers to the latter as his 'brother' and another document (p. 303) from May 1737 in which Daniel enters a plea to the Imperial court on behalf of his 'brother', now under arrest.

16 Stern, *Jud Süss*, p. 9; Haasis, *Joseph Süss Oppenheimer*, p. 16.

17 Haasis, *Joseph Süss Oppenheimer*, p. 33.

18 Schnee, *Die Hoffinanz und der moderne Staat*, iv, p. 113.

19 Stern, *Jud Süss*, p. 9; Haasis, *Joseph Süss Oppenheimer*, pp. 13–15.

20 Bernard, *Ausführlicher Diskurs mit Einem seiner Guten Freunde von allem, was Ihme in den drey letzten Tagen des unglücklichen Jud Süss Oppenheimers*, pp. 39–40; Stern, *Jud Süss*, p. 10; Elwenspoek, *Jew Süss Oppenheimer, The Great Financier, Gallant and Adventurer of the Eighteenth Century: A Study Based on Various Documents, Private Papers and Tradition*, p. 29, the latter citing Bernard as the source.

21 Stern, *Jud Süss*, p. 9; Schnee, *Die Hoffinanz und der moderne Staat*, iv, pp. 112–13.

22 Haasis, *Joseph Süss Oppenheimer*, pp. 17, 206, 207 claims that Jewish women married late though provides no source. This contradicts a very good source, Glückel of Hameln (1646/47–1724), whose memoirs, rare for a woman during this period and unique for a Jewish woman, were published almost two centuries later at the end of the nineteenth century: *The Life of Glückel of Hameln 1646–1724 Written by Herself*. Married at the age of 14, as were her daughters, Glückel at no point suggests that this was unusual. Jewish females in Hamburg, according to Davis, *Women on the Margins*, pp. 11, 224 n.20, married at a younger age than Christian females, a practice 'not uncommon among better-off Jews in Central and Eastern Europe'.

23 Haasis, *Joseph Süss Oppenheimer*, p. 15; Emberger and Ries, 'Der Fall Joseph Süss Oppenheimer', pp. 34–5. See also Schnee, *Die Hoffinanz und der moderne Staat*, iv, p. 113.

24 Bernard, *Erinnerung ausführlicher Diskurs*, p. 23.

25 Stern, *Jud Süss*, pp. 15, 206.

26 Cser, 'Zwischen Stadtverfassung und absolutischem Herrschaftsanspruch (1650 bis zum Ende der Kurpfalz 1802)', pp. 46–153.

27 Ibid.

28 Haasis, *Joseph Süss Oppenheimer*, pp. 16, 206.

29 Stern, *Jud Süss*, pp. 187–8; Emberger and Ries, 'Der Fall Joseph Süss Oppenheimer', p. 34.

30 Stern, *Jud Süss*, p. 139; Stern, *The Court Jew, A Contribution to the History of the Period of Absolutism in Central Europe*, p. 73; Haasis, *Joseph Süss Oppenheimer*, pp. 19–20.

31 Ibid., p. 19.

32 Rieger, *Sicherer Bericht von dem Juden Joseph Süss Oppenheimer Welcher an*

1738. Den 4. Febr. bey Stuttgard executirt wurde, p. 2; Haasis, *Joseph Süss Oppenheimers Rache*, p. 106.

33 Haasis, *Joseph Süss Oppenheimer*, p. 274; Schnee, *Die Hoffinanz und der moderne Staat*, iv, p. 113.

34 Haasis, *Joseph Süss Oppenheimer*, pp. 239–47.

35 *The Life of Glückel of Hameln*, esp. p.139.

36 Davis, *Women on the Margins*, pp. 11, 224 n.20.

37 Emberger and Ries, 'Der Fall Joseph Süss Oppenheimer', p. 36.

38 Haasis, *Joseph Süss Oppenheimer*, p. 248.

39 There seems little agreement about the correct spelling of this name: Stern, *Jud Süss*, pp. 10ff spells it Heidersdorf while Baumgart, 'Joseph Süss Oppenheimer: Das Dilemma des Hofjuden im absoluten Fürstenstaat', p. 99 spells it Heidersdorff as does Schnee, *Die Hoffinanz und der moderne Staat*, iv, p. 113, while Krauss in his entry on Süss in the *Allgemeine deutsche Biographie*, p. 181 spells it Heydersdorff and Haasis, *Joseph Süss Oppenheimer*, pp. 8, 17 spells it Heddersdorf.

40 Stern and Jewish historians dismiss the legend (Stern, *Jud Süss*, p. 10). Others, like Elwenspoek, *Jew Süss Oppenheimer*, pp. 27–31 and Zimmermann, *J. Süss Oppenheimer, ein Finanzmann des 18. Jahrhunderts: Ein Stück Absolutismus-und Jesuitengeschichte. Nach den Vertheidigungs-Akten und den Schriften der Zeitgenossen bearbeitet von* … accept it as does Schnee, *Die Hoffinanz und der moderne Staat*, iv, p. 113 who claims that it does appear in the archives and cites as his source an account by the examining judge (Regierungsrat) Philipp Friedrich Jäger, 'Species facti den Jud Süssen und dessen complicend betreffend', in A 53I. B11. See also Gerber, *Jud Süss: Aufstieg und Fall im frühen 18. Jahrhundert: ein Beitrag zur historischen Antisemitismus-und Rezeptionsforschung*, pp. 25, 309–10 n.90.

41 Blanning, *The Pursuit of Glory*, p. 55.

42 Haasis, *Joseph Süss Oppenheimer*, pp. 15, 206; Schnee, *Die Hoffinanz und der moderne Staat*, iv, p. 113.

43 Stern, *Jud Süss*, p. 10.

44 Ibid., pp. 14, 142.

45 Ibid., pp. 13, 14.

46 Ibid., pp. 16ff; Schnee, *Die Hoffinanz und der moderne Staat*, iv, p. 114.

47 Haasis, *Joseph Süss Oppenheimer*, pp. 20ff; Emberger and Ries, 'Der Fall Joseph Süss Oppenheimer', p. 35.

48 Haasis, *Joseph Süss Oppenheimer*, pp. 20-1; Emberger and Ries, 'Der Fall Joseph Süss Oppenheimer', p. 35; Schnee, *Die Hoffinanz und der moderne Staat*, iv, p.114.

49 Stern, *Jud Süss*, pp. 16–17 claims he visited 'relatives' in Vienna.

50 Ibid.

Notes to Chapter 2: Württemberg's Court Jew (1733–1737)

1 Israel, *European Jewry in the Age of Mercantilism, 1550–1750*, p. 115; Carsten, 'The Court Jews: prelude to emancipation', pp. 127–31.
2 Israel, *European Jewry*, p. 114.
3 Ibid., pp. 141–2; Stern, *Jud Süss*, p. 116.
4 Carsten, 'The Court Jews', p. 141.
5 Gerber, *Jud Süss*, p. 99.
6 Stern, *The Court Jew*, pp. 75–6.
7 Ibid., p. 232; Cohen and Mann, 'Melding Worlds: Court Jews and the Art of the Baroque', p. 101.
8 Ibid., p. 232; Carsten, 'The Court Jews', p. 138.
9 Carsten, 'The Court Jews', p. 139.
10 Emberger and Ries, 'Der Fall Joseph Süss Oppenheimer', p. 37; Haasis, *Joseph Süss Oppenheimer*, p. 33.
11 Stern, *Jud Süss*, pp. 7–20, 23.
12 Ibid., p. 29; Emberger and Ries, 'Der Fall Joseph Süss Oppenheimer', p. 37.
13 Stern, *Jud Süss*, p. 20.
14 Stern, *The Court Jew*, pp. 25, 26, 116–17.
15 Stern, *Jud Süss*, pp. 27–9.
16 Ibid., pp. 25, 189.
17 Ibid., p. 190; Emberger and Ries, 'Der Fall Joseph Süss Oppenheimer', p. 37.
18 Stern, *Jud Süss*, p. 191; Schnee, *Die Hoffinanz und der moderne Staat*, iii, p. 202.
19 Wilson, 'Der Favorit als Sündenbock', p. 162; Stern, *The Court Jew*, pp. 44–8.
20 Stern, *Jud Süss*, p. 9; Schnee, *Die Hoffinanz und der moderne Staat*, (Berlin Duncker & Humblot, 1963), iv, p. 112.
21 Schnee, *Die Hoffinanz und der moderne Staat*, iii, p. 202; (1967) vi, pp. 61–2; Stern, *The Court Jew*, pp. 29, 117, 218.
22 Stern, *Jud Süss*, pp. 45–6; Osswald-Bargende, *Die Mätresse, der Fürst und die Macht: Christina Wilhelmina von Grävenitz und die höfische Gesellschaft*, p. 17; Osswald-Bargende, 'Sonderfall Mätresse? Beobachtungen zum Typus des Favoriten aus geschlechtergeschichtlicher Perspektive am Beispiel der Christina Wilhelmina von Grävenitz', p. 151; Wilson, *War, State and Society in Württemberg, 1677–1793*; Wilson, 'Women in Imperial Politics: the Württemberg Consorts 1674–1757', pp. 238–9.
23 Wilson, *War, State and Society*, pp. 154–62.
24 Stern, *Jud Süss*, p. 23.
25 Haasis, *Joseph Süss Oppenheimer*, p. 95; Wilson, 'Der Favorit als Sündenbock', p. 161.
26 Vann, *The Swabian Kreis: Institutional Growth in the Holy Roman Empire, 1648–1715*, pp. 30–6.
27 Stern, *Jud Süss*, p. 33; Blanning, *The Pursuit of Glory*, p. 277.
28 Wilson, *War, State and Society*, p. 46.

29 Asch, 'Corruption and Punishment? The Rise and Fall of Matthäus Enzlin (1556–1613) Lawyer and Favourite', p. 98.

30 Gerber, *Jud Süss*, p. 78.

31 Wilson, 'Der Favorit als Sündenbock', p. 166.

32 Carsten, 'The Empire after the Thirty Years War', p. 98.

33 Wilson, *War, State and Society*, p. 160.

34 Emberger and Ries, 'Der Fall Joseph Süss Oppenheimer', p. 38.

35 Vann, *The Making of a State: Württemberg 1593–1793*, pp. 216–19.

36 Wilson, *War, State and Society*, pp. 171, 75–7.

37 Stern, *Jud Süss*, p. 49; Vann, *The Making of a State*, p. 224; Wilson, *War, State and Society*, p. 176.

38 Wilson, 'Der Favorit als Sündenbock', p. 164.

39 Wilson, *War, State and Society*, p. 165.

40 Wilson, 'Women in Imperial Politics', p. 307.

41 Wilson, *War, State and Society*, p. 165.

42 Blanning, *The Pursuit of Glory*, p. 57.

43 Carl Alexander to Süss 17 September, 1734, and 18 March 1735 cited in Stern, *Jud Süss*, pp. 206, 212. See also pp. 28–29, 142–3.

44 Wilson, *War, State and Society*, p. 164.

45 Wilson, 'Der Favorit als Sündenbock', pp. 165–6.

46 Blanning, *The Culture of Power*, p. 73.

47 Vann, *The Making of a State*, p. 218.

48 Wilson, 'Der Favorit als Sündenbock', pp. 165–7.

49 Stern, *The Court Jew*, p. 117.

50 Stern, *Jud Süss*, pp. 200–2; Wilson, 'Der Favorit als Sündenbock', p. 157.

51 Robertson, *The 'Jewish Question' in German Literature: Emancipation and its Discontents*, p. 9.

52 Emberger and Ries, 'Der Fall Joseph Süss Oppenheimer', p. 37; Haasis, *Joseph Süss Oppenheimer*, pp. 91–5.

53 Schnee, *Die Hoffinanz und der moderne Staat*, iv, pp. 120–1; Haasis, *Joseph Süss Oppenheimer*, p. 97.

54 Stern, *Jud Süss*, pp. 201–2; Haasis, *Joseph Süss Oppenheimer*, pp. 100–1.

55 Ibid., pp. 200–2; Stern, *The Court Jew*, pp. 76–7.

56 Haasis, *Joseph Süss Oppenheimer*, p. 96.

57 Ibid., pp. 72–3, 92, 96.

58 Stern, *Jud Süss*, p. 105; Wilson, 'Der Favorit als Sündenbock', p. 157.

59 Wilson, 'Women in Imperial Politics', pp. 238–9; Stern, *Jud Süss* pp. 45, 46; Schnee, *Die Hoffinanz und der moderne Staat*, iv, p. 141.

60 Wilson, 'Der Favorit als Sündenbock', p. 163; Stern, *Jud Süss*, p. 46.

61 Wilson, 'Der Favorit als Sündenbock', p. 168.

62 Stern, *The Court Jew*, pp. 99, 200, 240; Schnee, *Die Hoffinanz und der moderne Staat*, iv, p. 132; Gerber, *Jud Süss*, p. 100.

63 Emberger and Ries, 'Der Fall Joseph Süss Oppenheimer', p. 48.

64 Haasis, *Joseph Süss Oppenheimer*, p. 100.
65 Wilson, 'Der Favorit als Sündenbock', pp. 158, 176.
66 Gerber, *Jud Süss*, pp. 100, 128.
67 Stern, *Jud Süss*, pp. 46, 105, 112; Blanning, *The Pursuit of Glory*, p. 215.
68 Wilson, 'Der Favorit als Sündenbock,' p. 157.
69 Ibid., pp. 157–8.
70 Ibid., p. 157.
71 Stern, *Jud Süss*, pp. 46, 105, 112; Schnee, *Die Hoffinanz und der moderne Staat*, iii, pp. 203–4; iv, pp. 132–33; Wilson, 'Der Favorit als Sündenbock'. In using the term 'favourite', Wilson lends support to Stern's position rather than Schnee's.
72 Gerber, *Jud Süss*, p. 138.
73 Vann, *The Making of a State*, p. 224–5; Wilson, 'Der Favorit als Sündenbock', p. 169.
74 Ibid., pp. 159–70.
75 Vann, *The Making of a State*, pp. 231–2; Schnee, *Die Hoffinanz und der moderne Staat*, iv, pp. 130–2; Wilson, 'Der Favorit als Sündenbock', p. 180.
76 Vann, *The Making of a State*, pp. 231–2.
77 Ibid., pp. 232–3; Haasis, *Joseph Süss Oppenheimer*, p. 330.
78 Stern, *Jud Süss*, pp. 75–6, 117–24; Schnee, *Die Hoffinanz und der moderne Staat*, iv, pp. 131–2.
79 Gerber, *Jud Süss*, p. 74.
80 Stern, *Jud Süss*, p. 129; Stern, *The Court Jew*, pp. 164–5; Schnee, *Die Hoffinanz und der moderne Staat*, iv, p. 132.
81 Haasis, *Joseph Süss Oppenheimer*, p. 82–3.
82 Schnee, *Die Hoffinanz und der moderne Staat*. iv, p. 139.
83 Vann, *The Making of a State*, p. 226; Schnee, *Die Hoffinanz und der moderne Staat*, iv, p. 135.
84 Stern, *Jud Süss*, pp. 91–3; Vann, *The Making of a State*, p. 227; Schnee, *Die Hoffinanz und der moderne Staat*, iv, pp. 137–8; Wilson, *War, State and Society*, p. 180.
85 Vann, *The Making of a State*, p. 232; Stern, *Jud Süss*, pp. 78–9; Stern, *The Court Jew*, p. 158.
86 Stern, *Jud Süss*, pp. 76, 77, 81.
87 Fleischhauer, *Barock im Herzogtum Württemberg*, p. 257.
88 Walker, *Johann Jakob Moser and the Holy Roman Empire of the German Nation*, p. 81.
89 Ibid., pp. 240–2; Emberger and Ries, 'Der Fall Joseph Süss Oppenheimer', p. 39.
90 Vann, *The Making of a State*, pp. 226–7.
91 Schnee, *Die Hoffinanz und der moderne Staat*, iv, 138–9; Wilson, 'Der Favorit als Sündenbock', p. 181; Vann, *The Making of a State*, p. 226.
92 Stern, *The Court Jew*, p. 126.
93 Vann, *The Making of a State*, p. 225.

94 Ibid., pp. 225–6.
95 Wilson, *War, State and Society*, p. 132.
96 Ibid., p. 181; Stern, *Jud Süss*, pp. 99–104; Schnee, *Die Hoffinanz und der moderne Staat*, iv, pp. 139–40.
97 Vann, *The Making of a State*, p. 224; Stern, *Jud Süss*, pp. 99–104; Schnee, *Die Hoffinanz und der moderne Staat*, iv, pp. 139–40.
98 Wilson, 'War, State and Society, p. 181; Schnee, *Die Hoffinanz und der moderne Staat*, iv, p. 141.
99 Schnee, *Die Hoffinanz und der moderne Staat*, iv, p. 141.
100 Ibid.
101 Haasis, *Joseph Süss Oppenheimer*, p. 96.
102 Vann, *The Making of a State*, p. 230; Stern, *Jud Süss*, pp. 82, 146.
103 Vann, *The Making of a State*, p. 224.
104 Stern, *Jud Süss*, p. 91; Stern, *The Court Jew*, pp. 214, 240; Schnee, *Die Hoffinanz und der moderne Staat*, iv, p. 136.
105 Vann, *The Making of a State*, p. 235; Schnee, *Die Hoffinanz und der moderne Staat*, iv, pp. 87–109.
106 Haasis, *Joseph Süss Oppenheimer*, p. 296.
107 Ibid., p. 216.
108 Gerber, *Jud Süss*, p. 130.
109 Stern, *Jud Süss*, pp. 133, 222–3; Haasis, *Joseph Süss Oppenheimer*, pp. 239–41; Schnee, *Die Hoffinanz und der moderne Staat*, iv, pp. 132–3.
110 Gerber, *Jud Süss*, p. 103.
111 Haasis, *Joseph Süss Oppenheimer*, pp. 98, 240–1; Schnee, *Die Hoffinanz und der moderne Staat*, iv, pp. 142, 341.
112 Gerber, *Jud Süss*, p. 103.
113 Stern, *Jud Süss*, pp. 288–97; Haasis, *Joseph Süss Oppenheimer*, pp. 269–71; Emberger, 'Verdruss, Sorg und Widerwärtigkeiten: Die Inventur und Verwaltung des Jud Süsschen Vermögens 1737–1772', pp. 371–3.
114 Cohen and Mann, 'Melding Worlds', p. 110.
115 Haasis, *Joseph Süss Oppenheimer*, pp. 281–2; Stern, *Jud Süss*, pp. 298–303.
116 Haasis, *Joseph Süss Oppenheimer*, p. 93.
117 Ibid., pp. 173–5.
118 Schnee, *Die Hoffinanz und der moderne Staat*, iv, p. 141.
119 Ibid., iv, p. 141; Haasis, *Joseph Süss Oppenheimer*, pp. 173–6. The items from his Württemberg residences appears in Emberger, 'Verdruss, Sorg und Widerwärtigkeiten', p. 371–2 and from his Frankfurt residence in Stern, *Jud Süss*, pp. 288–302.
120 Haasis, *Joseph Süss Oppenheimer*, p. 272; Haasis, *Joseph Süss Oppenheimers Rache*, p. 89.
121 Wilson, 'Der Favorit als Sündenbock', pp. 158–9.
122 Ibid., pp. 164–5; Stern, *Jud Süss*, pp. 157–8; Stern, *The Court Jew*, pp. 133–4.
123 Wilson, 'Der Favorit als Sündenbock', pp. 158–9.

124 Gerber, *Jud Süss*, p. 107.
125 Ibid., p. 158; Haasis, *Joseph Süss Oppenheimer*, p. 118 n. 3.
126 Stern, *Jud Süss*, pp. 14, 142, 158 claims that they were not good while Haasis, *Joseph Süss Oppenheimer*, p. 300 claims that they were good.
127 Stern, *Jud Süss*, pp. 216–17; Wilson, 'Der Favorit als Sündenbock', p. 172.
128 Wilson, 'Der Favorit als Sündenbock', p. 172.
129 Stern, *Jud Süss*, pp. 145–6 and pp. 240–2 for the letter from the Duke to Süss dated as early as 30 June 1736 which also mentions an Absolutorium; Emberger, 'Joseph Süss Oppenheimer: Vom Günstling zum Sündenbock', p. 42.
130 Haasis, *Joseph Süss Oppenheimer*, p. 301. The announcement appeared in the *Wochentliche Anzeige von Neuigkeiten Stuttgardt* [*sic*], 15 February 1737 and is reproduced in Elwenspoek, *Jew Süss Oppenheimer*, p. 184.
131 Stern, *Jud Süss*, pp. 145–6, 281–2; Haasis, *Joseph Süss Oppenheimer*, p. 301.
132 Elwenspoek, *Jew Süss Oppenheimer*, p. 182.

Notes to Chapter 3: Trial and execution

1   Haasis, *Joseph Süss Oppenheimer*, p. 302.
2   *Hamburg Relations Courier* cited in Gerber, *Jud Süss*, p. 192.
3   Stern, *Jud Süss*, p. 160.
4   Haasis, *Joseph Süss Oppenheimer*, p. 302; Elwenspoek, *Jew Süss Oppenheimer*, p. 193.
5   Elwenspoek, *Jew Süss Oppenheimer*, pp. 191–2.
6   Stern, *Jud Süss*, p. 159; Elwenspoek, *Jew Süss Oppenheimer*, pp. 191–2; Haasis, *Joseph Süss Oppenheimer* p. 302.
7   Stern, *Jud Süss*, p. 159.
8   Haasis, *Joseph Süss Oppenheimer*, pp. 155, 301.
9   Ibid., p. 302.
10 Ibid., pp. 216–17, 289, 298, 302.
11 Ibid., p. 302.
12 Elwenspoek, *Jew Süss Oppenheimer*, pp. 194–5. Stern, *Jud Süss*, p. 160 mentions that Süss attempted an escape one week later, though others writing on the subject, do not mention this.
13 Haasis, *Joseph Süss Oppenheimer*, p. 216; Wilson, 'Women in Imperial Politics', p. 242. On the other hand Stern, *Jud Süss* p. 63; Elwenspoek, *Jew Süss Oppenheimer*, p. 107.
14 *Des Procopii Vessadiensis Anecdota von dem Alemannischen Hofe* (1740), cited in Gerber, *Jud Süss*, p. 130. Procopius Vessadiensis was the pseudonym used by Pfau, according to many accounts. However, a recent study, which is not actually concerned with Süss, refers to this pseudonym as being used by Heinrich August Krippendorf, an official who was cabinet secretary during the period of Duke Eberhard Ludwig and acted as secretary for his powerful mistress Wilhelmine

von Würben, the Countess Grävenitz. As Pfau himself had been associated
with the Grävenitz circle he may have taken over this pseudonym, based on
the original Procopius account of the scandals at the early Byzantine court
of Justinian. Krippendorf produced a manuscript which covered the period
up to the death of Eberhard Ludwig. See Osswald-Bargende, 'Eine jüristische
Hausaffäre: Einblicke in das Geschlechterverhältnis der höfischen Gesellschaft
am Beispiel des Ehezerwürfnisses zwischen Johanne Elisabeth und Eberhard
Ludwig von Württemberg', p. 68 n.16 and Osswald-Bargende, *Die Mätresse, der
Fürst und die Macht*, pp. 49, 110, 318. Pfau may have adopted this pseudonym
for his own account which covers the later reign of Carl Alexander. He would
have had contact with Krippendorf when he belonged to the to the so-called
Grävenitz clique.

15 Haasis, *Joseph Süss Oppenheimer*, pp. 216–17.
16 Ibid., p. 301.
17 Wilson, 'Women in Imperial Politics', p. 242.
18 Ibid.
19 Haasis, *Joseph Süss Oppenheimer*, p. 301.
20 Ibid.
21 Emberger and Ries, 'Der Fall Joseph Süss Oppenheimer', p. 40.
22 Wilson, 'Women in Imperial Politics', p. 243.
23 Ibid.
24 Ibid., p. 242.
25 Haasis, *Joseph Süss Oppenheimer*, p. 305.
26 Ibid.
27 Peter H. Wilson, *War, State and Society, 1677–1793*, p. 185.
28 Wilson 'Der Favorit als Sündenbock', p. 173.
29 Stern, *Jud Süss*, p. 160 mentions this removal as the consequence of an attempt
    by Süss to escape though others do not mention such an attempt. See Emberger
    and Ries, 'Der Fall Joseph Süss Oppenheimer', p. 40.
30 Stern, *Jud Süss*, p. 162; Haasis, *Joseph Süss Oppenheimer*, pp. 422–3.
31 Bernard, *Erinnerung ausführlicher Diskurs*.
32 Emberger, 'Verdruss, Sorg und Widerwärtigkeiten', pp. 369–75.
33 Wilson, 'Der Favorit als Sündenbock', pp. 173–4.
34 Haasis, *Joseph Süss Oppenheimer*, p. 360.
35 Ibid., p. 430.
36 Haasis, *Joseph Süss Oppenheimers Rache*, p. 79.
37 Ibid., p. 309 n. 3; Emberger and Ries, 'Der Fall Joseph Süss Oppenheimer',
    p. 41.
38 Emberger and Ries, 'Der Fall Joseph Süss Oppenheimer', p. 41; Stern, *Jud Süss*,
    p. 163. Emberger, 'Vom Günstling zum Sündenbock', p. 39.
39 Stern, *Jud Süss*, pp. 42 n. 50, 163.
40 Emberger and Ries, 'Der Fall Joseph Süss Oppenheimer', pp. 41, 42.
41 Ibid. p. 41.

42 Stern, *Jud Süss*, p. 163.
43 Ibid.
44 Haasis, *Joseph Süss Oppenheimer*, pp. 254–5.
45 Schlumborn, 'Grenzen des Wissens: Verhandlungen zwischen Arzt und Schwangeren', pp. 131–2 and Duden, 'Zwischen "wahrem Wissen" und Prophetie: Konzeptionen des Ungeboren', pp. 41–2.
46 Haasis, *Joseph Süss Oppenheimer*, p. 405; Duden, 'Zwischen "wahrem Wissen" und Prophetie', pp. 41–2.
47 Schnee, *Die Hoffinanz und der moderne Staat*, iv, p. 143; Wilson, 'Der Favorit als Sündenbock'; p. 156.
48 Haasis, *Joseph Süss Oppenheimer*, pp. 234–5.
49 Ibid., pp. 235–6.
50 Ibid., p. 234.
51 Both letters from the film company are reproduced in *Jud Süss: Propagandafilm im NS-Staat* (*Catalogue zur Ansstellung*), p. 21.
52 Ibid., p. 42 n50.
53 Ibid., p. 44.
54 Emberger and Ries, 'Der Fall Joseph Süss Oppenheimer', p. 42.
55 Wilson, 'Der Favorit als Sündenbock', pp. 155–7.
56 Ibid., p. 155.
57 Emberger and Ries, 'Der Fall Joseph Süss Oppenheimer', pp. 45.
58 Ulbricht, 'Criminality and Punishment of Jews in the Early Modern Period', p. 68.
59 Haasis, *Joseph Süss Oppenheimer*, p. 410.
60 Ibid., p. 43.
61 Elwenspoek, *Jew Süss Oppenheimer*, p. 209; Haasis, *Joseph Süss Oppenheimer*, p. 358.
62 Emberger and Ries, 'Der Fall Joseph Süss Oppenheimer', pp. 46–7.
63 Haasis, *Joseph Süss Oppenheimer*, p. 209.
64 Ibid., p. 210; Schnee, *Die Hoffinanz und der moderne Staat*, iv, pp. 114, 144–5.
65 Haasis, *Joseph Süss Oppenheimer*, pp. 211–12; 358, 408, 416.
66 Ibid., p. 211.
67 Emberger and Ries, 'Der Fall Joseph Süss Oppenheimer', p. 45.
68 Ibid., p. 43.
69 Ibid., p. 44; Haasis, *Joseph Süss Oppenheimer*, pp. 317–18.
70 Emberger and Ries, 'Der Fall Joseph Süss Oppenheimer', p. 44; Stern, *Jud Süss*, p. 166.
71 Haasis, *Joseph Süss Oppenheimer*, p. 354.
72 Ulbricht, 'Criminality and Punishment', p. 54; van Dülmen, *Theatre of Horror: Crime and Punishment in Early Modern Germany*, p. 64.
73 Rieger, *Sicherer Bericht*, p. 4; Stern, *Jud Süss*, pp. 168–9; Elwenspoek, *Jew Süss Oppenheimer*, p. 222; Haasis, *Joseph Süss Oppenheimer*, p. 403.
74 Emberger and Ries, 'Der Fall Joseph Süss Oppenheimer', p. 46.

75 Haasis, *Joseph Süss Oppenheimer*, p. 419; Dizinger, *Beiträge zur Geschichte Württembergs und seines Regentenhauses zur Zeit der Regierung Herzogs Karl Alexander und während der Minderjährigkeit seines Erstgebornen. Zum grossen Theile nach ungedruckten Archival-Urkunden*, I, pp. 160–1; and Pfaff, *Geschichte des Fürstenhauses und Landes Wirtemberg*, iv, p. 235.

76 Stern, *Jud Süss*, p. 170; Elwenspoek, *Jew Süss Oppenheimer*, p. 232.

77 Württembergischer Geschichts und Altertums-Verein, *Herzog Karl Eugen und seine Zeit*, i, p. 363; Walker, *Johann Jakob Moser*, p. 101; Elwenspoek, *Jew Süss Oppenheimer*, p. 263.

78 van Dülmen, *Theatre of Horror*, p. 2.

79 Ibid., p. 3.

80 Haasis, *Joseph Süss Oppenheimer*, pp. 414–15.

81 Gerber, *Jud Süss*, p. 258.

82 Ibid., p. 260.

83 Haasis, *Joseph Süss Oppenheimer*, p. 416.

84 Ibid., p. 417.

85 Elwenspoek, *Jew Süss Oppenheimer*, p. 236.

86 Haasis, *Joseph Süss Oppenheimer*, p. 420.

87 Stern, *Jud Süss*, pp. 173–4; Haasis, *Joseph Süss Oppenheimer*, pp. 427–30.

88 Haasis, *Joseph Süss Oppenheimer*, p. 421.

89 Ibid., p. 420.

90 Ibid., p. 428.

91 Elwenspoek, *Jew Süss Oppenheimer*, pp. 226–7.

92 Ulbricht, 'Criminality and Punishment', p. 53.

93 Haasis, *Joseph Süss Oppenheimer*, pp. 305, 422.

94 Haasis, *Joseph Süss Oppenheimer*, pp. 305, 421–2. Bernard, *Erinnerung ausführlicher Diskurs*, pp. 25–6.

95 Stern, *Jud Süss*, pp. 46, 74; Stern, *The Court Jew*, p. 73.

96 Haasis, *Joseph Süss Oppenheimer*, p. 422; Gerber, *Jud Süss*, p. 410 n. 202.

97 Emberger and Ries, 'Der Fall Joseph Süss Oppenheimer', p. 48; Haasis, *Joseph Süss Oppenheimer*, pp. 422, 423.

98 Bernard, *Erinnerung ausführlicher Diskurs*, p. 10.

99 Ibid., passim.

100 Gerber, *Jud Süss*, p. 268. The ban appears in Bernard's second pamphlet, *Der in den Lüfften schwebende neue Jüdische Heilige Joseph Süss Oppenheimer, oder Das von der Würtembergischen Judenschafft herausgegebene merckwürdige Canonisations-Manifest, Worinn dieselbe gemeldeten unglücklichen Juden ihren gesamten Glaubens-Genossen so wohl, also auch der leicht glaubigen und falsch-berichteten Christenheit Als einen Heiligen aufzubürden Sich unterstanden*. The title makes clear Bernard's purpose and can be translated as follows: 'The new Jewish Saint: Joseph Süss Oppenheimer, hovering in the air or the Remarkable Manifesto of Canonization issued by Württemberg Jewry, whereby the same mentioned unfortunate Jews dared to Impose as a Saint on their fellow Believers

as well as on those of slight Faith and misinformed Christianity'. See also Bernard, *Erinnerung ausführlicher Diskurs*, p. 50; Stern, *Jud Süss*, p. 175; Elwenspoek, *Jew Süss Oppenheimer*, pp. 267–8.

101 Haasis, *Joseph Süss Oppenheimer*, p. 424.
102 Ibid., p. 436.
103 Ibid., p. 437.
104 Ibid., p. 445; Stern, *Jud Süss*, p. 175.
105 Emberger and Ries, 'Der Fall Joseph Süss Oppenheimer', p. 46; Haasis, *Joseph Süss Oppenheimer*, p. 445.
106 Haasis, *Joseph Süss Oppenheimer*, p. 437.
107 Ibid., p. 444.
108 Stern, *Jud Süss*, p. 175; Haasis, *Joseph Süss Oppenheimer*, p. 442.
109 Haasis, *Joseph Süss Oppenheimer*, p. 445.
110 Elwenspoek, *Jud Süss Oppenheimer*, p. 250.
111 Stern, *Jud Süss*, p. 175; Haasis, *Joseph Süss Oppenheimer*, pp. 443–4.
112 Haasis, *Joseph Süss Oppenheimer*, p. 444.
113 Elwenspoek, *Jew Süss Oppenheimer*, p. 250.
114 Ibid., p. 248.
115 Ibid., p. 251.
116 Ibid., p. 273.
117 Schnee, *Die Hoffinanz und der moderne Staat*, iv, pp. 281–3; Elwenspoek, *Jew Süss Oppenheimer*, p. 251.
118 Elwenspoek, *Jew Süss Oppenheimer*, p. 278.

Notes to Chapter 4: The legend

1 Anon., *Curieuser Nachrichten Aus Dem Reich der Beschnittenen, Zweyter Theil, Darinnen die Unterredung zwischen Sabathai Sevi und dem fameusen Judden Süssen*, i, p. 25; Gerber, *Jud Süss*, p. 27.
2 Bernard, *Erinnerung ausführlicher Diskurs*, p. 39.
3 *Grosses vollständiges Universal-Lexikon aller Wissenschaften und Künste*, xli, 157; Gerber, *Jud Süss*, p. 28.
4 Dendl, 'Leben und Sterben des Joseph Süss Oppenheimer, *genannt* "Jud Süss" nach der Darstellung des "Grossen vollständigen Universal Lexikons', p. 7, citing Arnoldus Liberius, *Vollkommene Historie und Lebensbeschreibung des fameusen und berüchtigten Württembergishen Aventuriers, Jud Joseph Süss Oppenheimer* (Franckfurth und Leipzig, 1738).
5 Schnee, *Die Hoffinanz und der moderne Staat*, iv, p. 113 cites as his source an account by the examining judge, the government adviser (Regierungsrat) Philipp Friedrich Jäger, in 'Species facti den Jud Süssen und dessen complicend betreffend', in A 53I. B11 in the Hauptstaatsarchiv, Stuttgart.
6 Gerber, *Jud Süss*, pp. 25, 309–10 n.90.

7   Elwenspoek, *Jew Süss Oppenheimer, The Great Financier, Gallant and Adventurer of the Eighteenth Century: A Study Based on Various Documents, Private Papers and Traditions*, p. 27.

8   Stern, *Jud Süss*, p. 10; Haasis, *Joseph Süss Oppenheimer*, pp. 10–11.

9   Stern, *Jud Süss*, (frontispiece).

10 Gerber, *Jud Süss*, pp. 28, 31; Mann, 'Images of "Jud Süss" Oppenheimer, An Early Modern Jew', p. 258.

11 Cohen and Mann, 'Melding Worlds', p. 107.

12 Mann, 'Images of "Jud Süss"', p. 274.

13 Ibid., p. 258.

14 Gerber, *Jud Süss*, pp. 27, 28.

15 Cohen and Mann, 'Melding Worlds', p. 109.

16 Ibid., p. 105.

17 Ibid., p. 106; Haasis, *Joseph Süss Oppenheimers Rache*, pp. 258–60.

18 Mann, 'Images of "Jud Süss"', pp. 262–3; Ulbricht, ' Criminality and Punishment', pp. 49, 50; Gerber, *Jud Süss*, pp. 58–63.

19 Gerber, *Jud Süss*, pp. 264–5; Stern, *Jud Süss*, p. 293.

20 Mann, 'Images of "Jud Süss"', p. 264.

21 Rieger, *Sicherer Bericht*.

22 Elwenspoek, *Jew Süss Oppenheimer*, p. 262, citing Georg Conrad Rieger, *Gute Arbeit gibt herrlichen Lohn, In einer Predigt, über das Evangelium am Sonntage Septuagesimae, Matth. XX. V.1–16, in der Kirche zu St. Leonhard in Stuttgardt*, 1738, subsequent editions published in Esslingen by Gottlieb Maentleren (no date).

23 Ibid., p. 266. The two works are: Casparson's *Leben und Tod des Berüchtigten Juden Joseph Süss Oppenheimers, aus Heidelberg* (*Life and Death of the infamous Jew Joseph Süss Oppenheimer from Heidelberg*) and *Curieuser Nachrichten Aus dem Reich der Beschnittenen* though in the latter this image does not appear in the copy in the British Library.

24 Haasis, *Joseph Süss Oppenheimer*, pp. 435, 444.

25 Ibid., p. 417.

26 Ibid., Mann, 'Images of "Jud Süss"', p. 265.

27 Ibid.

28 Ibid., pp. 270–1, also Figure 8; Cohen and Mann, 'Melding Worlds', p. 221.

29 Mann, 'Images of "Jud Süss"', pp. 267, 273.

30 Cohen and Mann, 'Melding Worlds', pp. 106–7, 220, 'Les Regrets du Serail du Juif Süss', a copy of 'Lamentierendes Jud Süssisches Frauen-Zimmer' ('Jud Süss' Wailing Women').

31 Mann, 'Images of "Jud Süss"', p. 272.

32 Ibid., pp. 272–3.

33 Cohen and Mann, 'The Court Jew', p. 215, citing Arnoldus Liberius, *Vollkommene Historie und Lebensbeschreibung des fameusen und berüchtigten*

Württembergischen Aventuriers, Jud Joseph Süss Oppenheimer; Gerber, *Jud Süss*, plate IV.

34 Ibid.
35 Ibid., p. 188, citing *Dess justificierten Juden: Joseph Süss Oppenheimers Geist* (Frankfurt and Leipzig), 1738.
36 Ibid., p. 187.
37 Ibid., p. 188.
38 Ibid.; Gerber, *Jud Süss*, p. V, plate 5a.
39 Ibid., p. 170. The source is Anon., *Curieuser Nachrichten*, iv, p. 74.
40 Gerber, *Jud Süss*, p. 169.
41 Ibid., p. 173. See also plates 5a and 5b.
42 Ibid., p. 182.
43 Ibid., pp. 78, 230.
44 Ibid., pp. 130–1.
45 Ibid., p. 120.
46 Gerber, *Jud Süss*, pp. 131–3, 138; Stern, *The Court Jew*, p. 179.
47 Gerber, *Jud Süss*, p. 105; Haasis, *Joseph Süss Oppenheimer*, p. 264.
48 Gerber, *Jud Süss*, pp. 87, 219, 230, citing Casparson, *Leben und Tod des Berüchtigten Juden Joseph Süss Oppenheimers, aus Heidelberg*.
49 Ibid., pp. 54, 226.
50 Ibid., p. 72.
51 Ibid., pp. 57, 92.
52 Ibid., p. 603, citing Liberius, *Vollkommene Historie und lebensbeschreibung des fameusen und berüchtigten Württembergischen Aventuriers Jud Joseph Süss Oppenheimer*.
53 Ibid., p. 230.
54 *Zweyhundert Fünff und zwangstigse Entrevué, Zwischen Dem letzt-verstorbenen regierenden Hertzog von Würtemberg-Stuttgardt, Carol. Alexandro, und dem letzt verstorbenen Hertzog von Curland, Ferdinando.*
55 Ibid., p. 56, citing *Merckwürdige Staats-Assemblée In Dem Reiche derer Todten, Zwischen einem gantz besonderen Klee-Blat; Oder, Dreyen unartigen Staats-Ministern, Nemlich Dem Duc De Ripperda, Dem Grafen von Hoymb, Und dem Juden Süss Oppenheimer* (Amsterdam: Herman von der Haue, 1738).
56 Anon., *Curieuser Nachrichten Aus Dem Reich der Beschnittenen*, n.p.
57 Anon. (presumably Johann Casparson), *Gespräch in dem so gennanten Reiche der Todten, zwischen Carl Alexandern, dem letzt verstorbenen Regierenden Herzoge von Würtemberg, Kayserlicher wie auch des H. R. Reichs und Schwäbischchen Crayses General Feld-Marschalle etc. Und Johann Gaston, gewesenen letzten Gross-Herzoge von Toscana, aus dem Hause der Mediceer, etc.*
58 Rieger, *Nachricht Von denen letzten Stunden Des Juden Süss Oppenheimers, Wie sich dieser Jude in denselben so wohl zu Hohen-Aschberg, als auch zu Stuttgard auf dem Herren-Hauss und beym Gericht gegen die Herren Geistliche, Als: Herrn M.*

Georg Cunrad [sic] *Rieger, Herr M. Repet. Hoffmann, Herr M. Christoph Cunrad Heller.*

59 Gerber, *Jud Süss*, p. 606, citing Georg Conrad Rieger, *Gute Arbeit gibt herrlichen Lohn, In einer Predigt, über das Evangelium am Sonntage Septuagesimae, Matth. XX. V.1–16,* in der Kirche zu St. Leonhard in Stuttgardt, 1738, subsequent editions published in Esslingen by Gottlieb Maentleren (no date).

60 Ibid., pp. 241–4, 246, 268.

61 Bernard, *Der in den Lüfften.*

62 This apparently was reprinted by Helmut Haasis, ed., *Beilage zu in Salomon Schächter, Relation von des Joseph Süss Seel. Gedächtnus (1738)*, Fürth and Stuttgart, 1994) but it would seem not to be available.

63 Gerber, *Jud Süss*, p. 268.

64 Ibid, p. 194, citing *Hamburg Relations Courier.*

65 Ibid., pp. 192–3, citing *Hamburgischen Unpartheyischen Correspondenten.*

66 Ibid., p. 194.

67 Ibid., p. 196.

68 Ibid. pp. 192–3.

69 Ibid. p. 198.

70 Ibid., p. 197.

71 Cohen and Mann, 'Melding Worlds', p. 109; Dendl, 'Leben und Sterben', p. 2.

Notes to Chapter 5: Wilhelm Hauff's Jud Süss

1 Krauss, 'Spiegelungen des Karl Eugenschen Zeitalters in Schillers Jugenddramen', 14, pp. 112–13.

2 Sharpe, *Friedrich Schiller: Drama, Thought and Politics,* pp. 28–9.

3 Anon. [Schiller], *Die Räuber: ein Schauspiel,* Act II, Sc.3, p. 105; same as the second edition, Schiller *Werke,* iii, p. 70. Finanzrat and Finanzienrat for financial adviser seem to have been used interchangeably at that time and subsequently.

4 Terra Catalogue, pp. 5–6.

5 Hinz, *Hauff,* pp. 113–14, 120.

6 von Glasenapp, 'Literarische Popularisierungsprozesse eines antijudischen Stereotyps: Wilhelm Hauffs Jud Süss', p. 126.

7 Hinz, *Hauff,* pp. 9, 10.

8 Ibid.

9 Gerber, *Jud Süss*, p. 534 n.3.

10 Hinz, *Hauff,* p. 11.

11 Ibid., p. 10.

12 Ibid., p. 83.

13 Gerber, *Jud Süss*, p. 533 n.2; Arnsberg, 'Demokraten, "Ultraliberale" und sonstige Staatsfeinde zur württembergischen military-und Zivilverschwörung von 1831 bis 1833', pp. 76–7, 81–2, 84–6.

14 Hinz, *Hauff*, pp. 66–81.
15 Pulzer, *Jews and the German State: The Political history of a Minority, 1848–1933*, p. 15.
16 Gerber, *Jud Süss*, p. 296.
17 Ibid.
18 Feuchtwanger, 'Über "Jud Süss"', p. 380.
19 Chase, 'The Wandering Court Jew and the Hand of God: Wilhelm Hauff's *Jud Suss* as Historical Fiction,' p. 727.
20 Sheffi, 'Jud Süss', p. 428.
21 von Glasenapp, 'Literarische Popularisierungsprozesse', p. 126, citing Jürgen Landwehr, '"Jud Süss"' – Hauffs Novelle als literarische Legitimation eines Justizmordes und als Symptom und (Mit)-Erfindung eines kollektiven Wahns' in Ulrich Kittstein, ed., Wilhelm Hauff: Aufsätze zu seinem poetischen Werk (Mannheimer Studien zur Literatur-und Kulturwissenschaft, 28, St. Ingbert, 2002), p. 140.
22 Hinz, *Hauff*, pp. 53–5.
23 Frenzel, *Judengestalten auf der deutschen Bühne. Ein notwendiger Querschnitt durch 700 Jahre Rollengeschichte*, pp. 80–2.
24 Krobb, *Die schöne Jüdin: jüdische Frauengestalten in der deutschsprachigen Erzählliteratur vom 17. Jahrhundert bis zum Ersten Weltkrieg*, p. 128.
25 Hauff, *Jud Süss*, p. 195.
26 von Glasenapp, 'Literarische Popularisierungsprozesse', p. 131, citing Albert Mannheimer, Die Quellen von Hauffs Jud Süss (Giessen, 1909).
27 Gerber, *Jud Süss*, pp. 534, n3.
28 Hinz, *Hauff*, pp. 11,12.
29 Krobb, *Die schöne Jüdin*, pp. 123–8.
30 Hauff, *Jud Süss*, p. 156.
31 Ibid.
32 Ibid.
33 Ibid.
34 Ibid., p. 158.
35 Ibid., p. 163.
36 Ibid., pp. 164–5.
37 Ibid., p. 165.
38 Ibid., p. 166.
39 Ibid., pp. 166–7.
40 Ibid., p. 168.
41 Ibid., p.169.
42 Ibid., p. 171.
43 Ibid., p. 178.
44 Ibid.
45 Ibid., pp. 179–80.
46 Ibid., p. 180.

47 Ibid.
48 Ibid., p. 181.
49 Ibid., p. 189.
50 Ibid., p. 190.
51 Ibid., p. 191.
52 Ibid., p. 193.
53 Ibid., p. 194.
54 Ibid.
55 Ibid., pp. 196–8.
56 Ibid., p. 200.
57 Ibid.
58 Ibid., pp. 200–1.
59 Ibid., p. 204.
60 Ibid., pp. 204–5.
61 Ibid., p. 208.
62 Ibid., pp. 209–10.
63 Ibid., p. 214.
64 Ibid., p. 215.
65 Ibid., p. 216.
66 Ibid.
67 Ibid., p. 217.
68 Ibid., p. 220.
69 Ibid., p. 221.
70 Ibid., p. 222.
71 Ibid., p. 221.
72 Hauff, 'Abner, der Jude, der nichts gesehen hat', p. 237.
73 Ibid., p. 222.

Notes to Chapter 6: After Hauff

1 Ziel, 'Albert Dulk: Sein Leben und seine Werke', i, pp. 23–4.
2 Fraenkel, 'Albert Dulk'.
3 Rieber, 'Das Sozialistengesetz: Die Kriminalisierung einer Partei', pp. 181–3.
4 Ziel, 'Albert Dulk', i, p. 69.
5 Dulk, 'Jud Süss', p. 388.
6 Ibid., p. 482.
7 Ibid., pp. 484–5.
8 Ibid.
9 Ibid., p. 473.
10 Ibid., pp. 487–8.
11 Eller, *The Prime Minister of Würtemburg*.
12 Eller, *Ingatherings*.

13 Gerber, *Jud Süss*, p. 283.
14 Ibid.
15 Ibid.; *Allgemeine Zeitung des Judentums* (16 October 1860), p. 42 n. 623.
16 Lehmann, *Süss Oppenheimer: eine jüdische Erzählung*.
17 Ibid.; Gerber, *Jud Süss*, p. 537 n.14 gives other examples.
18 Gerber, *Jud Süss*, p. 283.
19 Lehmann, *Süss Oppenheimer*, chap. XVIII.
20 Krobb, *Selbstdarstellungen: Untersuchungen zur deutsch-jüdischen Erzahlliteratur im neunzehnten Jahrhundert*, pp. 61–2, 68–9.
21 Kohn, *Ein deutscher Minister: Roman aus dem Achtzehnten Jahrhundert*, i, p. 25.
22 Ibid., vol. ii, p. 213; Gerber, *Jud Süss*, p. 296.
23 Ibid., p. 284; Hollstein, *Jud Süss und die Deutschen: antisemitische Vorurteile im nationalsozialistischen Spielfilme*, p. 327 n.168 cites Elisabeth Frenzel mentioning a production in Breslau on 18 November 1930.

Notes to Chapter 7: The historians

1 Iggers, *The German Conception of History*, p. 64.
 2 Vierhaus, 'Historiography between Science and Art', pp. 62–3.
 3 Benzoni, 'The Venetian *Relazioni*: Impressions with Allusion to late Venetian Historiography', p. 45.
 4 Gerber, *Jud Süss*, pp. 22; 307 n. 59, citing Christoph J. Wagenseil, 'Süss Oppenheimer', *Geschichte gefallener Minister, Feldherren und Staatsmänner*, 2, p. 236, n.
 5 Dizinger, *Beiträge zur Geschichte Württembergs*, 2, Heft, p. v.
 6 Ibid.
 7 Ibid., p. 163.
 8 Ibid., p. xiii.
 9 Ibid., pp. 28–9.
10 Ibid., p. 154.
11 Haasis, *Joseph Süss Oppenheimers Rache*, p. 79.
12 Dizinger, *Beiträge zur Geschichte Württembergs*. p. 160; Haasis, *Joseph Süss Oppenheimer, genannt Jud Süss*, p. 419.
13 Pfaff, *Geschichte des Fürstenhauses und Landes Wirtemberg*, ii, pp. 198–237.
14 Ibid., p. 200.
15 Ibid., p. 210.
16 Ibid.
17 Ibid., p. 213.
18 Ibid., p. 235.
19 Belschner, *Geschichte von Württemberg in Wort und Bild*, p. 437.
20 Schön, 'Balthasar Friedrich Wilhelm Zimmermann', pp. 299–300; http://www.vormaerz.de/index.html.

21   Green, *Fatherlands: State-Building and Nationhood in nineteenth-century Germany*, p. 318.

22   Zimmermann, *J. Süss Oppenheimer, ein Finanzmann des 18 Jahrhunderts: Ein Stück Absolutismus- und Jesuitengeschichte. Nach den Vertheidigungs-Akten und den Schriften der Zeitgenossen bearbeitet.* This was based on his Jena dissertation, 'Versuch des Umsturzes einer süddeutschen Verfassung im 18. Jahrhundert', as cited in Schnee, *Die Hoffinanz und der moderne Staat*, iv, p. 279.

23   Blanning, *The Pursuit of Glory*, p. 215.

24   Gerber, *Jud Süss*, p. 23; Stern, *Jud Süss: ein Beitrag zur deutschen und zur Jüdischen Geschichte* (Berlin: Akademie, 1929), p. x. Stern overlooked Dizinger, wrongly claiming that this was the first study based on archival research.

25   Zimmermann, *J. Süss Oppenheimer*, p. 59.

26   Ibid., p. 10.

27   Ibid., p. 11.

28   Ibid., p. 14.

29   Ibid., p. 6.

30   Ibid., p. 32.

31   Feuchtwanger, 'Über "Jud Süss"', p. 381.

32   *Allgemeine Deutsche Biographie*, xxxvii, pp. 181–3.

33   Krauss, 'Spiegelungen', 14, pp. 112–13.

34   *Neue Deutsche Biographie*, xii, p. 720.

35   *Biographische Enzyklopädie*, 2nd edition (Munich: Saur, 2006), p. 39.

36   Kohut, *Geschichte der deutschen Juden: Ein Hausbuch für die jüdische Familie*, pp. 670–1.

37   Gerber, *Jud Süss*, pp. 23, citing 'Joseph Süss Oppenheimer' in *Jahrbuch für jüdische Geschichte und Literatur* (1902), pp. 138ff.

38   Kroner, 'Josef Süss-Oppenheimer'.

39   Ibid., pp. 14–15; Stern, *Jud Süss*, p. x.

40   Elwenspoek, *Jew Süss Oppenheimer*, p. 11.

41   Kroner, 'Josef Süss-Oppenheimer', p. 14.

42   Emberger and Ries, 'Der Fall Joseph Süss Oppenheimer', p. 53.

43   Hayn, 'Süss-Oppenheimer-Bibliographie: ein Beitrag zur Kuriositäten-Literatur', pp. 448–52; Freimann, 'Bibliographie der Flugschriften über Joseph Süss Oppenheimer' ix, 2 (1905) pp. 56–5, 79–81 and 10, 4 (1906) pp. 106–13; Gotthell, 'Bibliography of the Pamphlets Dealing with Joseph Suess Oppenheimer'.

44   Elwenspoek, *Jud Süss Oppenheimer*.

45   *Der Spiegel*, 15 August 1958, pp. 12, 33; *Jew Süss Oppenheimer: Great Financier, Gallant* and *Adventurer of the Eighteenth Century*, trans. Edward Cattle.

46   Ibid., p. 26.

47   Stern, 'Historische Romane'; Sassenberg, *Selma Stern*, p. 175.

48   Stern, *Anacharsis Cloots, der Redner des Menschengeschlechts: ein Beitrag zur Geschichte der Deutschen in der französischen Revolution*.

49 Brenner, *Propheten der Vergangenheit: Jüdische Geschichtschreibung*, p. 187.
50 Sassenberg, *Selma Stern*, pp. 71–2; Brenner, *Propheten der Vergangenheit*, p. 190.
51 Stern, *Der preussische Staat und die Juden*.
52 Stern, *Jud Süss*, p. 180.
53 Brenner, *Propheten der Vergangenheit*, p. 190.
54 Ibid., p. 189.
55 Ibid., p. 196.
56 Aue, '"Jud Süss" und die Geschichtswissenschaft', pp. 63–4.
57 Stern, 'Historische Romane'.
58 Ibid.
59 *Berliner Tageblatt*, 4 July 1930 (Beiblatt), 227.
60 Brenner, *Propheten der Vergangenheit*, p. 190.
61 Sassenberg, *Geschichtsentwürfe einer Historikerin*, p. 183.
62 Feuchtwanger, 'Jud Süss historisch: Zu dem Buch Selma Stern', p. 65.
63 Sassenberg, *Geschichtsentwürfe einer Historikerin*, p. 175; Stern, 'Historische Romane'.
64 Aue, '"Jud Süss" und die Geschichtwissenschaft', p. 65.
65 Stern, Der Preussische Staat und die Juden.
66 Sombart, Die Juden und das Wirtschaftsleben.
67 Schnee, 'Die Judenfrage in Geschichte und Gegenwart', pp. 367ff. For a full account of Schnee's career see Laux, 'Ich bin der Historiker der Hoffaktoren: Zur antisemitischen Forschung von Heinrich Schnee (1895–1968)'.
68 Schnee, *Die Hoffinanz und der moderne Staat*.
69 I am grateful to Ludwig Feuchtwanger's son, Edgar, for this information. See also Laux, 'Ich bin der Historiker der Hoffaktoren, pp. 485–513.
70 Laux, 'Ich bin der Historiker der Hoffaktoren,'pp. 489–91.
71 Steinweis, *Studying the Jew: Scholarly Antisemitism in Nazi Germany*, pp. 158–9.
72 Laux, 'Ich bin der Historiker der Hoffaktoren', p. 492, citing Winfried Ekkehart [Schnee], *Rasse und Geschichte, Grundzüge einer rassewertended Geschichtsbetrachtung von der Urzeit bis zur Gegenwart*.
73 Schnee, *Bürgermeister Karl Lueger: Leben und Wirken eines grossen deutsche; George Ritter von Schönerer: ein Kämpfer für Alldeutschland: Mit ausgewählten Zeugnissen aus Schönerers Kampfzeit für deutsche Einheit und deutsche Reinheit*.
74 Laux, 'Ich bin der Historiker der Hoffaktoren', p. 495; Schnee, 'Heinrich Heine's Ahnen als Hofjuden im deutschen Fürstenhöfe', *Der Weltkampf 2* (1944), pp. 91–4.
75 Deeg, *Hofjuden, Juden, Judenverbrechen und Judengesetze in Deutschland von der Vergangenheit bis zur Gegenwart*.
76 Hitler, *Mein Kampf*, trans. Ralph Manheim, p. 282.
77 Schnee, *Hofjuden*, iii, pp. 262–3; iv, pp. 109–48, 277–84, 341; vi, pp. 57–70.
78 Rohrbacher, 'Jüdischer Geschichte', p. 167.

79 Carsten, Review of Heinrich Schnee's *Das Hoffaktorum in der deutschen Geschichte*, vol. 1.
80 Ibid.
81 Laux, 'Ich bin der Historiker der Hoffaktoren', p. 487.
82 Ibid., iv, p. 113.
83 Ibid. iv, p. 110. In support of Heidersdorf's paternity Schnee cites other historians in whose work Süss figures only marginally: Schnabel, *Das 18. Jahrhundert in Europa* and Schulte, *Wilhelm von Baden und der Reichskrieg gegen Frankreich 1693–1697*.
84 Schnee, *Hofjuden*, iv, p. 280.
85 In particular, the biography by Hellmut Haasis (*Joseph Süss Oppenheimer*) and the work on Württemberg by Peter H. Wilson, especially ('Der Favorit als Sündenbock', and *War State and Society in Württemberg 1777–1793*).

Notes to Chapter 8: Lion Feuchtwanger's Jew Süss

1   Feuchtwanger, *Jud Süss* (Munich: Drei Maskenverlag, 1925).
2   von Sternberg, *Lion Feuchtwanger: ein deutsches Schriftstellerleben*, p. 188.
3   Feuchtwanger, *Die hässliche Herzogin Margarete Maultasch*.
4   Dahlke, *Lion Feuchtwanger, Dramen*, ii, p. 686; Dietschreit, *Lion Feuchtwanger*, p. 2.
5   Fuegi, *The Life and Lies of Bertolt Brecht*, pp. 123–4, 126–7, 132–3.
6   Knilli and Zielinski, 'Lion Feuchtwangers "Jud Süss" und die Filme von Lothar Mendes und Veit Harlan', pp. 103–4.
7   Feuchtwanger, *Power*, trans. Willa and Edwin Muir (New York: Viking, 1926); Feuchtwanger, *Jew Süss*, trans. Willa and Edwin Muir (London: Martin Secker, 1926).
8   *Evening Standard*, 13 January 1927.
9   *Times Literary Supplement*, 6 January 1927.
10 *Daily Mail*, 19 December 1927.
11 Spalek, '*Jud Süss*: Anatomy of a Best Seller', p. 126.
12 von der Luhe, 'Lion Feuchtwangers Roman "Jud Süss" und die Entwicklung des jüdischen Selbstbewusstseins in Deutschland', p. 36.
13 Gerber, *Jud Süss*, p. 284.
14 Dahlke, *Lion Feuchtwanger, Dramen*, ii, pp. 686–7; Dietschreit, *Lion Feuchtwanger*, p. 2.
15 Pulzer, *Jews and the German State*, pp. 205–6.
16 Feuchtwanger, 'Über "Jud Süss"', p. 36.
17 Knilli and Zielinski, 'Lion Feuchtwangers "Jud Süss"', p. 101; Dahlke, *Lion Feuchtwanger, Dramen*, i, p. 644.
18 Knilli and Zielinski, 'Lion Feuchtwangers "Jud Süss"', p. 101, citing *Neue Münchener Tageblatt*, 15 October 1917.

19 Ibid., pp. 101–2.

20 Ibid., p. 102.

21 Ibid., p. 102, citing Wolfgang Berndt, 'Die früh historischen Romane Lion Feuchtwanger' (PhD thesis, Berlin, 1953), p. 50.

22 Haumann, *Paul Kornfeld, Leben, Werk, Wirkung*, p. 620, citing Feuchtwanger, 'Vom Schicksal des Buches "Jud Süss": einige Fakten'.

23 Specht, *Die Feuchtwangers: Familie, Tradition und jüdisches Selbstverständnis im deutsch-jüdischen Bürgertum des 19. und 20. Jahrhunderts*, pp. 40, 75; Dietschreit, *Lion Feuchtwanger*, p. 30; Feuchtwanger, *Ebenbilder Gottes*, pp. 54, 56 (this is subtitled *Ein Roman* – a novel, but is clearly autobiographical).

24 von Sternburg, *Lion Feuchtwanger: Ein Deutsches Schriftstellerleben*, p. 30; Haasis, *Joseph Süss Oppenheimer*, p. 432.

25 Feuchtwanger, *Jud Süss, Schauspiel in drei Akten (vier Bilder)*, pp. 139–42; Feuchtwanger, *Jew Süss*, pp. 430–2.

26 Sammons, *Heinrich Heine: A Modern Biography*, p. 94; Krobb, 'Macht die Augen zu, Sarah, Heinrich Heines Rabbi von Bacharach', pp. 169–70.

27 Sammons, *Heinrich Heine*, pp. 180–1.

28 Feuchtwanger, *Jud Süss, Schauspiel in drei Akten (vier Bilder)*, pp. 68–9.

29 Ibid., pp. 122–42.

30 Feuchtwanger, 'Vom Sinn und Unsinn des historischen Romans'; von Sternberg, *Lion Feuchtwanger*, p. 188.

31 Moore, 'From Buddhism to Bolshevism: Some Orientalist Themes in German Thought', p. 29; Robertson, 'Urheimat Asien: The Re-Orientation of German and Austrian Jews 1900–1925', p. 183.

32 Feuchtwanger, 'Vom Sinn und Unsinn', p. 497.

33 Ibid.

34 von Sternberg, *Lion Feuchtwanger*, p. 323. Later known as the *Wartesaal Trilogie*, the novels were *Erfolg: Drei Jahre Geschichte einer Provinz* (1930); *Die Geschwister Oppermann* (1933) – earlier title, *Die Geschwister Oppenheim*; *Exil* (1940).

35 Feuchtwanger, 'Die drei Sprünge des Wang-lun', p. 328.

36 Dahlke, *Lion Feuchtwanger, Dramen*, i, p. 640–2; Haumann, *Paul Kornfeld*, p. 621 n103.

37 Döblin, 'Der historische Roman und Wir', p. 177.

38 Feuchtwanger, 'Über "Jud Süss"', p. 381.

39 Ibid.

40 Robertson, 'Urheimat Asien', p. 183, citing Herder; Marchand, *German Orientalism in the Age of Empire: Religion, Race, and Scholarship*, pp. 43–52, 300–2.

41 Kalmar and Penslar, *Orientalism and the Jews*, p. xviii.

42 Robertson, 'Urheimat Asien', p. 188.

43 Feuchtwanger, *Jew Süss*, p. 357.

44 Dahlke, *Lion Feuchtwanger, Dramen*, i, p. 336, citing letter from Lion Feuchtwanger to Ludwig Ganghofer, 2 December 1917.

45 Feuchtwanger, *Jud Süss* (1917), p. 136; Feuchtwanger, *Jud Süss* (1925), pp. 351–2, 359.
46 Haasis, *Joseph Süss Oppenheimer*, p. 296; Wilson, *War, State and Society*, pp. 179 n.79, 185.
47 *Biographische Enzyklopädie*, vol. viii, p. 399.
48 Ibid.
49 Ibid., p. 353.
50 Feuchtwanger, 'Über "Jud Süss"', p. 380.
51 Feuchtwanger, *Jew Süss*, p. 424.
52 Feuchtwanger, 'Jud Süss historisch', p. 65.
53 Dukes, *The Scene is Changed*, pp. 131–2.
54 Ibid., p. 132.
55 Ibid., pp. 132–3.
56 Ibid., p. 133.
57 *Sunday Express*, 22 September 1929.
58 Michael Billington, *Peggy Ashcroft*, pp. 34–7.
59 *Jewish Chronicle*, 4 October 1929.
60 *Daily Express* 22 September 1929.
61 *Daily Mail*, 20 September 1929.
62 Singer, *Le Juif Süss et la Propagande nazie*, p. 64.
63 Feuchtwanger, *Nur eine Frau*, pp. 226–7.
64 Dukes, *The Scene is Changed*, p. 134.
65 Knilli and Zielinski, 'Lion Feuchtwangers "Jud Süss"' p. 105.
66 Singer, *Le Juif Süss*, p. 65.
67 Ibid., p. 134; Ritchie, 'Ashley Dukes and the German Theatre between the Wars', p. 101; Ritchie, 'Die Jud Süss-Dramatisierung von Ashley Dukes', p. 132.
68 Feinberg, 'Leopold Jessner: German Theatre and Jewish Identity', p. 124.
69 Ibid., p. 110–33.
70 Rühle, *Theater für die Republik, 1917–1933, im Spiegel der Kritik*, p. 1108.
71 Singer, *Le Juif Süss*, p. 65.
72 Aurich, *Theo Lingen*, pp. 117, 128; Rathkolb, *Führertreu und gottbegnadet: kunsterleiten im Dritten Reich*, pp. 20, 36, 142, 170, 178.
73 Haumann, *Paul Kornfeld*, pp. 601–2.
74 Haasis, *Joseph Süss Oppenheimer* pp. 126, 218, 227.
75 Ibid., p. 613.
76 Kornfeld, 'Jud Süss: Tragödie in drei Akten und einem Epilog', p. 140. The play, based on its 1988 Nuremberg production, which had some cuts, is also published in *Theater Heute* (1988), 2, pp. 29–55.
77 Rühle, *Theater für die Republik*, p. 34; Haumann, *Paul Kornfeld*, p. 604.
78 Ibid., p. 125.
79 Feinberg, 'Leopold Jessner', p. 125, citing Hollaender, 'Kornfelds "Jud Suss"' in *8-Uhr-Abendblatt*, 8 October 1930; Haumann, *Paul Kornfeld*, p. 605.
80 Haumann, *Paul Kornfeld*, pp. 612–13.

81 Ibid. p. 607.
82 Knilli and Zielinski, 'Lion Feuchtwangers "Jud Süss"', p. 105; Pazi, 'Zwei kaum bekannte Jud Süss-Theaterstücke', pp. 100ff; Singer, *Le Juif Süss*, p. 68.
83 *Daily Express* 7 October 1940, p. 1. For details on the escape see also *Manchester Guardian* 2 October 1940, p. 5 and *New York Times*, 6 October 1940.
84 Lion Feuchtwanger, 'To my Friends, the Actors', *Atlantic Monthly* (April, 1941), pp. 500–1.
85 Bundesarchiv, BA R109 I/1568 Correspondence of Marta Feuchtwanger to Lübeck Criminal Polizei, 17 December 1959; and of her lawyer, George Bronfen, to Ufa 12 Oct. 1961 and 6 November 1961.

Notes to Chapter 9: The British film Jew Süss *(1934)*

1 British Board of Film Censors Scenario Reports (1933), B[ritish] F[ilm] I[nstitute], London, p. 154.
2 *The Times*, 9 May 1933.
3 British Board of Film Censors Scenario Reports (1933), p. 162.
4 Robertson, *The British Board of Film Censors: Film Censorship in Britain, 1896–1950*, pp. 92–4; Richards, *The Age of the Dream Palace, Cinema and Society in Britain 1930–1939*, p. 128.
5 Ibid., p. 52.
6 Ibid.; Richards, 'The British Board of Film Censors and Content Control in the 1930s: Foreign Affairs', pp. 40–1.
7 Ibid.
8 Robertson, *The British Board of Film Censors*, p. 94.
9 British Board of Film Censors Scenario Reports (1934), p. 230.
10 *Kinematograph*, 25 December 1927; C. A. Lejeune, *Observer*, 7 October 1934.
11 *Kinematograph*, 25 December 1927.
12 *Die Filmwoche*, 12 February 1930. Two months later *Film-Journal* (Berlin) 17, 2 (13 April, 1930) had a large advertisement for Gold-Film (the distributors) announcing the Conrad Wiene-Produktion for the German version. Filming for a 'Pathé-Natan-Superproduktion' was to begin that June. According to Hollstein, *Jud Süss und die deutschen: Antisemitische Vorurteile im Nationalsozialistischen Spielfilm*, p. 326, Kortner's widow had no recollection of this.
13 Betts, *Jew Süss*, p. ix.
14 Ibid., p. x.
15 Ibid., p. xi.
16 *Picturegoer Weekly*, 7 April 1934; 12 January 1934.
17 Low, *The History of British Film: Film Making in 1930s Britain*, p. 138.
18 Betts, *Jew Süss*, p. x.
19 Erens, *The Jew in American Cinema*, esp. pp. 148–52; Friedman, *Hollywood's Image of the Jew*, pp. 55–87; Shindler, *Hollywood in Crisis; Cinema and American*

Society: 1929-1939, pp. 59–63; Carr, *Hollywood and Anti-Semitism: A Cultural History up to World War*, esp. pp. 182–92; Welky, *The Moguls and the Dictators: Hollywood and the Coming of World War II*, pp. 20–6.

20 Balcon, *Michael Balcon Presents … A Lifetime in Films*, p. 99.

21 Betts, *The Private Life of Henry VIII*.

22 Ibid., p. 89.

23 Ibid., p. 124.

24 Low, *The History of the British Film*, p. 141 gives £100,000 while *Picture Goer Weekly*, 20 October and *Manchester Sunday Chronicle*, 7 October 1934 give £125,000.

25 Bergfelder, 'The Producer Designer and the *Gesamtkunstwerk*: German Film Technicians in the British Film Industry of the 1930s', pp. 27–9.

26 Gough Yates 'Jews and Exiles in British Cinema', xxxvii, p. 523; Betts, *Jew Süss*, pp. xiii, xiv.

27 Ibid., p. x.

28 Harper, '"Thinking Forward and Up": The British Films of Conrad Veidt', p. 123.

29 Betts, *Jew Süss*, p. x.

30 Balcon, *A Lifetime in Films*, pp. 75–6; Fraenkel, *Unsterblicher Film*, pp. 100–2; Allen, *Conrad Veidt: From Caligari to Casablanca*, pp. 208–14.

31 Balcon, *A Lifetime in Films*, pp. 75–76; Fraenkel, *Unsterblicher Film* pp. 100–2; Allen, *Conrad Veidt*, pp. 126–48; Holba, 'From Caligari to Hollywood, Conrad Veidt', pp. 27–46.

32 *Film Weekly*, 5 October 1934.

33 Harper, '"Thinking Forward and Up"', p. 123.

34 Isherwood, *Christopher and his Kind*, p.128.

35 Ibid., pp. 128–9.

36 Ibid.

37 I am grateful to Lucie Skeaping for providing this information at a talk I gave on the film on 26 March 2003 as her father was one of the boys.

38 Betts, *Jew Süss*, p. 2.

39 Ibid., p. 6.

40 Feuchtwanger, *Jew Süss*, trans. Willa and Edwin Muir, p. 428.

41 *Daily Sketch*, 5 October 1934; *The Times*, 5 October 1934.

42 Sedgwick, 'The Market for Feature Films in Britain in 1934: a Viable National Cinema', pp. 19, 34.

43 *Daily Telegraph*, 8 October 1934; *The Sunday Times*, 7 October 1934; *Daily Mail*, 5 October 1934.

44 *The Times*, 5 October 1934; *Spectator*, 12 October 1934.

45 *Cinema Quarterly* (1934), ii, pp. 44–5; Fielding, *The American Newsreel: 1911–1967*, pp. 138–41.

46 *Observer*, 7 October 1934. This review does not appear in the published collection of Lejeune's reviews though an earlier report (7 January, 1934) on the film when in production does. Lejeuene, ed., *The C. A. Lejeune Reader*, p. 93.

47 Ibid.
48 Atkinson, *Era*, 10 October 1934, British Film Institute cuttings.
49 *Spectator*, 12 October 1934.
50 Agate, *Around Cinemas*, pp. 104–6.
51 *Punch*, 17 October 1934.
52 Atkinson, *Era*, 10 October 1934.
53 *Daily Telegraph*, 8 October 1934.
54 *Motion Picture Daily*, 4 October 1934 reported $15,480 takings in one day (Sunday).
55 *Hollywood Reporter*, 8 October 1934, cutting in Balcon Collection Scrapbook, British Film Institute.
56 *Film Daily*, 5 October 1934, cutting in Balcon Collection Scrapbook, British Film Institute.
57 *Showmen's Round Table*, 13 October 1934, cutting in Balcon Collection Scrapbook, British Film Institute.
58 Erens, *The Jew in American Cinema*, 148ff; Friedman, *Hollywood's Image of the Jew*, pp. 64ff, 78ff.
59 *Time*, 15 October 1934, cutting in Balcon Collection Scrapbook, British Film Institute.
60 *New York Herald Tribune*, 5 October 1934.
61 *New York Times*, 5 October 1934.
62 *Variety*, 9 October 1934.
63 Wise, *Challenging Years: The Autobiography of Stephen Wise*, pp. 159–60, 175.
64 *American*, 15 October 1934, cutting in Michael Balcon Collection Scrapbook, British Film Institute.
65 Ibid.
66 Wise, *Challenging Years*, pp. 166–79; Friedländer, *The Years of Extermination: Nazi Germany and the Jews: 1939–1945*, pp. 85–6, 304, 460–2, 595.
67 Singer, *Le Juif Suisse*, p. 302.
68 Freidenreich, *Jewish Politics in Vienna: 1918–1938*, pp. 86–113; Clare, (London: Macmillan, 1981), p. 105.
69 Carsten, *Fascist Movements in Austria: Schönerer to Hitler*, p. 284.
70 *Variety*, 24 April 1934 found this surprising.
71 *Oestereichische Abendzeitung*, 16, 17 October 1934; *Neues Wiener Reichspost* and *Wiener Zeitung*, 19 October 1934.
72 Hostile newspapers include the official (government-owned): *Wiener Zeitung*, 19 October 1934; *Reichspost*, 17 October 1934 and *Neuigkeits-Welt-Blatt*, 19 October and 23 October 1934. There were mixed reviews in *Neues Wiener Journal*, 18 October 1934 and favourable ones in *Neue Freie Presse*, 18 October 1934, *Das Echo*, 17 October 1934 and *Neue Wiener Tageblatt*, 17 October 1934.
73 *Reichspost*, 16 October 1934; 17 October 1934.
74 *Wiener Zeitung*, 19 October 1934.
75 *Neuigkeits-Welt-Blatt*, 19 October 1934.

76 *Ibid.*, 23 October 1934.
77 Pulzer, *The Rise of Political Antisemitism in Germany and Austria*, p. 69. The exception was the Polna case in 1899 with Thomas Masaryk defending. Tried twice, the accused was eventually convicted of murder rather than ritual murder and pardoned almost thirty years later by the emperor.
78 Carsten, *Fascist Movements in Austria*, p. 28.
79 Ecksteins, 'War, Memory and Politics: The Fate of the film *All Quiet on the Western Front*', p. 71.
80 National Archives, Kew, PRO FO120/1092 Edgar Granville to Sir Walford Selby 24 October 1934 and Selby to Granville 7 November 1934.
81 PRO FO120/1092 Despatch no. 217, R. H. Hadow to Sir John Simon, 7 November 1934.
82 PRO FO120/1092 Note Verbale (Translation) Federal Chancery, Austrian Department of Foreign Affairs to British Legation, 31 October 1934.
83 PRO FO120/1092 British Legation Vienna to Federal Chancery, Department of Foreign Affairs, 24 October 1934.
84 PRO FO120/1092 Note Verbale (Translation) Federal Chancery, Austrian Department of Foreign Affairs to British Legation, 31 October, 1934.
85 *Neuigkeits-Welt-Blatt* 19 October 1934.
86 *Die Neue Freie Presse*, 23 Oct 1934; *Neue Wiener Tageblatt*, 23 October 1934.
87 Oesterreichisches Staatsarchiv, Vienna: Archiv der Republik: Bundeskanzleramt 261.652.
88 *Oesterreichische Abendzeitung*, 16, 17, 18 October 1934.
89 Oesterreichisches Staatsarchiv hereafter ÖSt.A., Vienna, Archiv der Republik: Bundeskanzleramt 261.652; National Archives, Kew, PRO FO120/1092 7 W. H. Hadow to Sir John Simon, 7 November 1934.
90 Ibid.
91 ÖSt.A. Vienna, Archiv der Republik, Bundeskanzleramt 261.652. Bundes-polizeidirektion in Wien to Bund der Filmindustriellen in Oesterreich, 11 Nov 1934.
92 PRO FO120/1092, W. H. Hadow to Sir John Simon, 7 November 1934.
93 PRO FO120/1092, Note Verbale, 24 October 1934.
94 PRO FO120/1092 British Legation Vienna to Federal Chancery, Department of Foreign Affairs, 24 October 1934.
95 Ibid.
96 *Wiener Zeitung*, 26 October 1934.
97 *Reichspost*, 23 October 1934.
98 *Der gute Film*, 26 October 1934.
99 *Deutsche Filmzeitung*, 4 November 1934.
100 *Deutsche Zeitung*, 19 and 24 October 1934, Deutsches Institut für Filmkunde, Frankfurt.
101 Reichsfilmarchiv, 1934, 2744.

Notes to Chapter 10: Veit Harlan's Jud Süss: *in production (1939–1940)*

1 The judges' summing up at Harlan's trials in Bundesarchiv (hereafter BArch): Z38/392; *Filmpress* (Hamburg), 22 July 1950.

2 *Tagesspiegel*, p. 23 March 1949. For a perceptive portrait of Engel see Zuckmayer, *Geheimreport*, pp. 128–30.

3 This is taken from the judges' summary of the evidence at the trial of Veit Harlan. BArch Z38/392 which also appears in *Filmpress* (Hamburg) 22 July 1950.

4 Prawer, *Between Two Worlds: The Jewish Presence in German and Austrian Film: 1910–1933*.

5 Tegel, *Nazis and the Cinema*, pp. 49–74.

6 Ibid., pp. 99–102.

7 Ibid., pp. 102–6.

8 Ibid., pp. 106–11; Wright, *The Visible Wall: Jews and other Ethnic Outsiders in Swedish Film*, pp. 51–4.

9 Tegel, *Nazis and the Cinema*, pp. 205–7.

10 Fröhlich, *Die Tagebücher von Joseph Goebbels: Sämtliche Fragmente*, pt 1, vol. viii, p. 195 (27 June 1940).

11 Harlan, *Im Schatten meiner Filme*, p. 117. See also Tegel, *Nazis and Cinema*, p. 259, n57.

12 Staatsanwaltschaft bei dem Landgericht Hamburg, Strafverfahren gegen Veit Harlan, AZ 14JS/555/48, hereafter SLH, 23 April 1949, II, p. 23ff; Buchloh, *Veit Harlan: Goebbels Starregisseur*, pp. 199–200.

13 Drewniak, *Der deutsche Film 1938–1945: ein Gesamtüberblick*, p. 431.

14 BArch, Berlin Document Center, hereafter BDC, RKK 2703013124 Kreisverlag, Metzger's account given 7 August 1946; Hamburg: Staatsanwaltschaft be idem Landgericht, Ebbecke, iv, p. 340.

15 *Filmpress*, 22 July 1950, p. 1: SLH, AZ 14, iv, p. 340 (Ebbecke).

16 Harlan, *Im Schatten*, pp. 809–90; BArch, BDC, RKK 2100 Teichs file.

17 Fröhlich, *Die Tagebücher von Joseph Goebbels*, pt 1, vol. viii, p. 417 (14 November 1940).

18 Schmitt, 'Der Fall Veit Harlan', 12, p. 20; BArch, BDC, 2100, Adolf Teichs file; SLH, Teichs testimony, ii, p. 207ff; Hamburg Staatsarchiv, Misc. 6911 Veit Harlan, Teichs letter 28 July 1947.

19 *Filmpress*, 22 July 1950, p. 2; Harlan, *Im Schatten Meiner Filme*, p. 89ff; SLH (Ebbecke testimony), IV, p. 340; Hans-Joachim Beyer testimony, IV, p. 301.

20 *Frankfurter Allgemeine*, 5 April 1950; *Film & Mode Revue*, 12, p. 20.

21 BArch, BDC, Greven file.

22 Ibid. Greven entered the party in December 1931, left September 1932, re-entered September 1934.

23 SLH, Wolf von Gordon testimony, III, p. 231 (copy at Institut für Zeitgeschichte, Munich); *Filmpress* (22 July 1950, p. 2.

24 *Jud Süss, Propagandafilm im NS-Staat, Catalogue zur Ausstellung*, p. 21.

25 Haasis, *Joseph Süss Oppenheimer, genannt Jud Süss*, pp. 234–6.
26 Hippler, *Die Verstrickung: Einstellungen und Rückblenden von Fritz Hippler, ehem. Reichsfilmintendant unter Joseph Goebbels*, p. 197; Hamburg St.A, Brauer Testimony, II, p. 204; Fröhlich, *Die Tagebücher von Joseph Goebbels*, pt 1, vol. vi, pp. 252–3 (9 February 1939).
27 *Filmwelt*, 28 July 1939.
28 Terra Catalogue.
29 Ibid.
30 *Lichtbild-Bühne*, 18 July 1939.
31 Ibid, 25 October 1939.
32 *Hamburg Tageblatt*, 18 November 1939.
33 *Lichtbild-Bühne*, 18 July 1939.
34 BArch, BDC, RKK 3545 Gordon file, Metzger file.
35 Institut für Zeitgeschichte, Munich, 7841/90 Sp44 Fall Hippler; SLH (Teich testimony) II, pp. 208–8, (Gordon Testimony) III, p. 231; National Archives, Kew (Public Record Office) F01060/1233, Anklageschrift gegen Veit Harlan, 15 July 1948, p. 11.
36 Institut für Zeitgeschichte, Munich, 784/90 Sp 44 Fall Hippler; Staatsanwaltschaft Fritz Hippler, pp. 207–8.
37 *Lichtbild-Bühne* 25 October 1939.
38 *Hamburg Tageblatt*, 18 November 1939.
39 Harlan, *Im Schatten meiner Filme*, p. 90; BArch, R109 11568, Letter of Harlan, 27 November 1961. A letter dated 6 August 1948, BDC, RKK 2703 0171 Kreisverlag. File 3 complains that the actors were more harshly dealt with than Möller, a scriptwriter. For a portrait of Möller see Baird, *To Die for Germany*, but he is wrong in claiming (p. 245) that Möller wrote the script, rather than an earlier draft.
40 Harlan, *Im Schatten meiner Filme*, p. 90.
41 SLH (Gordon Testimony), iii, p. 231.
42 Ibid., Ebbecke testimony, iv, p. 340.
43 *Lichtbild-Bühne*, 25 Oct 1939.
44 BArch, BDC, RKK 10703 0131 24 Kreisverlag. He claimed to have received RM4000 for the script, an additional RM40000 plus RM2000 for a treatment, when an average script fee was RM 8,000–15,000 and a top scriptwriter like Thea von Harbou received RM 80,000.
45 BArch, BDC, RKK 2703 0131 24 Kreisverlag.
46 BArch, BDC, RKK, Veit Harlan.
47 Eberhard Wolfgang Möller and Ludwig Metzger, 'Jud Süss: ein historischer Film'. Stiftung Deutsche Kinemathek, Berlin.
48 *Lichtbild-Bühne*, 25 October 1939.
49 Ibid.
50 Möller and Metzger, 'Jud Süss: ein historischer Film', scene 46.
51 *Lichtbild-Bühne*, 25 October 1939.

52 Fröhlich, *Die Tagebücher von Joseph Goebbels*, pt 1, vol. vii, p. 177 (2 November 1939).
53 Ibid., pt. 1, vol. vii, p. 220 (5 December 1939).
54 Harlan, *Im Schatten meiner Filme*, p. 93.
55 Ibid.
56 Ibid.
57 Ibid., pp. 91–2.
58 Fröhlich, *Die Tagebücher von Joseph Goebbels*, pt 1, vol. vii, p. 149 (11 Oct. 1939).
59 Ibid., pt 1, vol. vii, p. 220 (5 Dec 1939).
60 BArch, BDC, Harlan file; Buchloh, *Veit Harlan: Goebbels Starregisseur*, p. 7.
61 Riess, *Das Gab's Nur Einmal*, p. 626.
62 Harlan, *Im Schatten meiner Filme*, p. 83.
63 Fröhlich, *Die Tagebücher von Joseph Goebbels*, pt 1, vol. vii, p. 46 (17 August 1938).
64 Zwicker, '*Nationale Märtyer' Albert Leo Schlageter und Julius Fucik: Heldenkult, Propaganda und Erinnerungskultur* (Paderborn: Schöningh, 2006), p. 87.
65 Billington, *Peggy Ashcroft*, pp. 69–71.
66 Fröhlich, *Die Tagebücher von Joseph Goebbels*, pt 1, vol. iv, p. 48 (12 March 1937).
67 Staatsarchiv Hamburg, Marian's Account, 20 September 1945 also reproduced in *Filmpress*, (22 July 1950), p. 2.
68 Krauss, *Das Schauspiel meines Lebens*, pp. 199–200.
69 Söderbaum, *Nichts bleib immer so: Rückblenden auf ein Leben vor und hinter der Kamera*, p p. 152.
70 Feuchtwanger, 'To my Friends, the Actors', *Atlantic Monthly*.
71 Harlan, *Im Schatten meiner Filme*, pp. 120–1.
72 Boelcke, *Kriegspropaganda Geheime Ministerkonferenzen im Reichspropagandaministerium 1939–1941*, p. 526.
73 Knilli, *Ich War Jud Süss*, p. 75; see Tegel, *Nazis and the Cinema*, p. 257, n16.
74 Harlan, *Im Schatten meiner Filme*, pp. 225–6; Söderbaum, *Nichts bleib immer so*, pp. 149–50; see Tegel, *Nazis and the Cinema*, p. 257, n16.
75 BArch, Sammlung Sänger Zsg 113/102/62 Kulturkonferenz 12 April 1940. On June 1939 Goebbels had banned the term antisemitic. See Welch, *Propaganda and the German Cinema 1933–1945*, p. 239.
76 *Jud Süss*: ein historischer Film, scene 78; *Jud Süss*: ein historischer Film, scene 407.
77 SLH, 14 JS4/48, Conny Carstensson testimony, i, p. 73.
78 Ibid., p. 70; Mondi sworn statement, i, pp. 64–5; Harlan, *Im Schatten meiner Filme*, pp. 115ff.
79 SLH, 14 JS4/48, Carstenson Testimony i, p. 69ff.
80 Harlan, *Im Schatten meiner Filme*, pp. 116.
81 BArch, Sammlung Brammer, 17 January 1940.
82 BArch, Zsg.101/15; Zeitschriften-Dienst 40:1705, 26 January 1940.

83 SLH 14 JS 4/48, I, p. 72; Schmitt, 'Der Fall Veit Harlan', 18, p. 29; National Archives, Kew PRO, FO 1060, p. 13.

84 Schmitt, 'Der Fall Veit Harlan', 18, p. 29; SLH 14/JS4/48 Letter, 3 February 1948 from Židovská Nábóženká Obec v Praze to Central Committee of Liberated Jews in British Zone; see Susan Tegel, '"The Demonic Effect": Veit Harlan's Use of Jewish Extras in Jud Süss 91940' in *Holocaust and Genocide Studies*, 14 (2000), p. 228.

85 Staatsarchiv Hamburg, Veit Harlan, Misc, Harlan, 'My Attitude to National Socialism' (typescript), pp. 4, 5.

86 Harlan, *Im Schatten meiner Filme*, p. 116; Harlan, 'My Attitude to National Socialism', pp. 5–6.

87 Schmitt, 'Der Fall Veit Harlan', No. 18, p. 29.

88 Ibid.

89 SLH, 14/Js4/48, I, pp. 145–6 Bedrich Dostal.

90 Ibid.; Schmitt, 'Der Fall Veit Harlan', No. 18, p. 29.

91 SLH, 14/Js 4/48 Chasin sworn statement, iii, pp. 44–9, 266.

92 Ibid.

93 Veit Harlan, 'Wie es War … Erlebnis eines Filmregisseurs unter seinem aller höchtsten Chef, dem Schirmherrn des deutschen Films, Dr. Goebbels', typescript, c. 1960, Schriftliche Abteilung der Bayerischen Staatsbibliothck, Munich, p. 209.

94 Fröhlich, *Die Tagebücher von Joseph Goebbels*, pt 1, vol.viii, p. 279 (18 August 1940).

Notes to Chapter 11: Veit Harlan's Jud Süss: *on screen*

1 Schulte-Sasse, 'The Jew as Other under National Socialism: Veit Harlan's Jud Süss', p. 24.

2 Feuchtwanger, 'To my Friends, the Actors'.

3 Ferro, 'Dissolves in Jud Süss', pp. 139–41.

4 Harlan, *Im Schatten meiner Filme*, p. 93.

5 I am grateful to Victor Tunkel for this information.

6 Haasis, *Joseph Süss Oppenheimer, genannt Jud Süss*, pp. 339 385, 387.

7 Bartov, *The 'Jew' in Cinema from The Golem to Don't Touch my Holocaust*, p. 13.

8 I am grateful to Victor Tunkel for this information.

9 Rothmüller, *The Music of the Jew*, pp. 231–4; Hirshberg, *Music in the Jewish Community of Palestine: 1880–1948*, p. 224.

10 Hollstein, *Jud Süss und die Deutschen*, p. 98, citing Eric Seifert, *Der Angriff*, 233 (26 September 1940, p. 1).

11 Haasis, *Joseph Süss Oppenheimer*, p. 235.

12 Harlan, *Im Schatten meiner Filme*, pp. 112–13; Krauss, *Das Schauspiel meines Lebens*, p. 202.

13 'Jud Süss: ein historischer Film. Regie Veit Harlan' Berlin, Stiftung Deutsche Kinemathek.
14 Hippler, *Betrachtungen zum Filmschaffen*, p. 107.

Notes to Chapter 12: Veit Harlan's Jud Süss: reception (1940–1945)

1 Rohdie, *Antonioni*, p. 29.
2 Ibid.
3 Kracauer, 'Cult of Distraction on Berlin's Picture Palaces', p. 323.
4 Fröhlich, *Die Tagebücher von Joseph Goebbels*, pt 1, vol. viii, p. 345 (25 Sept. 1940).
5 Albrecht, *Der Film im Dritten Reich: eine Dokumentation*, pp. 76, 77.
6 Hollstein, *Jud Süss und die Deutschen*, p. 81, citing *Berliner Lokalanzeiger*, 25 September 1940; Culbert, 'Essay', p. 9.
7 Bundesarchiv, Berlin, hereafter BArch, R56/132 Letter 30 September 1940; also cited in Wulf, *Theater und Film im Dritten Reich*, p. 452.
8 BArch, Decree dated 15 November 1940 in Ministerialblatt des Reichs und Preussischen Innern (Interior Ministry), vol. ii, p. 21166, 'Vorführung des Filmes *Jud Süss*'.
9 BArch, RA56/132 also reproduced in Wulf, *Theater und Film im Dritten Reich*, pp. 450–1.
10 BArch, Sicherheitsdienst Reports (28 November 1940); Boberach, *Meldungen aus dem Reich: Die Geheimen Lageberichte des Sicherheitsdienstes der SS, 1938–1945*, vol. vi, p. 1812, reproduced in Kulka and Jäckel, *Die Juden in den Geheimen NS-Stimmungsberichten*, pp. 437–8. See also Hollstein, *Jud Süss und die Deutschen*, p. 106; Welch, *Propaganda and the German Cinema*, p. 291 n. 118.
11 George, *Jud Süss* (Berlin: Terra, 1941).
12 von Arndt, *Aktuelle Filmbücher: Dem Drehbuch von Veit Harlan, E. W. Möller und Ludwig Metzger, Nacherzählt von Heinrich von Arndt*.
13 Proctor, *The Nazi War on Cancer*, p. 22.
14 Ibid.
15 *Frankfurter Zeitung*, 26 September 1940.
16 Wulf, *Theater und Film im dritten Reich*, p. 449.
17 *Filmwoche*, 9 October 1949.
18 Ernst von der Decken, '*Jud Süss* in Venedig' in *Deutsche Allgemeine Zeitung* (6 September 1940).
19 *Film-Kurier*, 25 September 1940.
20 *Völkischer Beobachter*, 26 September 1940.
21 Albrecht, *Der Film im dritten Reich*, p. 251; Welch, *Propaganda and the German Cinema*, pp. 277–81 indicates which films were commissioned by the state.
22 Knilli, *Ich War Jud Süss*, p. 143.
23 BArch, R055/00949; *Film-Kurier*, 6 March 1943.

24 Albrecht, *Der Film im dritten Reich*, p. 24.

25 *Der Film*, 9 November 1940.

26 BArch, 58/156; Hollstein, *Jud Süss*, pp. 104–6; Bankier, *The Germans and the Final Solution: Public Opinion under Nazism*, pp. 7–8; Nolzen, '"Hier sieht man den Juden wie er wirklich ist": Die Rezeption des Filmes *Jud Süss* in der deutschen Bevölkerung', p. 249.

27 BArch, R58/157, pp. 7–9 (January 1941) also cited in Boberich, *Meldungen aus dem Reich*, vi, no. 155, p. 1918.

28 Bucher, 'Die Bedeutung des Films als historische Quelle: *Der ewige Jude*', p. 317.

29 Reeves, *The Power of Film Propaganda*, pp.107, 132 n.67, citing David Welch.

30 Nolzen, 'Hier sieht man den Juden, wie er wirklich ist: Die Rezeption des Filmes *Jud Süss* in der deutschen Bevölkerung', p. 249; Bankier, *The Germans and the Final Solution*, pp. 7–23.

31 Lesch, *Heim ins Ufa-Reich? NS-Filmpolitik und die Rezeption deutscher Filme in Luxemburg 1933–1944*, p. 88.

32 Ibid.

33 Ibid.

34 Ibid., p. 88 n.298.

35 *Film-Kurier*, 20 February 1941; also reproduced in Wulf, *Theater und Film im Dritten Reich*, p. 453.

36 *Ibid.*, 23 July 1941.

37 *Film-Kurier*, 16 July 1941.

38 Ibid., 6 February 1941, p. 452–3.

39 Vande Winkel, 'German Influence on Belgian Cinema: From Low Profile Presence to Downright Colonisation', p. 74.

40 *Film-Kurier*, 16 July 1941; Singer, *Le Juif Süss*, p. 191.

41 Ibid.

42 *Film-Kurier*, 5 August 1943.

43 Wulf, *Theater und Film im dritten Reich*, p. 455; Hollstein, *Jud Süss*, pp. 106.

44 Langbein, *Der Auschwitz Prozess: Eine Dokumentation*, i, p. 208.

45 Haver, 'Film Propaganda and the Balance between Neutrality and Alignment: Nazi Films in Switzerland, 1933–1945', p. 280; Singer, *Le Juif Süss*, p. 191.

46 Culbert, 'Essay', p. 13 though according to BArch, *Zeitschriften-Dienst*, No. 5092 it was screened there.

47 Wright, 'Swedish Film and Germany', p. 268.

48 *Film-Kurier*, 16 May 1941 and 26 May 1941; see also Culbert, 'Essay', p. 13.

49 Culbert, 'Essay', p. 13; *Film-Kurier*, 16 July 1941; Drewniak, *Der deutsche Film 1938–1945: ein Gesamtüberblick*, p. 699.

50 BArch, *Zeitschriften-Dienst*, No. 5092.

51 *Film-Kurier*, 16 July 1941.

52 Ibid.

53 *Der Film*, 15 March 1941.

54 Culbert, 'Essay', p. 12, citing Frey.

55 BArch, R43II 389, Letter, 31 March 1941, Eugen Hadamovsky in the Propaganda Ministry to Dr Lammers Chef der Reichskanzlei.

56 BArch, R43II 389, Letter of Eugen Hadamovsky in the Propaganda Ministry to Dr Lammers, Chef der Reichskanzlei, 31 March 1941.

57 *Film-Kurier*, 31, 6 February 1941 cited in Wulf, *Theater und Film im Dritten Reich*, p. 452.

58 Fröhlich, *Tagebücher von Joseph Goebbels*, pt.1, vol. ix, p. 171 (8 March 1941).

59 Albrecht, *Nationalsozialistische Filmpolitik*, p. 499.

60 Nolzen, 'Hier sieht man den Juden', pp. 256–7.

61 Culbert, 'Essay', p. 12 cites Frey who has not been able to confirm whether this demonstration actually took place, but mentions the street protests by antisemitic student groups like the Turul Society which had previously done this for the premieres of other films relating to Jews.

62 BArch, R43II 389. Letter 31 March 1941, from Hadamovsky in the Propaganda Ministry to Dr Lammers, Chef der Reichskanzlei.

63 Culbert, 'Essay', pp. 12–13, citing Frey.

64 Ibid.

65 Singer, *Le Juif Süss*, pp. 197–9.

66 Ibid.

67 The evidence comes from the translation of 'Judenhure' (Jew's whore) which was translated into French as 'punaise à youtre' – punaise is French for bedbug while 'youtre' is best translated as 'Yid'. Presumably bedbug unlike the French word for whore, putain, is not gender-specific. See Garçon, 'Cinéma et Historie: Les Trois Discours du Juif Süss', p. 705 who cites the conclusion of R. Migeon who compared the French dialogue with the German.

68 *Le Petit Parisien*, 2 March 1941 cited in Singer, *Le Juif Süss*, p. 211.

69 *Film-Journal*, 27 April 1930.

70 Singer, *Le Juif*, reproducing Vinneuil, *Action Française*, 30 November 1934.
Süss, p. 302.

71 Bardèche and Brasillach, *Historie du cinema*, p. 360.

72 Bowles, 'Propaganda and its Backlash: Reception of *Le Juif Süss* en France, 1941–42'.

73 Ibid.

74 Ibid.

75 Bowles, 'German Newsreel Propaganda in France', p. 50.

76 Ibid.

77 Weekly Report of the Propaganda Abteilung, Referat Film, Aussenstelle Paris, March–October 1941, United States National Archives, Microfilm Reel no. T 141, frames 1074 and 1079.

78 Ibid.; Garçon, 'Nazi Propaganda in Occupied France', pp. 171–4.

79 Singer, *Le Juif Süss*, pp. 228–30.

80 Ibid., p. 218.

81 Ibid., p. 219.

82 Ibid.
83 Ibid., p. 220.
84 *The Times*, 24 October 2008.
85 Bowles, Propaganda and its Backlash', p. 6.
86 Singer, *Le Juif Süss*, p. 223.
87 Bowles, Propaganda and its Backlash', p. 6.
88 *Liberté*, 25 July 1941. (I am grateful to Brett Bowles for providing me with a copy of this.)
89 Bowles, 'Propaganda and its Backlash', pp. 1, 7.
90 Ibid., p. 7.
91 Domerus, *Hitler, Reden, Proklamationen 1932-1941*, i, p. 1064.
92 Hornshøy-Møller, *Der ewige Jude, quellenkritische Analyse eines antisemitischen Propagandafilms*, pp. 296-7.
93 Herf, *The Jewish Enemy: Nazi propaganda during World War II and the Holocaust*, p. 14.
94 Ibid.
95 Zuckmayer, *Briefe an Hans Schiebelhuth 1921-1936* (Göttingen: Wallstein, 2003), p. 225, citing Helmuth Kiesel, ed., *Ernst Junger/Carl Schmitt Briefe 1930-1983*, p. 105.
96 Hickethier, 'Der Audiovisuell Inszenierte Antisemitismus', pp. 236-8.
97 Stahr, *Volksgemeinschaft vor der Leinwand?: Nationalsozialistische Film und sein Publikum*, pp. 67-73.
98 Nolzen, 'Hier sieht man den Juden', pp. 257-8; the responses cited in Friedrich Knilli's biography of Ferdinand Marian are anecdotal. See Knilli, *Ich War Jud Süss*, pp. 156-7.
99 Lohmeier, 'Propaganda als Alibi', p. 217.
100 See especially Kershaw, 'How Effective was Nazi Propaganda?', pp. 180-205.
101 Rentschler, *The Ministry of Illusion: Nazi Cinema and its Afterlife*, p. 169.
102 Pardo and Schiffer, *Jud Süss. Historisches und juristisches Material zum Fall Veit Harlan*, p. 66, reproducing 'Open Letter of Veit Harlan to Lion Feuchtwanger'.

Notes to Chapter 13: Veit Harlan on trial (1945-1950)

1 Tegel, *Nazis and the Cinema*, pp. 187-90.
2 Staatsarchiv Hamburg, hereafter SH, Veit Harlan, Misc 6911, Letter dated 5 March 1945 of Kristina Söderbaum to Heinrich Himmler (at the request of a Swedish pastor to spare the lives of two young Swedish men).
3 Harlan, *Im Schatten meiner Filme* (Gütersloh: Sigbert Mohn, 1966), p. 209; SH, Veit Harlan Misc 6911, Letter to Zentralstelle für Berüfungsaussschuss, 17 August 1947.
4 SH, Veit Harlan Misc 6911, Veit Harlan, 'My Attitude to National Socialism', pp. 30-31; Letter of Frowein, 12 October 1944, copy in Bundesarchiv Berlin

(hereafter BArch) Berlin Document Center (hereafter BDC). The script can be found amongst the Erich Lüth papers, SH.

5   Ibid., p. 2.

6   Ibid.

7   Ibid.

8   Ibid., pp. 17–21.

9   BArch, R 109/111: Riefenstahl to Winkler, 18 June 1944; to Walter Müller-Goerne, 5 July 1944; to Hans Hinkler, 22 October 1944. For the making of *Tiefland* see Tegel, 'Leni Riefenstahl's Gypsy Question Revisited: The Gypsy Extras in "Tiefland"', pp. 21–43.

10 SH, Veit Harlan Misc. 6911, Letter from Harlan to Capt Phillips, 17 July 1945.

11 Hippler, *Die Verstrickung: Einstellungen und Ruckblenden*, pp. 253–5.

12 SH, Veit Harlan Misc 6911, Erich Kästner, 'Harlan oder die Weisse Mütze', *Die Neue Zeitung*, 30 November 1945 (copy); the same Kästner piece also appears later under the title 'Veit Harlan ein Charakter' in *Pitt's Künstlerpost*, 25 January 1946.

13 BArch, BDC, letter 6 January 1946. (The letter is wrongly dated due to a typographical error which should read 6 January 1947 as it is date-stamped 7 January 1947 though the typist has given 1946).

14 SH, Veit Harlan Misc 6911, Harlan's statement to the Central Denazification Panel, 26 November 1947.

15 SH, Veit Harlan Misc 6911 Letter of Secretariat of Central Denazification Panel, 13 November 1947 to Buckland-Smith, Hamburg.

16 SH, Misc. 6911. Veit Harlan. Käutner to Zentral Ausschuss 22 November 1947; BArch, BDC, Memo 13 January 1948.

17 BArch, BDC, Harlan file, Letter, H. L. Ormond to Sely, 17 December 1947.

18 Ibid.

19 Ibid.; SH, Veit Harlan Misc 6911, Letters of Hans Vetter, 22 December 1947 and Richard Schäuble, 15 December 1947; *Hamburger Echo*, 19 December 1947.

20 *Die Weltbühne*, September 1947.

21 Lion Feuchtwanger, 'To my Friends, the Actors', pp. 500–1.

22 SH, Veit Harlan Misc 6911, Harlan to Lion Feuchtwanger, 12 December 1947 also reprinted in Pardo, etc.

23 Buchloh, *Veit Harlan: Goebbels Starregisseur*, p. 188.

24 BArch, BDC, Letter (undated) on behalf of the Association of Film Producers in the US zone, signed Eberhard Klagemann and Josef von Baky.

25 BArch, BDC, Veit Harlan, Sely to Ramsbothom (Hamburg Intelligence), Letter, 22 December 1947, BDC, RKK 2703 0082, File 35.

26 Clare, *Berlin Days 1946–47*, p. 68.

27 BArch, BDC, Harlan file, Sely to Ramsbothom, 22 December 1947.

28 BArch, BDC, Ormond to Sely 17 December 1947 Prisc BArch, BDC; Clare, *Berlin Days*, p. 152.

29 *Tagesspiegel*, 5 January 1948.

30 BArch, BDC, Veit Harlan file. Memo, 13 January 1948.
31 Staatsanwaltschaft bei dem Landgericht Hamburg, hereafter SLH Ermittlungs-akten gegen Harlan, Veit wegen Verbrechen gegen die Menschlichkeit. AZ 14JS/555/48.
32 Ibid. Hippler testimony; I, p. 147, iii; pp. 44–49.
33 Ibid. Chasan testimony, I, p. 45.
34 SH, Veit Harlan Misc. 6911 Memo, 4 March 1948.
35 Schmitt, 'Der Fall Veit Harlan', 13, pp. 17–18.
36 SH, Veit Harlan Misc. 6911, Letter of Braun to Zippel, 5 July 1946; Harlan, *Im Schatten meiner Filme*, p. 186.
37 SLH, Carstensson, i, p. 69.
38 SH, Veit Harlan Misc 6911, Letter of Harlan to Capt Phillips, 17 July 1945; letter of Irene Meyer-Hanno, 3 January 1947; Harlan, *Im Schatten meiner Filme*, pp. 186, 199.
39 Harlan to Capt Philips 17 July 1945.
40 Tegel, *Nazis and the Cinema*, p. 124.
41 Harlan, *Im Schatten meiner Filme*, pp. 91–5, 100–3.
42 Laregh, *Heinrich George, Komödiant seiner Zeit*, p. 290ff.
43 Krauss, *Das Schauspiel meines Lebens*, p. 228.
44 Pardo and Schiffner, *Jud Süss: Historisch und Juristisch*.
45 Laux, 'Ich bin der Historiker der Hoffaktoren', p. 490.
46 Schmidt, 'Der Fall Veit Harlan', XV, pp. 18–19.
47 Liebert, 'Vom Karrierstreben'; BArch, Z38/392 fol. 1 Akten des Obersten Gerichtshofs für die Britische Zone in Köln, 22 April 1949; National Archives, Kew, PRO FO1060/1233.
48 Liebert, 'Vom Karrierstreben', pp. 142–3.

Filmography

Jew Süss (Power)

Production company: Gaumont British
Director: Lothar Mendes
Producer: Michael Balcon
Script:
Adaptation: Dorothy Farnum (assisted by Heinrich Fraenkl)
Scenario and Dialogue: Arthur Richard Rawlinson
Photography: Roy Kellino, Bernard Knowles,
Art director (sets): Alfred Junge
Music director: Louis Levy
Editor: Otto Ludwig
Recordist: William Salter
Costumes and period adviser: Herbert Norris
Unit production adviser Herbert Norris
Studio: Gainsborough Studios
Cast:

Joseph Süss Oppenheimer	Conrad Veidt
Duchess Marie Auguste	Benita Hume
Duke Carl Alexander	Frank Vosper
Rabbi Gabriel	Cedric Hardwicke
Weissensee	Gerald du Maurier
Landauer	Paul Graetz
Magdalene Sybille	Joan Maude
Naemi	Pamela Ostrer
Michele Süss	Haidée Wright
Jantje	Eva Moore
Prince of Thurn and Taxis	Campbell Gullan
Harprecht	Sam Livesey
Seligman	Joseph Markovitch
Frau Seligman	Selma Vaz Dias
Ottman	Lucius Blake
Graziella	Marcelle Rogez

Schoolmaster   Randle Ayrton
Judge   P. Kynaston Reeves
Censor: (completed film): 14 June 1934 'A' (adult viewing)
Premiere: 4 October 1934 Tivoli Theatre, London; Radio City Music Hall, New York.

Jud Süss

Production Company: Terra (State-commissioned)
Director: Veit Harlan
Script: Veit Harlan, Eberhard Wolfgang Möller and Ludwig Metzger
Camera: Bruno Mondi
Producer: Otto Lehmann
Sets: Otto Hunte and Karl Vollbrecht
Music: Wolfgang Zeller
Cast:

Jud Süss	Ferdinand Marian
Duke Karl Alexander	Heinrich George
The Duchess	Hilde von Stolz
Werner Krauss	Levy, Secretary to Süss
	Rabbi Loew
	Butcher
	Old man at the window
Landschaft Councillor Sturm	Eugen Klöpfer
Dorothea Sturm	Kristina Söderbaum
Faber, her fiancé	Malte Jaeger
Röder	Albert Florath
von Remchingen	Theodor Loos
Fiebelkorn	Walter Werner
Frau Fiebelkorn	Charlotte Schulz
Minchen Fiebelkorn	Anny Seitz
Frederike Fiebelkorn	Ilse Buhl
Luziana, Süss' mistress	Else Elster
Hans Bogner, a smith	Emil Hess
Bogner's wife	Käte Joken-König
Councillor of the Consistory	Jacob Tiedtke
Adviser's wife	Erna Morena
Ballerina	Ursula Deinert
Master of the Smiths	Erich Dunskus
Chairman of the Court	Otto Henning
Von Neuffer	Heinrich Schroth
Maid in Sturm household	Hannelore Benzinger
Faber's friend	Wolfgang Staudte

Gatekeeper   Hans Meyer-Hanno
Censor: 6 September 1940
Premiere: 24 September 1940 Ufa-Palast am Zoo, Berlin
Category: of special political and artistic value, valuable for youth

Bibliography

Archival Sources

ARCHIV DER STIFTUNG DEUTSCHE KINEMATHEK, BERLIN.
Jud Süss: ein historischer Film (Endgültige Fassung). Eberhard Wolfgang Möller and Ludwig Metzger, Regie Dr. Peter Paul Brauer, Typescript (n.d.).
Jud Süss: ein historischer Film. Regie: Veit Harlan, Terra Filmkunst, Typescript (n.d.).

BAYERISCHE STAATSBIBLIOTHEK, HANDSCHRIFTLICHE ABTEILUNG, MUNICH.
Veit Harlan, 'Wie es war ... Erlebnis eines Filmregisseurs unter seinem aller höchsten Chef, dem "Schirmherrn des deutschen Films"', Dr Goebbels', typescript (n.d.).

BAYERISCHES HAUPTSTAATSARCHIV, MUNICH.
Sammlung, Rehse, 7008, Eberhard Wolfgang Möller, Veit Harlan, 'Wie es war ... Erlebnis eines Filmregisseurs unter seinem aller höchsten Chef, dem "Schirmherrn des deutschen Films"', Dr Goebbels', typescript, *c.*1960.

BRITISH FILM INSTITUTE.
British Board of Film Censors Scenario Reports, 1933, London.
Michael Balcon Collection Scrapbook.

BUNDESARCHIV, BERLIN.
R43II/389; 810b; R55; R 56; R58; R109 I/1568, R109/II, R109/III/16 Ufa Bestand; Z38/392; Zeitschriften-Dienst; ZSg 102/62; Sammlung Sänger; ZSg. 101/ Sammlung Bramner; SG 101/15; Sammlung Sänger, Zsg.102/62; R109 I, Ufa Bestände; Berlin Document Center, (RKK).

DEUTSCHES INSTITUT FÜR FILMKUNDE, FRANKFURT AM MAIN.
Jud Süss file (cuttings and catalogue).
Reichsfilmarchiv, 1934, 2744.

NATIONAL ARCHIVES, PUBLIC RECORD OFFICE, KEW.
FO120/1092; FO1060/1233.

OESTERRICHSCHEN STAATSARCHIV, VIENNA: ARCHIV DER REPUBLIK.
Bundeskanzleramt 261:652.

STAATSANWALTSCHAFT BEI DEM LANDGERICHT HAMBURG.
Strafverfahren gegen Veit Harlan, AZ 14JS.

STAATSARCHIV HAMBURG.
Misc 6911, Veit Harlan; Erich Lüth papers.

UNITED STATES NATIONAL ARCHIVES.
Weekly Report of the Propaganda Abteilung, Referat Film, Aussenstelle Paris, 1941
(Microfilm Reel Number T141, March–October 1941).

Journals, Newspapers

Allgemeine Zeitung des Judentums
Cinema Quarterly
Daily Express
Daily Mail
Daily Sketch
Daily Telegraph
Das Echo
Der Angriff
Der Film
   Reichspost
Der deutsche Film
Der gute Film
Deutsche Allgemeine Zeitung
Deutsche Filmzeitung
Deutsche Zeitung
Die Filmwoche
Die neue Freie Presse
Die Welt
Evening Standard
Film-Journal
Film-Kurier
Filmpress
Filmwelt
Filmwoche
Frankfurter Zeitung
Hamburger Tageblatt
Hollywood Reporter

Jewish Chronicle
Kinematograph
Lichtbild-Bühne
Manchester Guardian
Motion Picture Daily
Neue Freie Presse
Neue Wiener Tageblatt
Neues Wiener Journal
Neuigkeits-Welt-Blatt, Neues Wiener
New York Herald Tribune
New York Times
The Observer
Oestereichische Abendzeitung
Picturegoer Weekly
Punch
Reichspost
Spectator
Sunday Express
Sunday Times
Tagespiegel
The Times
The Times Literary Supplement
Time
Variety
Völkischer Beobachter
Wiener Zeitung

Primary Sources

Published

Anon., *Curieuser Nachrichten Aus Dem Reich der Beschnittenen*. In the British
Library copy Books i, iii and iv claim to have been published in Cana in Galilee

in 1738, while Book III appears as published in 'Frankfurth und Leipzig' in 1738 though no publisher is mentioned).

Anon. [Johann Casparson] *Gespräch in dem so gennanten Reiche der Todten, zwischen Carl Alexandern, dem letzt verstorbenen Regierenden Herzoge von Würtemberg, Kayserlicher wie auch des H. R. Reichs und Schwäbischchen Crayses General Feld-Marschalle etc. Und Johann Gaston, gewesenen letzten Gross-Herzoge von Toscana, aus dem Hause der Mediceer*, etc. Franckfurt am Mayn: Heinrich Ludwig Brunner, 1738.

Anon. [Friedrich Schiller] *Die Räuber*. Frankfurt and Leipzig: n.p., 1781.

Bernard, Christoph David, *Erinnerung … Ausführlicher Diskurs mit Einem seiner Guten Freunde von allem, was Ihme in den drei letzten Tagen des unglücklichchen Jud Süss Oppenheimers vornemlich von seiner Beicht, Glaubens-Bekanntniss, und Ablass, auch zukünftigen Sünden, und andern merckwürdigen Vorfallenheiten bekannt worden*, etc. Tübingen: Joseph Sigmund, 1738.

Bernard, Christoph David, *Der in den Lüfften schwebende neue Jüdische Heilige Joseph Süss Oppenheimer, oder Das von der Würtembergischen Judenschafft herausgegebene merckwürdige Canonisations-Manifest, Worinn dieselbe gemeldeten unglücklichen Juden ihren gesamten Glaubens-Genossen so wohl, also auch der leicht glaubigen and falschberichteten Christenheit Als einen Heiligen aufzubürden Sich unterstunden*. Tübingen: Johann Georg Cotta, 1738.

Boberach, Heinz, *Meldungen aus dem Reich: Die Geheimen Lageberichte des Sicherheitsdienstes der SS, 1938–1945*. Herrsching: Pawlak, 1984.

Boelcke, Willi, ed., *Kriegspropaganda Geheime Ministerkonferenzen im Reichspropagandaministerium 1939–1941*. Stuttgart: Deutsche Verlag-Anstalt, 1966.

Dahlke, Hans, ed., *Lion Feuchtwanger, Dramen*. Berlin and Weimar: Aufbau, 1984. 2 vols.

Domerus, Max, ed., *Hitler, Reden und Proklmationen*. 2 vols in 5 parts. Munich: Löwit, 1963.

Döblin, Alfred. 'Der historische Roman und Wir', in *Aufsätze zur Literatur*. Olten and Freiburg: Walter, 1963.

Dukes, Ashley, *The Scene is Changed*. London: Macmillan, 1942.

Eller, or A. E. Ellerman (pseudonym), *The Prime Minister of Würtemburg*. London: Andrews & Co., 1897.

Eller, Ingatherings. London: Andrews & Co, 1897.

Feuchtwanger, Lion, 'Die drei Sprünge des Wang-lun', in Feuchtwanger, Lion, *Ein Buch nur für meine Freunde*. Frankfurt am Main: Fischer, 1984 (originally published as *Centum Opuscula*, Rudolstadt, 1956).

Feuchtwanger, Lion, *Die hässliche Herzogin Margarete Maultasch*. Berlin: Wegweiser, 1923.

Feuchtwanger, Lion, *Jud Süss, Schauspiel in drei Akten (vier Bilder)*. Munich; Georg Müller, 1917.

Feuchtwanger, Lion, *Jud Süss*. Munich: Drei Maskenverlag, 1925.

Feuchtwanger, Lion, *Jud Süss*. trans. Willa and Edwin Muir. London: Martin Secker, 1926.

Feuchtwanger, Lion, 'Jud Süss historisch: Zu dem Buch Selma Stern' in *Berliner Tageblatt*. (4 July 1930).

Feuchtwanger, Lion, 'To my Friends, the Actors', *Atlantic Monthly*. (April, 1941), pp. 735–9.

Feuchtwanger, Lion, 'Über "Jud Süss"', Freie deutsche Bühne, (Das blaue Heft) xi, 1 95 (5 January 1929), reprinted in Lion Feuchtwanger, Ein Buch nur für meine Freunde (Frankfurt am Main: Fischer, 1984), originally published as *Centum Opuscula*, Rudolstadt, 1956).

Feuchtwanger, Lion, 'Vom Sinn und Unsinn des historischen Romans' in Lion Feuchtwanger, *Ein Buch nur für meine Freunde*. Frankfurt am Main, 1984 (originally published as *Centum Opuscula*, Rudolstadt, 1956).

Feuchtwanger, Marta, *Nur eine Frau*. Munich: Langen Müller, 1983.

Feuchtwanger, Martin, *Ebenbilder Gottes*. Tel Aviv: Edition Olympia, 1952.

Fröhlich, Elke ed., *Die Tagebücher von Joseph Goebbels: Sämtliche Fragmente*. 25 vols. Munich: Saur, 1987–2005.

George, J. R., (pseudonym for Hans Hömberg) *Jud Süss*. Berlin: Terra, 1941.

Hauff, Wilhelm, 'Abner, der Jude, der nichts Gesehen Hat', in Bernhard Zeller, ed., *Hauff, Märchen*. Frankfurt: Insel, 1976.

Hauff, Wilhelm, *Jud Süss* in Hermann Engelhard, ed., *Novellen, Prosastücke, Briefe*, ii. Stuttgart: J. G. Cotta, 1962.

Hippler, Fritz, *Betrachtungen zum Filmschaffen*. Berlin: Max Hesses, 1942.

Hippler, Fritz, *Die Verstrickung: Einstellungen und Rückblenden von Fritz Hippler ehem. Reichsfilmintendant unter Joseph Goebbels*. Düsseldorf: Mehr Wissen, 1982.

Hitler, Adolf, *Mein Kampf*. trans. Ralph Manheim. London: Pimlico, 1992.

Isherwood, Christopher, *Christopher and his Kind*. London: Eyre Methuen, 1976.

Kohn, Salomon, *Ein deutscher Minister: Roman aus dem Achtzehnten Jahrhundert*. Cincinnati: Bloch, 1886, 2 vols

Kornfeld, Paul, 'Jud Süss: Tragödie in drei Akten und einem Epilog' (playscript, Rowohlt). Also published with cuts in *Theater Heute*. 1988, 2, pp. 29–55.

Kracauer, Siegfried, 'Cult of Distraction – on Berlin's Picture Palaces' in *The Mass Ornament*. trans. Thomas Y. Levin, Cambridge, MA.: Harvard, 1995.

Krauss, Werner, *Das Schauspiel meines Lebens*. Stuttgart: Henry Govert, 1958.

Kulka, Otto Dov and Jäckel, Eberhard, eds., *Die Juden in den Geheimen NS-Stimmungsberichten*. Düsseldorf: Droste, 2004.

Langbein, Hermann, ed., *Der Auschwitz Prozess: Eine Dokumentation*. I, Frankfurt am Main: Neue Kritik, 1995.

Lehmann, Markus, *Süss Oppenheimer: eine jüdische Erzählung*. Mainz: Johann Wirth'sche Hofdrückerei, 1872 and serialized from January to April 1872 in *Der Israelit*.

Lejeuene, Anthony, ed., *The C. A. Lejeune Reader*. London: Carcanet, 1991.

Rieger, Georg Conrad, *Sicherer Bericht von dem Juden Joseph Süss Oppenheimer*

Welcher an 1738 den 4. Febr. bey Stuttgart executirt wurde. Augsburg: Elias Beck, 1738.

Rieger, Georg Conrad, *Nachricht Von denen letzten Stunden Des Juden Süss Oppenheimers, Wie sich dieser Jude in denselben so wohl zu Hohen-Aschberg, als auch zu Stuttgard auf dem Herren-Hauss und beym Gericht gegen die Herren Geistliche, Als: Herrn M. Georg Cunrad [sic] Rieger, Herr M. Repet. Hoffmann, Herr M. Christoph Cunrad Heller.* Frankfurt: Wolfgang Christof Mulzen, 1738.

Schiller, Friedrich, *Die Räuber: ein Schauspiel* in Schiller, *Werke*, iii, Weimar; H. Böhlaus, 1953.

Wulf, Josef, *Musik im Dritten Reich.* Frankfurt: Ullstein, 1983.

Wulf, Josef, *Theater und Film im Dritten Reich.* Frankfurt: Ullstein, 1983.

Reference works

Allgemeine Deutsche Biographie. xxxvii. Leipzig: Duncker & Humblot, 1894.

Catalogues

Jud Süss: Propagandafilm im NS-Staat. Catalogue zur Ansstellung. Stuttgart: Haus der Geschichte Baden-Württemberg, 2007.

Terra Catalogue, Institut für Filmkunde, Frankfurt (also reprinted in *Film Press.* 22 July 1950).

Memoirs

Balcon, Michael, *Michael Balcon Presents … A Lifetime in Films.* London: Hutchinson, 1969.

Clare, George, *Berlin Days 1946–1947.* London: Macmillan, 1989.

Glückel, von Hameln, *The Life of Glückel of Hameln 1646–1724, Written by Herself,* trans. Beth-Zion Abrahams. London: East and West Library, 1962.

Harlan, Veit, *Im Schatten meiner Filme.* Gütersloh: Sigbert Mohn, 1966.

Hippler, Fritz *Die Verstrickung: Einstellungen und Ruckblenden.* Düsseldorf: Mehr Wissen, 1981.

Isherwood, Christopher, *Christopher and his Kind.* London: Methuen, 1976.

Söderbaum, Kristina, *Nichts bleibt immer so: Rückblenden auf ein Leben vor und hinter der Kamera.* Bayreuth: Hestia, 1983.

Wise, Stephen, *Challenging Years: The Autobiography of Stephen Wise.* London: East and West Library, 1951.

Zuckmayer, Carl, *Briefe an Han Schiebelhuth 1921–1936.* Göttingen: Wallstein, 2003.

Zuckmayer, Carl, *Geheimreport.* Göttingen: Wallstein, 2002.

DVDs

Moeller, Felix, *In the Shadow of Jew Süss,* 2008

Jud Süss, International Historic Films; 2007
David Culbert, 'Essay', on DVD Jud Süss.

Secondary sources

Reference works

Allgemeine deutsche Biographie. xlv, Leipzig: Duncker & Humblot, 1900.
http://www.vormaerz.de/index.html
Biographische Enzyklopädie. 2nd edn, Munich: Saur, 2006.
Grosses Vollständiges Universal-Lexikon aller Wissenschaften und Künste. Leipzig and
  Halle: Heinrich Zedler, 1744.
Jahrbuch für Geschichte Neue Deutsche Biographie. Berlin: Duncker & Humblot,
  1979.

Unpublished

Bowles, Brett, 'Propaganda and its Backlash: Reception of Le Juif Süss en France,
  1941–42', unpublished paper.

Books and articles

Agate, James, *Around Cinemas*. 2nd series. London: Home & Van Thal, 1948.
Albrecht, Gerd, *Der Film im Dritten Reich: eine Dokumentation*. Karlsruhe: Doku
  Verlag, 1979.
Albrecht, Gerd, *Nationalsozialistische Filmpolitik. Eine soziologische. Untersuchung
  über die Spielfilme des Dritten Reiches*. Stuttgart: Ferdinand Enke, 1969.
Allen, Jerry, *Conrad Veidt: From Caligari to Casablanca*. Pacific Grove, CA:
  Boxwood, 1993.
Arndt, Heinz, von, *Aktuelle Filmbücher: Dem Drehbuch von Veit Harlan, E. W.
  Möller and Ludwig Metzger, Nacherzählt von Heinrich von Arndt*. Berlin; Carl
  Curtius, 1940.
Arns, Alfons, 'Fluchtpunkt Antisemitismus: Die Organisation des Raums in Otto
  Huntes Entwürfen zu Jud Süss', in *Otto Hunte: Architekt für den Film*. Frankfurt
  am Main: Filmmuseum, 1996.
Arns, Alfons, 'Fatale Korrespondenzen: Die Jud-Süss-Filme von Lothar Mendes
  und Veit Harlan im Vergleich in Jüdische Figuren' in Cilly Kugelmann and Fritz
  Backhaus, eds., *Film und Karikatur: Die Rothschilds und Joseph Süss Oppenheimer*.
  Sigmaringen and Frankfurt: Jan Thorbecke, 1996)
Arnsberg, Gad, 'Demokraten, "Ultraliberale" und sonstige Staatsfeinde zur
  württembergischen military-und Zivilverschwörung von 1831 bis 1833' in Haus
  der Geschichte Baden-Württemberg in Verbindung mit der Landeshauptstadt,
  Politische Gefangene in Südwestdeutschland. Stuttgart: Silberburg, 2001.

Asch, Ronald, 'Corruption and Punishment? The Rise and Fall of Matthäus Enzlin (1556–1613) Lawyer and Favourite' in J. H. Elliott and L. W. B. Brockliss, eds., *The World of the Favourite*. New Haven, Conn. and London: Yale University Press, 1999.

Ascheid, Antje, *Hitler's Heroines: Stardom and Womanhood in Nazi Cinema*. Philadelphia: Temple University Press, 2003.

Aue, Irene, '"Jud Süss" und die Geschichtswissenschaft: Das Beispiel Selma Stern', in Alexandra Przyrembel and Jörg Schonert, eds., *Jud Süss: Hofjude, literarische Figur, antisemitisches Zerrbild*. Frankfurt, New York: Campus, 2006.

Auge, Oliver, 'Holzinger, Enslin, Oppenheimer: Günstlingfälle am spätmittelälterlichen und frühneuzeitlichen Hof der Württemberg', in Jan Hirschbiegel and Werner Paravicini, eds., *Der Fall des Günstlings. Hofparteien in Europa vom 13. bis zum 17. Jahrhundert*. Ostfildern: Thorbecke, 2004.

Aurich, Rolf, *Theo Lingen*. Berlin: Aufbau, 2008.

Baird, Jay, *To Die for Germany: Heroes in the Nazi Pantheon*. Bloomington, Ind: Indiana University Press, 1992.

Bankier, David, *The Germans and the Final Solution: Public Opinion under Nazism*. Oxford: Blackwell, 1992.

Bardèche, Maurice and Brasillach, Robert, *Historie du Cinéma*. Paris: Denoel & Steele, 1943.

Bartov, Omer, *The 'Jew' in Cinema From The Golem to Don't Touch My Holocaust*. Bloomington, Indiana University Press: 2005.

Baumgart, Peter, 'Joseph Süss Oppenheimer: Das Dilemma des Hofjuden im absoluten Fürstenstaat' in Karlheinz Müller und Klaus Wittstadt, eds., *Geschichte und Kultur des Judentums: eine vorlesungsreihe an der Julius Maximilians-Universität*. Würzburg: Schöningh, 1988.

Belschner, Christian, *Geschichte von Württemberg in Wort und Bild*. Stuttgart: Zeller & Schmidt, 1902.

Benzoni, Guido, 'The Venetian *Relazioni*: Impressions with Allusion to late Venetian Historiography' in George Iggers and James Powell, eds., *Leopold von Ranke and the Shaping of the Historical Discipline*. Syracuse, NY: Syracuse University, 1990.

Bergfelder, Tim, 'The Producer Designer and the *Gesamtkunstwerk*: German Film Technicians in the British Film Industry of the 1930s' in Andrew Higson, ed., *Dissolving Views: Key Writings in British Cinema*. London: Cassell, 1996.

Betts, Ernest, *Jew Süss*. London: Methuen, 1935.

Betts, Ernest, ed., *The Private Life of Henry VIII*. London: Methuen, 1934.

Billington, Michael, *Peggy Ashcroft*. London: John Murray, 1989.

Blanning, T. W. J., *The Culture of Power and the Power of Culture: Old Regime Europe 1660–1789*. Oxford: OUP, 2004.

Blanning, Tim, *The Pursuit of Glory*. London: Penguin, 2007.

Bowles, Brett, 'German Newsreel Propaganda in France', *Historical Journal of Film, Radio and Television* 2004, 24, 45–68.

Bowles, Brett, 'Propaganda and its Backlash: Reception of Le Juif Süss in France', (unpublished).

Bowles, Brett, 'The Attempted Nazification of French Cinema 1933–1944' in Roel Vande Winkel and David Welch, eds., *Cinema and the Swastika: the International Expansion of Third Reich Cinema*. 2nd edn. Basingstoke: Palgrave Macmillan, 2011.

Brenner, Michael, *Propheten der Vergangenheit: Jüdische Geschichtschreibung*. Munich: Beck, 2006.

Bucher, Peter, 'Die Bedeutung des Films als historische Quelle: Der ewige Jude' in Heinz Duchardt and Manfred Schlenke, eds., *Festschrift für Eberhard Kessel zum 75. Geburtstag*. Munich: Wilhelm Fink, 1982.

Buchloh, Ingrid, *Veit Harlan: Goebbels' Starregisseur*. Paderborn: Ferdinand Schöningh, 2010.

Carr, Steven, *Hollywood and Anti-Semitism: A Cultural History up to World War II*. Cambridge: Cambridge University Press, 2001.

Carsten, Francis, 'The Court Jews: prelude to emancipation', *Leo Baeck Yearbook*,. III, 1958, republished in Francis Carsten, *Essays in German History*. London: Hambledon, 1985.

Carsten, Francis, 'The Empire after the Thirty Years War' in F. L. Carsten, *Essays in German History*.

Carsten, Francis, Review of Heinrich Schnee's *Das Hoffaktorum in der deutschen Geschichte*, vol. 1, *English Historical Review* 1953, 68, p. 646.

Carsten, Francis, *Fascist Movements in Austria: Schönerer to Hitler*. London, Sage, 1977.

Chase, Jefferson. 'The Wandering Court Jew and the Hand of God: Wilhelm Hauff's *Jud Suss*. as Historical Fiction'. *The Modern Language Review* 1998, 93, pp. 724–40.

Cohen, Richard I. and Mann, Vivian B., 'Melding Worlds: Court Jews and the Arts of the Baroque' in Richard I. Cohen and Vivian B. Mann, eds., *From Court Jews to the Rothschilds: Art, Patronage, and Power 1600–1800*. Munich and New York: Prestel, 1996.

Cohen, Richard I. and Mann, Vivian B., 'The Court Jew' in Vivian B. Mann and Richard I. Cohen, eds., *From Court Jews to the Rothschilds: Art, Patronage and Power 1600–1800*. Munich and New York: Prestel, 1996.

Cser, Andreas, 'Zwischen Stadtverfassung und absolutischem Herrschaftsanspruch (1650 bis zum Ende der Kurpfalz 1802)', in Andreas Cser et al, *Geschichte der Juden in Heidelberg*. Heidelberg: B. Guderjahn, 1996.

Culbert, David, 'Essay' in DVD *Jud Süss*. International Historic Films, Chicago, 2008.

Davis, Nathalie Zemon, *Women on the Margins: three seventeenth-century lives*. Cambridge, MA.: Harvard University Press, 1996.

Deeg, Peter, *Hofjuden, Juden, Judenverbrechen und Judengesetze in Deutschland von der Vergangenheit bis zur Gegenwart*. Nüremberg: Der Stürmer, 1938.

Dendl, Jörg, 'Leben und Sterben des Joseph Süss Oppenheimer, *genannt* "Jud Süss" nach der Darstellung des '"Grossen vollständigen Universal Lexikons' von Johann Heinrich Zedler'. Available at http://www.aillyacum.de/Dt/18-Jh/Oppenheimer. html.

Dietschreit, Frank, *Lion Feuchtwanger*. Stuttgart: J. B. Metzler, 1988.

Dizinger, Karl Friedrich, *Beiträge zur Geschichte Württembergs und seines Regentenhauses zur Zeit der Regierung Herzogs Karl Alexander und während der Minderjährigkeit seines Erstgebornen. Zum grossen Theile nach ungedruckten Archival-Urkunden,*. 2 vols. Tübingen: Heinrich Laupp, 1834.

Drewniak, Boguslaw, *Der deutsche Film 1938–1945: ein Gesamtüberblick*. Düsseldorf: Droste, 1987.

Duden, Barbara, 'Zwischen "wahrem Wissen" und Prophetie: Konzeptionen des Ungeboren', in Barbara Duden, Jürgen Schlumborn, Patrice Veit, eds., *Geschichte des Ungeborenen: zur Erfahrungs-und Wissenschaftsgeschichte der 17.-20. Jahrhundert*. Göttingen: Vandenhoeck & Ruprecht, 2002

Dülmen, Richard van, *Theatre of Horror: Crime and Punishment in Early Modern Germany,*. trans. Elisabeth Neu. Oxford: Polity, 1990.

Ekkehart, Winfried [Heinrich Schnee], *Rasse und Geschichte, Grundzüge einer rassewertenden Geschichtsbetrachtung von der Urzeit bis zur Gegenwart*. Bochum: Ferdinand Kamp, 1936.

Ecksteins, Modris, 'War, Memory and Politics: The Fate of the film *All Quiet on the Western Front*', *European History* 1980, 13, pp. 60–82.

Elwenspoek, Curt, *Jew Süss Oppenheimer, The Great Financier, Gallant and Adventurer of the Eighteenth Century: A Study Based on Various Documents, Private Papers and Traditions*. trans. E. Cattle. London: Hurst & Blackett, 1931.

Elwenspoek, Curt, *Jud Süss Oppenheimer: Der grosses Finanzier und galante Abenteurer des 18. Jahrhunderts*. Stuttgart: Süddeutsches Verlagshaus, 1926. (*Great Financier, Gallant and Adventurer of the Eighteenth Century: A Study Based on Various Documents, Private Papers and Traditions*, trans. Edward Cattle. London: Hurst and Blackett, 1931).

Elwenspoek, Curt, *Der Spiegel*. 15 August 1958, pp. 12, 33.

Emberger, Gudrun, 'Joseph Süss Oppenheimer: Vom Günstling zum Sündenbock' in Gad Arnsberg, et al, *Politische Gefangen in Südwestdeutschland*. Tübingen: Silberburg, 2001.

Emberger, Gudrun, 'Verdruss, Sorg und Widerwärtigkeiten: Die Inventur und Verwaltung des Jud Süsschen Vermögens 1737–1772' in *Zeitschrift für Württembergische Landesgeschichte* 1981, 40, pp 369–75.

Emberger, Gudrun, 'Review of Haasis, Joseph Süss Oppenheimer' in *Zeitschrift für Württembergische Landesgeschichte* 1999, 58, pp. 437–41.

Emberger, Gudrun, and Ries, Rotraud, 'Der Fall Joseph Süss Oppenheimer' in Alexandra Przyrembel and Jörg Schonert, eds., *Jud Süss: Hofjude, literarische Figur, antisemitisches Zerrbild*. Frankfurt am Main and New York: Campus, 2006).

Erens, Patricia, *The Jew in American Cinema*. Bloomington: Indiana University Press, 1984.

Feinberg, Anat, 'Leopold Jessner: German Theatre and Jewish Identity', *Leo Baeck Yearbook* 2003, XLVIII, pp. 110–33.

Ferro, Marc, 'Dissolves in Jud Süss', in Marc Ferro, *Cinema and History*. trans. Naomi Green. Detroit: Wayne State University, 1988.

Fielding, Raymond, *The American Newsreel: 1911–1967*. 2nd ed. Jefferson N. C. and London: McFarland, 2006.

Fleischhauer, Werner, *Barock im Herzogthum Württemberg*. 2nd edition Stuttgart: W. Kohlhammer, 1981.

Fox, Jo, *Filming Women in the Third Reich*. Oxford, Berg, 2000.

Fox, Jo, *Film Propaganda in Britain and Nazi Germany*. Oxford and New York: Berg, 2007.

Fraenkel, Heinrich, *Unsterblicher Film*. Munich: Kindler, 1957.

Fraenkel, Ludwig Julius, 'Albert Dulk', in *Allgemeine Deutsche Biographie* 1905. Available at http://de.Wikisource.org/wiki/ADB:Dulk,_Albert.

Freidenrich, Harriet, *Jewish Politics in Vienna: 1918–1938*. Bloomington, Ill.: Indiana University Press: 1991.

Freimann, A., 'Bibliographie der Flugschriften über Joseph Süss Oppenheimer', *Zeitschrift für Hebräische Bibliographie* 1905, ix, 2, pp. 56–58, 79–81 and X 1906, pp. 106–113.

Frenzel, Elisabeth, *Judengestalten auf der deutschen Bühne. Ein notwendiger Querschnitt durch 700 Jahre Rollengeschichte*. Munich: Deutscher Volksverlag, 1942.

Friedländer, Saul, *The Years of Extermination: The Years of Persecution 1933–1939*. London: Weidenfeld & Nicolson, 1997.

Friedländer, Saul, *The Years of Extermination: Nazi Germany and the Jews: 1939–1945*. London: Weidenfeld & Nicolson, 2007.

Friedman, Lester, *Hollywood's Image of the Jew*. New York: Frederick Unger, 1982.

Friedman, Régine Mihal, *L'Image et son Juif*. Paris: Payot, 1983.

Friedman, Régine Mihal, 'Male Gaze and Female Reaction: Veit Harlan's Jew Süss' (1940), in Sandra Frieden, Richard W. McCormick, Vibeke R. Petersen snd Laurie Melissa Vogelsang, eds., *Gender and German Cinema: Feminist Interventions*. ii, Providence, RI, 1993; Oxford: Berg, 1993.

Friedman, Régine Mihal, 'Mein Tag mit Kristina', *Frauen und Film* 1988, pp. 44–45, pp. 104–08.

Fuegi, John, *The Life and Lies of Bertolt Brecht*. London: Harper Collins, 1994.

Garçon, François, '*Cinéma et Historie: Les Trois Discours du Juif Süss*', *Annales* 1979, pp. 694–720.

Garçon, François, 'Nazi Film Propaganda in Occupied France' in David Welch, ed., *Nazi Propaganda*. Beckenham: Croom Helm, 1983.

Gerber, Barbara, *Jud Süss: Aufstieg und Fall im frühen 18. Jahrhundert: Ein Beitrag zur historischen Antisemitismus-und Rezeptionsforschung*. Hamburg: Christians, 1990.

Glasenapp, Gabriela von, 'Literarische Popularisierungsprozesse eines antijudischen Stereotyps: Wilhelm Hauffs Jud Süss', in Alexandra Przrembel and Jörg Schönert, eds., *Jud Süss, Hofjude, literarische Figur, antisemitisches Zerrbild*. Frankfurt am Main: Campus, 2006.

Gough Yates, Kevin, 'Jews and Exiles in British Cinema', *Leo Baeck Institute Yearbook* 1992, xxxvii, pp. 571- 41.

Gotthell, Richard, 'Bibliography of the Pamphlets Dealing with Joseph Suess Oppenheimer' *Zeitschrift für Hebräische Bibliographie* 1905, 9 and 10, pp. 106–13.

Green, Abigail, *Fatherlands: State-Building and Nationhood in nineteenth century Germany*. New York: Cambridge University Press, 2001.

Haasis, Hellmut, *Joseph Süss Oppenheimer, genannt Jud Süss Finanzier, Freidenker Justizopfer*. Hamburg/Reinbek: Rowohlt, 1998.

Haasis, Hellmut, *Joseph Süss Oppenheimers Rache*. Steinbach: Gollenstein, 1994.

Harper, Sue, '"Thinking Forward and Up": The British Films of Conrad Veidt' in Jeffrey Richards, ed., *The Unknown 1930: an alternative history of the British cinema 1929–39*. London: I. B. Tauris, 1998.

Haumann, Wilhelm, *Paul Kornfeld, Leben, Werk, Wirkung*. Würzburg: Königshäusen & Neumann, 1996.

Haver, Gianni, 'Film Propaganda and the Balance between Neutrality and Alignment: Nazi Films in Switzerland, 1933–1945' in Roel Vande Winkel and David Welch, eds., *Cinema and the Swastika: the International Expansion of Third Reich Cinema*. 2nd edn Basingstoke: Palgrave Macmillan, 2011.

Hayn, Hugo, 'Süss-Oppenheimer-Bibliographie: Ein Beitrag zur Kuriositäten – Literature' in *Zeitschrift für Bücherfreunde* 1904–5, viii, ii, pp. 448–52.

Henne, Thomas, 'Der Umgang der Justiz mit Harlans *Jud Süss* seit den 1950er Jahren: Prozesse. Legenden, Verdikte' in Alexandra Przyrembel and Jörg Schönert, eds. *Jud Süss: Hofjude, literarische Figur, antisemitisches Zerrbild*. Frankfurt and New York: Campus, 2006.

Herf, Jeffrey, *The Jewish Enemy: Nazi Propaganda during World War II and the Holocaust*. Cambridge, MA and London: Belknap, Harvard University Press, 2006.

Hickethier, Knut, 'Der Audiovisuell Inszenierte Antisemitismus' in Alexandra Przrembel and Jörg Schönert, eds., *Jud Süss, Hofjude, literarische Figur, antisemitisches Zerrbild*. Frankfurt am Main: Campus, 2006.

Hinz, Ottmar, *Hauff*. Hamburg: Rowohlt, 1989.

Hirschberg, Jehoash, *Music in the Jewish Community of Palestine: 1880–1948*. Oxford, Clarendon, 1995.

Holba, H., 'From Caligari to Hollywood, Conrad Veidt', *Focus on Film* 1975, 21, pp. 27–46.

Hollstein, Dorothea, 'Dreimal Jud Süss: Zeugnisse, "schmählichster Barbarei", Hauffs Novelle, Feuchtwangers Roman and Harlans Film in vergleichender Betrachtung', *Deutschunterricht* 1985, 37:3, 42–54.

Hollstein, Dorothea, *Jud Süss und die deutschen: Antisemitische Vorurteileimnationalsozialistischen Spielfilme*. Berlin: Ullstein, 1983.

Hornshøy-Møller, Stig, *Der ewige Jude, quellenkritische Analyse eines antisemitischen Propagandafilms*. Göttingen: Institut fur den Wissenschaftlichen Film, 1995.

Hull, David Stewart, *Film in the Third Reich: A Study of the German Cinema 1933–1945*. Berkeley and Los Angeles: University of California Press, 1969.

Iggers, George, *The German Conception of History*. Middletown, Conn.: Wesleyan University Press, 1968.

Israel, Jonathan, *European Jewry in the Age of Mercantilism, 1550–1750*. 3rd edn. London: Vallentine Mitchell, 1998.

Jersch-Wenzel, Steffi. 'Jewish economic activity in early modern times' in Ronald Po-Chia Hsia and Hartmut Lehmann. eds. *In and Out of the Ghetto: Jewish–Gentile Relations in late Medieval and Early Modern Germany*. Washington: Cambridge University Press, 1995.

Kalmar, Ivan Davidson and Penslar, Derek, eds., *Orientalism and the Jews*. Hanover, NH: University Press of New England, 2005.

Kanzog, Klaus, '*Staatspolitisch besonders wertvoll': Ein Handbuch zu 30. deutschen Spielfilmen der Jahre 1934 bis 1945*. Munich: Diskurs Film, 1994.

Kater, Michael, *The Twisted Muse*. New York: Oxford University Press, 1997.

Kershaw, Ian, 'How Effective Was Nazi Propaganda?' in David Welch, ed., *Nazi Propaganda*. Beckenham: Croom Helm, 1983.

Klotz, Marcia. 'Epistemological Ambiguity and the Fascist Text: Jew Süss, Carl Peters and Ohm Krüger,' *New German Critique*. 1998, 74, pp. 91–124.

Knilli, Friedrich, *Ich War Jud Süss: die Geschichte des Filmstars Ferdinand Marian*. Berlin: Henschel, 2000.

Knilli, Friedrich and Zielinsky, Siegfried. 'Lion Feuchtwangers "Jud Süss" und die Filme von Lothar Mendes und Veit Harlan', *Text und Kritik* 1983, 79–80, 99–121.

Knilli, Friedrich, Maurer, Thomas, Radevagen, Thomas, and Zielinski, Siegfried, *Jud Süss' Film protokoll, Programmheft und Einzelanalysen*. Berlin: Volker Spiess, 1983.

Kohut, Adolf, *Geschichte der deutschen Juden: Ein Hausbuch für die jüdische Familie*. Berlin: Deutsche, 1898–99.

Israel, Jonathan, *European Jewry in the Age of Mercantilism, 1550–1750*. 3rd edn. London: Vallentine Mitchell, 1998.

Krauss, Rudolf, '*Spiegelungen des Karl Eugenschen Zeitalters in Schillers Jugenddramen*', *Württembergische Vierteljahrshefte für Landesgeschichte*), 14.

Krauss, Rudolf, 'Süss' in *Allgemeine deutsche Biographie*. vol. 37,. Leipzig: Duncker & Humblot, 1894.

Krobb, Florian, *Die schöne Jüdin: jüdische Frauengestalten in der deutschsprachigen Erzählliteratur vom 17. Jahrhundert bis zum Ersten Weltkrieg*.Tübingen: Niemyer, 1994.

Krobb, Florian, 'Macht die Augen zu, Sarah, Heinrich Heines Rabbi von Bacharach', *German Life and Letters* 1994, 47, pp. 167–181.

Krobb, Florian, *Selbstdarstellungen: Untersuchungen zur deutsch-jüdischen Erzählliteratur im neunzehnten Jahrhundert*. Würzburg: Koenigshausen und Neuman, 2000.

Kroner, Theodor, 'Joseph Süss Oppenheimer', *Zeitschrift des Zentralvereins deutscher Staatsbürger judischen Glaubens', Im deutschen Reich* 1903, ix, pp. 14–43.

Laregh, Peter, *Heinrich George, Komödiant seiner Zeit*. Frankfurt: Ullstein, 1996.

Laux, Stephan, 'Ich bin der Historiker der Hoffaktoren: Zur antisemitischen Forschung von Heinrich Schnee (1895–1968)', in *Simon Dubnow Institute Yearbook* 2006, V, pp. 485–513.

Leiser, Erwin, trans. Gertrud Mander and David Wilson, *Nazi Cinema*. London: Secker & Warburg, 1974.

Lesch, Paul, *Heim ins Ufa-Reich? NS-Filmpolitik und die Rezeption deutscher Filme in Luxemburg 1933–1944*. trans George Hausmier. Trier: Wissenschaftlicher Verlag, 2002.

Levi, Erik, *Music in the Third Reich*. Basingstoke: Macmillan, 1994.

Liebert, Frank, 'Vom Karrierstreben zum "Nötigungsnotstand": Jud Süss, Veit Harlan und die deutsche Nachkriegsgesellschaft (1945–50)' in Thomas Henne and Arne Riedlinger, eds., *Das Lüth-Urteil aus (rechts-historischer Sicht: Die Konfllikt um Veit Harlan und die Grundrechtjudikatur des. Bundesverfassungsgerichts*. Berlin: BMW, 2005.

Lohmeier, Anke-Maria, 'Propaganda als Alibi' in Alexandra Przrembel and Jörg Schönert, eds., *Jud Süss, Hofjude, literarische Figur, antisemitisches Zerrbild*. Frankfurt am Main: Campus, 2006.

Low, Rachel, *History of the British Film: Film Making in 1930s Britain*. London: Routledge, 1985.

Luhe, Barbara von der, 'Lion Feuchtwangers Roman "Jud Süss" und die Entwicklung des jüdischen Selbstbewusstseins in Deutschland', in Rudolf Wolff, ed., *Lion Feuchtwanger, Werk und Wirkung*. Bonn: Bouvier, 1984.

Mann, Vivian B., 'Images of "Jud Süss" Oppenheimer, An Early Modern Jew' in Mitchell B. Merback, ed., *Beyond the Yellow Badge: Anti-Judaism and Antisemitism in Medieval and Early Modern Visual Culture*. Leiden and Boston: Brill, 2007.

Marchand, Suzanne, *German Orientalism in the Age of Empire: Religion, Race, and Scholarship*. Cambridge: Cambridge University Press, 2009.

Moeller, Felix, *The Film Minister: Goebbels and the Cinema in the 'Third Reich'*. Michael Robinson, trans. Stuttgart and London: Axel Menges, 2000.

Moore, Greg, 'From Buddhism to Bolshevism: Some Orientalist Themes in German Thought', *German Life and Letters* 2003, 56, pp. 20–42.

Noack, Frank, *Veit Harlan: Des Teuffelsregisseur*. Munich: Belleville, 2007.

Nolzen, Armin, 'Hier sieht man den Juden', in Alexandra Przrembel and Jörg Schönert, eds., *Jud Süss, Hofjude, literarische Figur, antisemitisches Zerrbild*. Frankfurt am Main: Campus, 2006.

Osswald-Bargende, Sybille, *Die Mätresse, der Fürst und die Macht: Christina Wilhelmina von Grävenitz und die höfische Gesellschaft*. Frankfurt am Main and New York: Campus, 2000.

Osswald-Bargende, Sybille, 'Eine jüristische Hausaffäre: Einblicke in das Geschlechterverhältnis der höfischen Gesellschaft am Beispiel des

Ehezerwürfnisses zwischen Johanne Elisabeth und Eberhard Ludwig von Württemberg' in Ulrike Weckel, Claudia Opitz, Olivia Hochstrasser und Brigitte Tolkemitt, eds., *Ordnung, Politik und Geselligkeit der Geschlechter im 18. Jahrhundert*. Göttingen: Wallstein, 1998.

Osswald-Bargende, Sybille, 'Sonderfall Mätresse? Beobachtungen zum Typus des Favoriten aus geschlechtergeschichtlicher Perspektive am Beispiel der Christina Wilhelmina von Grävenitz' in Michal Kaiser and Andreas Pecar, eds., *Der zweite Mann im Staat: Oberste Amtsträger und Favoriten im Umkreis der Reichsfürsten in der Frühen Neuzeit*. Berlin: Duncker & Humblot, 2003.

Palmier, Jean-Michel, 'Le Juif Süss de Veit Harlan 1940' in Maria-Antoninetta Macciochi, ed. *Éléments Pour Une Analyse Du Fascisme*, ii. Paris: Inédit, 1976.

Pardo, Herbert and Schiffer, Siegfried, *Jud Süss. Historisches und juristisches Material zum Fall Veit Harlan*. Hamburg: Auerdruck, 1949.

Pazi, Marguerita, 'Zwei kaum bekannte Jud Süss-Theaterstücke' in Walther Huder and Friedrich Knilli, eds., *Lion Feuchtwanger – für die Vernunft, gegen Dummheit und Gewalt*. Berlin: Publica, 1985.

Pfaff, Carl, *Geschichte des Fürstenhauses und Landes Wirtenberg*. [sic]. 2nd edn, vol. 4. Stuttgart: J. W. Metzlerschen, 1854. The first edition was published in 1839.

Prawer, S. S., *Between Two Worlds: The Jewish Presence in German and Austrian Film: 1910–1933*. New York and Oxford: Berghahn, 2005.

Prieberg, Fred, *Musik im NS-Staat*. Frankfurt: Fischer, 1982.

Proctor, Robert, *The Nazi War on Cancer*. Princeton: Princeton University Press, 1999.

Pulzer, Peter, *Jews and the German State: The Political History of a Minority, 1848–1933*. Oxford: Blackwell, 1992.

Pulzer, Peter, *The Rise of Political Antisemitism in Germany and Austria*. revised edn., London: Peter Halban, 1988.

Rathkolb, Oliver, *Führertreu und gottbegnadet: kunstlereliten im Dritten Reich*. Vienna: ÖBV, 1991.

Reeves, Nicholas, *The Power of Film Propaganda*. London: Cassell, 1999.

Reimer, Robert C. ed, *Cultural History through a National Socialist Lens*. Rochester: Camden House, 2000.

Rentschler, Eric, *The Ministry of Illusion: Nazi Cinema and its Afterlife*. Cambridge, Mass.: Harvard University Press, 1998.

Richards, Jeffrey, *The Age of the Dream Palace: Cinema and Society in Britain 1930–1939*. London: Routledge, 1984.

Richards, Jeffrey, 'The British Board of Film Censors and Content Control in the 1930: foreign affairs', *Historical Journal of Film, Radio and Television* 1982, 2, 39–48.

Rieber, Christof, 'Das Sozialistengesetz: Die Kriminalisierung einer Partei' in Gad Arnsberger ed., *Politische Gefangene in Südwestdeutschland*. Stuttgart: Silberburg, 2001.

Riess, Curt, *Das Gab's Nur Einmal*. Hamburg: Sternbucher, 1956.

Ritchie, J. M., 'Ashley Dukes and the German Theatre between the Wars' in R. W. Last, ed., *Affinities: Essays in German and English Literature*. London: Wolff, 1971.

Ritchie, James. 'Die Jud Süss-Dramatisierung von Ashley Dukes' in Walter Huder and Friedrich Knilli, eds., *Lion Feuchtwanger ... für die Vernunft, gegen Dummheit und Gewalt*. Berlin: Publica, 1985.

Ritchie, J. M., 'Ashley Dukes and the German Theatre between the Wars' in R. W. Last, ed., *Affinities: Essays in German and English Literature*. London: Wolff, 1971.

Robertson, James C., *The British Board of Film Censors: Film Censorship in Britain, 1896–1950*. London, Sydney, Dover: Croom Helm, 1985.

Robertson, James C., *The Hidden Cinema: British Film Censorship in Action*. London: Routledge, 1989.

Robertson, Ritchie, *The 'Jewish Question' in German Literature: Emancipation and its Discontents*. Oxford, Oxford University Press, 1999.

Robertson, Ritchie, 'Urheimat Asien: The Re-Orientation of German and Austrian Jews 1900–1925', *German Life and Letters* 1996, 49, pp. 182–92.

Rohdie, Sam, *Antonioni*. London: British Film Institute, 1990.

Rohrbacher, Stefan, 'Jüdischer Geschichte' in Michael Brenner and Stefan Rohrbacher, eds., *Wissenschaft vom Judentum: Annährerungenen nach den Holocaust*. Göttingen: Vandenhoek & Rupprecht, 2000.

Rothmüller, Aaron, *The Music of the Jew*. London: Vallentine Mitchell, 1953.

Rühle, Günther, *Theater für die Republik, 1917–1933, im Spiegel der Kritik*. Frankfurt am Main: S. Fischer, 1967.

Sammons, Jeffrey, *Heinrich Heine: A Modern Biography*. Princeton: Princeton University Press, 1979.

Sassenberg, Marina. *Selma Stern (1890–1981): das Eigene in der Geschichte: Selbstentwürfe und Geschichtsentwürfe einer Historikerin*. London and Tübingen: Mohr Siebeck, 2004.

Scherr, Lilly. 'Le Juif Süss', *Yod, Revue des Études hébraiques et Juives moderne et contemporaine* 1976, I, 53–72.

Schlumborn, Jürgen. 'Grenzen des Wissens: Verhandlungen zwischen Arzt und Schwangeren' in Barbara Duden, Jürgen Schlumborn, Patrice Veit, eds., *Geschichte des Ungeborenen: zur Erfahrungs-und Wissenschaftsgeschichte der 17.-20. Jahrhundert*. Göttingen: Vandenhoeck & Ruprecht, 2002.

Schmitt, Leonhard, 'Der Fall Veit Harlan', *Film und Mode Revue*. 1952.

Schnabel, Franz, *Das 18. Jahrhundert in Europa*. Berlin: Goetz W. Propyläen-Weltgeschichte, 1931.

Schnee, Heinrich, Bürgermeister Karl Lueger: *Leben und Wirken eines grossen Deutsche*. Paderborn, 1936.

Schnee, Heinrich, *Die Hoffinanz und der moderne Staat: Geschichte und System der Hoffaktoren an deutschen Fürstenhofen im Zeitalter des Absolutismus*. Nach archivalischen Quellen. 6 vols. Berlin: Duncker & Humblot, 1953–1967.

Schnee, Heinrich, 'Die Judenfrage in Geschichte und Gegenwart', *Deutsches Archiv. für Landes-und Volksforschung* 1944, viii.

Schnee, Heinrich, 'Heinrich Heine's Ahnen als Hofjuden im deutschen Fürstenhöfe', *Der Weltkampf* 1944, 2, pp. 91–94.

Schnee, Heinrich, *George Ritter von Schönerer: ein Kämpfer für Alldeutschland: Mit ausgewählten Zeugnissen aus Schönerers Kampfzeit für deutsche Einheit und deutsche Reinheit.* Reichenberg, 1940).

Schön, Theodor, 'Balthasar Friedrich Wilhelm Zimmermann' in *Allgemeine Deutsche Biographie.* xlv, Historischen Kommission bei der Bayerischen Akademie der Wissenschaften, Band 45. Leipzig: Duncker & Humblot, 1900. Available at http://de.wikisource.org/w/index.php.

Schulte-Sasse, Linda, *Entertaining the Third Reich: Illusions of Wholeness in Nazi Cinema.* Durham, NC: Duke, 1996.

Schulte-Sasse, Linda, 'The Jew as Other under National Socialism: Veit Harlan's *Jud Süss*', *German Quarterly* 1988, 61, pp. 22–49.

Schulte-Sasse, Linda, 'Courtier, Vampire or Vermin? Jew Süss's Contradictory Effort to Render the "Jew" Other' in Terri Ginsberg and Kristin Thompson, eds., *Perspectives on German Cinema.* New York and London: G. K. Hall-Macmillan, 1996.

Schulte, Alois, *Wilhelm von Baden und der Reichskrieg gegen Frankreich 1693–1697.* Karlsruhe: C. Winters Universitätbuchhandlung, 1892.

Sedgwick, John, 'The Market for Feature Films in Britain in 1934: a Viable National Cinema', *Historical Journal of Film, Radio and Television* 1994, 14;1, pp. 15–36.

Sharpe, Lesley, *Friedrich Schiller: Drama, Thought and Politics.* Cambridge: Cambridge University Press, 1991.

Sheffi, Na'ama, 'Jud Süss', in Étienne François and Hagen Schulze, eds., *Deutsche Erinnerungsorte.* Munich: Beck, 2001.

Shindler, Colin, *Hollywood in Crisis; Cinema and American Society: 1929–1939.* London and New York: Routledge, 1996.

Singer, Claude, *Le Juif Süss et la Propagande nazie.* Paris: Les Belles Lettres, 2003.

Sombart, Werner, *Die Juden und das Wirtschaftsleben.* Leipzig: Duncker & Homblot, 1911.

Spalek, John. 'Jud Süss: Anatomy of a Best Seller' in John Spalek, ed., *Lion Feuchtwanger, the Man, his Ideas and his Work.* Los Angeles: Hennessey & Ingalls, 1972.

Specht, Heike, *Die Feuchtwangers: Familie, Tradition und jüdisches Selbstverständnis im deutsch-jüdischen Bürgertum des 19. und 20. Jahrhunderts.* Göttingen: Wallstein, 2006.

Stahr, Gerhard, *Volksgemeinschaft vor der Leinwand?: Nationalsozialistische Film und sein Publikum.* Berlin: Hans Theissen, 2001.

Steinweis, Alan, *Studying the Jew: Scholarly Antisemitism in Nazi Germany.* Cambridge, Mass.: Harvard University Press, 2006.

Stern, Selma, *Anarcharsis Cloots, der Redner des Menschengeschlechts: ein Beitrag zur Geschichte der deutschen in der französischen Revolution.* Berlin: Ebering, 1914.

Stern, Selma, *The Court Jew, A Contribution to the History of the Period of Absolutism in Central Europe.* trans. Ralph Weiman. Philadelphia, PA: Jewish Publication Society, 1950.

Stern, Selma, 'Historische Romane' in *Der Morgen* 1925, i, pp. 716–18.

Stern, Selma, *Jud Süss: ein Beitrag zur deutschen und zur Jüdischen Geschichte.* Berlin: Akademie, 1929.

Stern, Selma, 'Jud Süss', *Korrespondenzblatt des gesamtvereins der deutschen Geschichts und Altertumsvereine* 1920–1930, 7, pp. 23–40.

Stern, Selma, *Der Preussische Staat und die Juden.* i,. Berlin: Akademie für des Wissenschaft des Judentums, 1925.

Stern, Selma, *Der Preussische Staat und die Juden.* ii. Berlin, 1938 and Tübingen, J. C. Mohr, 1962–75.

Sternberg, Wilhelm von, *Lion Feuchtwanger: ein deutsches Schriftstellerleben.* Frankfurt am Main: Ullstein, 1988.

Sternberg, Wilhelm von, ed., *Lion Feuchtwanger: Materialien zu Leben und Werk.* Frankfurt am Main: Fischer, 1989.

Tegel, Susan, 'Leni Riefenstahl's Gypsy Question Revisited: The Gypsy Extras in "Tiefland"', *Historical Journal of Film, Radio and Television* 2006, 26, pp. 21–43.

Tegel, Susan, *Jew Süss Jud Süss.* Trowbridge: Flicks, 1996.

Tegel, Susan, *Nazis and the Cinema.* London: Hambledon Continuum, 2007.

Tegel, Susan, '"The Demonic Effect": Veit Harlan's Use of Jewish Extras in "Jud Süss" (1940)', in *Holocaust and Genocide Studies* 2000, XIV, pp. 215–241.

Tegel, Susan, 'The Politics of Censorship: Britain's "Jew Süss" (1934)' in London, New York and Vienna, *Historical Journal of Film, Radio and Television* 1995, 15, pp. 219–44.

Tegel, Susan, 'Veit Harlan and the Origins of "Jud Süss", 1938–1939: Opportunism in the Creation of Nazi anti-Semitic film Propaganda' in *Historical Journal of Film, Radio and Television* 1995, 15, pp. 515–531.

Töteberg, Michael, 'Karriere im Dritten Rich: Der Regisseur Veit Harlan' in Hans-Michael Bock and Michael Töteberg, eds., *Das Ufa-Buch: Kunst und Krisen, Stars und Regisseure, Wirtschaft und Politik.* Frankfurt am Main: Zweitausendeins, 1992.

Ulbricht, Otto, 'Criminality and Punishment of the Jews in the Early Modern Period', in R. Po-chia Hsia and Hartmut Lehmann, eds., *In and Out of the Ghetto: Jewish–Gentile Relations in Late Medieval and Early Modern Germany.* Washington, DC: Cambridge University Press, 1995.

Vande Winkel, Roel, 'German Influence on Belgian Cinema, 1933–45: From Low Profile Presence to Downright Colonisation' in Roel Vande Winkel and David Welch, eds., *Cinema and the Swastika: the International Expansion of Third Reich Cinema.* 2nd edn Basingstoke: Palgrave Macmillan, 2011.

Vann, James Allen, *The Making of a State: Württemberg 1593–1793.* Ithaca and London: Cornell University Press, 1983.

Vann, James Allen, *The Swabian Kreis: Institutional Growth in the Holy Roman Empire, 1648–1715.* Brussels: Éditions de la Librairie Encylopédique, 1975.

Vierhaus, Rudolf, 'Historiography between Science and Art' in George Iggers and James Powell, eds., *Leopold von Ranke and the Shaping of the Historical Discipline*. Syracuse, NY: Syracuse University Press, 1990.

Walker, Mack, *Johann Jakob Moser and the Holy Roman Empire of the German Nation*. Chapel Hill, N.C: University of North Carolina Press, 1981.

Welch, David, *Propaganda and the German Cinema 1933–1945*. 2nd edn. London: I. B. Tauris, 2001.

Welky, David, *The Moguls and the Dictators: Hollywood and the Coming of World War II*. Baltimore: Johns Hopkins, 2008.

Wilson, Peter H., *Absolutism in Central Europe*. London: Routledge, 2000.

Wilson, Peter H., 'Der Favorit als Sündenbock' in Michael Kaiser and Andreas Pecar, eds., *Der zweite Mann im Staat: Oberste Amtsträger und Favoriten im Umkreis der Reichsfürsten in der Frühen Neuzeit*. Berlin: Duncker & Humblot, 2003.

Wilson, Peter H., *War, State and Society in Württemberg, 1677–1793*. Cambridge: Cambridge University Press, 1995.

Wilson, Peter H., 'Women in Imperial Politics: the Württemberg Consorts 1674–1757', in Clarissa Campbell-Orr, ed., *Queenship in Europe, 1660–1815*. Cambridge: Cambridge University Press, 2004.

Witte, Karsten H., 'Der Barocke Faschist': Veit Harlan und seine Film', in Karl Corino, ed., *Intellektuelle im Bann des Nationalsozialismus*. Hamburg: Hoffmann und Campe, 1980.

Witle, Karsten H., 'Film im Nationalsozialismus: Blendung und Überblendung' in Wolfgang Jacobsen, Anton Kaes and Hans Helmut Prinzler, eds., *Geschichte des deutschen Films*. Stuttgart:Verlag J. B. Metzler, 1993.

Württembergischer Geschichts und Altertums-Verein, eds., *Herzog Karl Eugen und seine Zeit*. Esslingen: Paul Neff, 1907.

Wright, Rochelle, 'Swedish Film and Germany' in Roel Vande Winkel and David Welch, eds., *Cinema and the Swastika: the International. Expansion of Third Reich Cinema*. 2nd edn Basingstoke: Palgrave Macmillan, 2011.

Wright, Rochelle, *The Visible Wall: Jews and other Ethnic Outsiders in Swedish Film*. Carbondale and Edwardsville, Il, 1998.

Württembergisches Geschichts und Altertumsverein Verein, *Herzog Karl Eugen und seine Zeit*. Esslingen: Paul Neff, 1907.

Ziel, Ernst, ed., 'Albert Dulk: Sein Leben und seine Werke' in Albert Dulk, *Sämmtliche Dramen*. i. Stuttgart: Dietz, 1893.

Zielinski, Siegfried, Veit Harlan: *Analysen und Materialien zur Auseinandersetzung mit einem Film-Regisseur des deutschen Faschismus*. Frankfurt: Rita G Fischer, 1981.

Zimmermann, Manfred, *J. Süss Oppenheimer, ein Finanzmann des 18. Jahrhunderts: Ein Stück Absolutismus-und Jesuitengeschichte. Nach den Vertheidigungs-Akten und den Schriften der Zeitgenossen bearbeitet von …* Stuttgart: Rieger'sche, 1874.

Zweyhundert Fünff und zwangstige Entrevué, Zwischen Dem letzt-verstorbenen regierenden Hertzog von Würtemberg-Stuttgardt, Carol. Alexandro, und dem letzt verstorbenen Hertzog von Curland, Ferdinando. Leipzig: Wolfgang Deer, 1737.

Zwicker, Stefan, *'Nationale Märtyer' Albert Leo Schlageter und Julius Fučik: Heldenkult, Propaganda und Erinnerungskultur.* Paderborn: Schöningh, 2006.

Index